innovative a⎪ ⎪ guide th e

Srini Pillay? In this heartfelt book Srini uses his own experience and insights as a physician, psychiatrist, counsellor and musician to profoundly speak to the way we live our lives and narrate a way of being that will bring all of us to use our 'beautiful brain'. A must-read for anyone determined to be inspiring, reflective and dynamic."
— Lynda Gratton, Professor of Management Practice, London Business School

"I highly recommend this book to anyone looking to accomplish more by doing less. It shows why relentless focus and a cultish adherence to overwork are counter-productive. And it explains how innovation and insight are more in our control than we might think. Read *Think Less* to strengthen both your ability and your resolve to slack off, strategically."
— Christine Carter, PhD, author of *The Sweet Spot*

"Dr. Srini Pillay's new book will help you create a new, fun, more playful destiny and unlock your brain's inner potential."
— Daniel G. Amen, co-author of *The Brain Warrior's Way*

"The story of how the brain takes the 'ingredients' of our lives – smells, sounds, experiences, memories – and spins them into new ideas, innovations, and creative inspirations is one of the most fascinating narratives I have read in some time. This book leaves me in awe of all that quietly goes on between our ears."
— John Assaraf, author of *Having It All* and chairman and CEO of NeuroGym

"This brilliant book shows how to harness a hidden neurological process that taps into your creativity, reducing stress while simultaneously boosting your productivity at work. When you learn how to manipulate your brain to alternate between intense concentration and deliberate mind-wandering you'll solve problems more quickly and experience more satisfaction in life."
— Mark Robert Waldman, co-author of *How God Changes Your Brain*

"Srini Pillay describes important strategies for purposeful focusing and, conversely, 'unfocusing' of our minds to improve resourcefulness, creativity, optimism, and mental well-being. As a lifelong business and social entrepreneur and survivor of a recent brain injury, I can attest to the great value of these practices."
— David Shaw, biotech entrepreneur and founder of Idexx

think
less

learn
more

unlock the power of the unfocused mind

DR SRINI PILLAY

First published in the United States with the
title *Tinker Dabble Doodle Try* by Ballantine Books,
an imprint of Random House, a division of Penguin
Random House LLC, New York.

Published in the United Kingdom in 2017 by Short Books,
Unit 316, ScreenWorks, 22 Highbury Grove,London, N5 2ER

Published by arrangement with Ballantine Books,
an imprint of Random House, a division of
Penguin Random House LLC. All rights reserved.

This is a work of nonfiction. Some names and identifying
details have been changed.

10 9 8 7 6 5 4 3 2 1

A CIP catalogue record for this book is available from the British Library.

ISBN: 978-1-78072-314-3

Cover design by asmithcompany.co.uk

Printed at CPI Group (UK) Ltd, Croydon, CR0 4YY

This book is dedicated to all of those people in the world who dare to tap into their ingenuity and brilliance – and to those who defy the naysayers to explore their greatest and most heartfelt possibilities.

CONTENTS

Introduction

LEAVING THE CULT OF FOCUS

"...For oft, when on my couch I lie
In vacant or in pensive mood,
They flash upon that inward eye
Which is the bliss of solitude;
And then my heart with pleasure fills,
And dances with the daffodils..."
William Wordsworth
"I Wandered Lonely as a Cloud"

One Friday night in 1983, a man and his girlfriend were driving down California Highway 128 from Berkeley to Mendocino where he was building a cabin in the woods. It was late at night, it was a long drive, and he was feeling a little tired and spacey. As his girlfriend dozed in the passenger seat, the man's mind wandered back to his work, in his case research on DNA.

As he put it, "My little silver Honda's front tyres pulled us through the mountains. My hands felt the road and the turns. My mind drifted back into the laboratory. DNA chains coiled and floated. Lurid blue and pink images of electric molecules injected themselves somewhere between the mountain road and my eyes."

Like an enthusiastic puppy just unleashed, his thoughts darted to and fro, mulling, comparing and connecting fragments of information. Suddenly, something new fell into place for him. He pulled off to the side of the road—mile marker 46.58 to be exact, he found himself noticing—and began to connect the dots of his thoughts. Science would never be the same again.

That man was Dr. Kary Banks Mullis—a biochemist who ten years later would win the Nobel Prize for chemistry for his invention of the polymerase chain reaction, also known as PCR. A way of making synthetic DNA, this has proven crucial in a wide range of disciplines, from obstetrics to forensics. It was on that restless, late-night journey that his mind collected ideas and put them together in new and strange ways. Later he would sort and hone what his wandering mind had pooled before him. The magic of that process—both the collecting and the sorting—is the stuff of this book.

As a physician, psychiatrist and executive coach, I am privy to people's hope for change and their yearning for change strategies. In every consultation—whether in a boardroom or on the therapeutic couch, whether about work-flow and workplace efficiency, leadership, learning, parenting, marriage, or trying to lose weight—everyone wants to figure out how to get over a hurdle, reach their goals and get ahead. Most people I talk to are convinced that more focus—maybe in the form of better organisation, more detailed plans or even getting an advanced degree—will be the solution to their issues. They use focusing tools—timetables, to-do lists, calendar reminders and noise-blocking headphones—though they often come to see that these technologies don't actually move the needle on the quality of their lives or productivity in quite the way they were hyped.

Some have read about meditation and mindfulness and how very healthy and productivity-inducing the development of these kinds of here-and-now "mental muscles" can be. They try to fit them into their daily lives, although not always successfully. Others come to me with the vague sense that they have distractibility, procrastination, attention deficit hyperactivity disorder (ADHD) or follow-through issues. Many even hope I'll make a formal diagnosis and prescribe medication to keep them on task. These people believe that their inability to focus and stay focused is what is getting in the way.

Often focus appears to be exactly what's needed (though medication is far too overused). Indeed, focus can be a tremendous change agent. It keeps you on target until a job is done, allowing you to coordinate your thinking, emotions and movement to execute and finish a job. Kids need it in quantity to sit through a traditional school day's worth of instruction. Leaders need it to unify people around a mission or objective. Businesses need it to build and grow their market share. Try to thread a needle or follow a recipe or build "some assembly required" furniture without it.

In the long run, focus can selectively—and often profitably—hone your interests. Except for polymath geniuses like Michelangelo (I have to pause to ask: would someone like him be medicated today?), having a wide range of interests may make you a jack-of-all-trades, but master of none. Focused specialisation gives you greater depth of understanding, insight, practice and experience. Over time, it gives you confidence in your abilities, and gives others confidence in you as well. If you had to have a heart bypass, wouldn't you choose the surgeon who has performed the specific surgery 1,000 times, rather than one who has performed 300 bypass-es, 300 gut resections and 400 brain surgeries? In the business realm, the company that focuses on one specific market need is often the company that meets the need best.

Neurologically, focusing plays an essential role in keeping information online in your brain, a process that has far-ranging—almost unquantifiable—value. While you are completing a task, your brain is busy relaying and conveying information to your short-term memo-ry, which is housed in a region called the dorsolateral prefrontal cortex (DLPFC). I like to call this region the "memory cup", because it collects information that you will need to access as you are completing a task. Focus is one of the key determinants (along with emotion and intuition) of what gets deemed relevant, which, in turn, can make you better/faster/smoother/smarter at that task in the future.

For all its "clear" benefits, however, I believe that too many of us have (unwittingly) bought into the idea of what I call the cult of focus: led to believe that focus is the capability above all capabilities, the core competency to strive for. In truth, focus, in isolation, will actually work against and disempower you.

Think of it this way: focus is your brain's flashlight. When you need to pay attention to something specific, a bright, narrow beam of light cast straight out in front of you is terrifically helpful. But what about your peripheral vision? Often you need to be aware of something important in the areas around that narrow beam. But a focused mind doesn't work like that. In the extreme, focus begets a kind of "blinker vision", which psychologists call inattentional blindness, a syndrome wherein you are blind to some things because you simply cannot pay attention to everything; your brain makes a choice about what to focus on, sometimes to your detriment.

For instance, in 1995, a police officer in Boston ran right past someone being viciously beaten while he was chasing a suspect in another crime. The officer claimed not to have seen the assault but jurors didn't believe he could possibly have been so blinkered—they convicted him of perjury and obstruction of justice and he was sentenced to more than two years in jail, plus a fine.

Interested in the possibility that the officer might have been experiencing inattentional blindness—in this case a kind of focus overload due to his zeal to catch a suspect—researchers simulated the scene and found that many test subjects would have missed the violence in their peripheral vision, too: at night only 35 per cent of experimental subjects noticed the fight; during the day 56 per cent noticed it.

A more fun example of how focus can compromise your ability to take in relevant information is brought to life through what's known as the invisible gorilla experiment. Look up "invisible gorilla" online and you can experience it yourself.

Studying the concept of "selective attention", researchers asked viewers to count how many times a group of people wearing white shirts on screen pass a basketball (there was also a team wearing black). You would be forgiven—and not at all unique—if you failed to notice a person in a gorilla suit walk right through the basketball drill. Focusing on the white shirts and on counting the passes preoccupies most people so much that they too miss seeing a man in a gorilla suit on the screen.

If focus makes you miss seeing a gorilla, what else are you missing in life?

Perhaps you are concentrating so hard on developing your company that you neglect to see the competition gathering momentum in the proverbial wings. Or you are so in love with someone that you don't notice changes in their behaviour until they break up with you. Or, if you are a psychiatrist, you may be so consumed with uncovering the emotional root of your patient's anxiety that you may neglect to investigate whether adrenal problems are causing it. As the saying goes, to the guy with a hammer (or medical speciality), everything looks like a nail (or biased diagnosis).

Related to blinker vision and selective attention, there is the issue of too much focus, or hyper-focus. Hyper-focus can make you miss out on what truly matters to you. You may, for example, become so absorbed in your academic pursuits that you "forget" to socialise or date through college and then find it difficult to meet potential life partners. This is something that I see a lot as a therapist. There's a scientific name for this too—it's called long-term discounting; it's your brain's tendency to minimise the importance of things in the future because they are too far off. Many studies now show us that this is the brain's default. In my opinion, it is one of the biggest reasons we come to regret things—not being able to shift into and out of the long-view as much as we need to.

Another consequence of hyper-focus is what psychologists refer to as a loss of caring. In one study of this phenomenon, subjects were asked to focus intently while watching a video of a woman talking. They were asked to ignore the bottom corner of the screen where words appeared every ten seconds and, if they were distracted, to quickly start watching the woman again. Others watched the video normally and more casually (no instruction not to look at the words). Later, after the viewing, all the subjects were asked to volunteer to help victims of a recent tragedy. Researchers found that those in the hyper-focused group were less likely to volunteer. Why were focused people less generous with their help?

When we hyper-focus, it depletes the brain's prefrontal cortex (PFC), which helps us make moral decisions. In other words, hyper-focus can drain your brain of the resources needed to balance your own tiredness with helping others.

Then there are ways that focus may stymie innovation. In an article in *Harvard Business Review*, business professor Rosabeth Moss Kanter pointed to some of the problems associated with limiting the scope of innovation or staying too focused. For example, she pointed out that the Gillette Company had a toothbrush unit (Oral B), an appliance unit (Braun), and a battery unit (Duracell) but failed to make a battery-powered toothbrush. Each division stayed too focused on its own products and practices. And yet our brains are wired to make these connections if we allow them to map similarities across apparently unrelated domains.

So how, exactly, do we do this? What's the sweet spot between focus that galvanises and focus that calcifies or exhausts your thinking? How do you achieve a workable balance between a "zoomed-in" perspective and a more panoramic view of the world? The answer lies in developing the capacity for what I call unfocus.

When I raise the idea of unfocus to clients and patients I often automatically get a little push-back: they think it means they should relax their standards or flit around aimlessly. They don't want to become (or continue to be) dilettantes; they want to be producers and problem-solvers. And in order to fulfil this desire, they feel that they have to think more and try harder. They prize grit, determination and perseverance above all. The mere mention of thinking "less" sounds lazy, unproductive and too "restful". At its best, it simply sounds like taking a break.

In this context, unfocus sounds like a negative. But disregard semantics for a moment and come back to the metaphor of a flashlight. Focus and unfocus are two different settings. Focus is the close and narrow beam that illuminates the path directly ahead. Unfocus is the beam that reaches far and wide, enabling your peripheral vision. Either beam in isolation is helpful only up to a point. Combining these settings will keep your battery charged the longest.

Many important discoveries have come from what appear to be unfocused career trajectories. If, for example, you wanted to emulate Dr. Mullis's path through life leading to his discovery, you might expect that, logically, you would need to do well enough at school to obtain a PhD in biochemistry, and then systematically approach the question of DNA duplication. Yet there is little in Dr. Mullis's history to suggest that this was how he arrived at his eureka moment. If anything, the journey to his goal was marked by deviations from the straight and narrow.

After obtaining his PhD, he left science to write fiction. Following that, he became a biochemist. Then he left to manage a bakery for two years. When he returned to science, he was anything but focused. Earlier in his life, he tried to make rockets before he made DNA.

Much of his life has been an emotional rollercoaster. He is currently on his fourth marriage. These are the parts of the story that we leave out, yet they are probably as important to his insights and intellectual development as his actual work in biochemistry. You couldn't mimic this. But in you, there is an unfocused story waiting to be told if it has not been told already.

Every experience contributes to your brain development. Deviations from the straight and narrow path can offer unanticipated insights, different perspectives on the same issue, and build the character you need to gain the fortitude to pursue your passions. There's no saying what would have happened if Dr. Mullis had become a biochemist sooner, stuck with his first marriage and never worked in a bakery. But there are few, if any, successful people who have such linear paths to their goals even if it seems that way in retrospect.

Nor may such a focused career path even be desirable. As London Business School professor Lynda Gratton points out in her book *The 100-Year Life*, in this age of longevity, we have to rethink how we build our lives. Focus may be a quick and dirty way to make sense of how people get to their goals. But in many cases, it is a powerful and persuasive fiction.

Learning to unfocus and focus will make you more effective, productive and nimble as a thinker and problem-solver. Getting into a new and conscious rhythm with them both is the key to the creativity, ingenuity or general happiness you seek. Indeed, one of the ironic byproducts of learning to unfocus is that doing so will sharpen your focus when you need it. And that's because they are two sides of the same mental coin. (By the way, if you've come to this book seeking validation for already being quite unfocused—perhaps it's the very thing people criticise you for the most—it'll likely be music to your ears that unfocus is a valuable skill. The key for you will be to learn to hone and harness it instead of letting it run quite so rampant in your life.)

Consider an orchestra. Each member has to practise (focus) to master his own individual part. But at concert time, orchestra members must be able to blend their expertise and sound into the greater whole (unfocus). They have to focus just enough to perform their music and keep track of the score, while also being unfocused enough to interact with and hear the other musicians (not to mention keep an intermittent eye on the conductor). Letting go of tight focus and melding your sound with others around you is indeed a skill.

So it is in sports. To be a great tennis player, for example (and assuming a good level of fitness), you need to practise a number of specific, focused skills: how to grip the racket for each kind of shot and where to follow through; the position of your feet in relation to your body; how high to toss the ball up when serving; how much power to put behind your strokes in order to place the ball where you want it to go. And you have to play the game repeatedly to develop a sense for ball placement in the first place. It takes hours and hours of focused practice to programme this, but all those hours of focus create a blueprint in your brain and if you trust it, at match time you simply need to watch the ball and let your body do what it has learned to do. This is you allowing unfocus to take over. And it's in that state of mind that your body will carry out the many tiny adjustments you will need to get the ball where it should go without you having to actively think them all through.

In the basest and broadest sense, unfocusing is the process of relaxing your brain so that it can be ready, recharged, coordinated and innovative when you need it to be. This isn't wishful thinking; its proven neurology. Unfocusing reduces amygdala activation and creates calmness. It activates the frontopolar cortex and enhances innovation. It increases anterior insula activity and strengthens a sense of self. It limits the grip of the part of the brain called the precuneus, the "observing ego" that makes you self-conscious (this, essentially, is the getting-out-of-your-own-way ability I'm talking about for the violinist or tennis player). It restores prefrontal cortex activity so that we can become re-energised in our thinking and have less burnout. It improves long-term memory and retrieval of relevant experience. And perhaps its most consistent and profound effect is that it increases activity in the default mode network (DMN)—a collection of brain regions that are active during rest and usually deactivate during focused tasks. We will also call the DMN the "unfocus network", although it is vitally important for focus too—if, for example, this network did not deactivate during focused tasks, it would interrupt your ability to focus.

This, tragically, is what happens in diseases like

Alzheimer's disease. Patients with this disease have a DMN that is not synchronised—its various components metaphorically shoot randomly in the dark. Reduced connectivity in the unfocus network has also been linked to problems in thinking in several other neurological and psychiatric disorders including autism, frontotemporal dementia, multiple sclerosis and vegetative states when people have severe brain damage and can be partially aroused but not aware. Studies indicate that if you build cognitive reserve by training your brain with *both* focused and unfocused activities, you have a backup should something go wrong. Simply put: unfocus can protect your thinking brain over the course of your life. And if you change your lifestyle and train your brain so that unfocus serves you, you are likely to see the changes sooner than you think.

In my opinion, there is nothing—absolutely nothing—more beautiful than the brain in action shifting between focus and unfocus. And in unfocus, when you're thinking less, the brain is more dynamic and active than ever. In fact, it consumes huge amounts of energy continuously, whether you're diligently balancing your budget or surfing the internet.

Brain scanners can photographically capture the flow of blood to and between engaged circuits and brain regions, the sure sign that the billions of neurons are working extra-hard. Think of neurons as modern dancers—moving around and coming together in unexpected ways, pushing off one another, and changing directions suddenly. Instead of just two arms and two legs, however, these lithe and shapely dancers have millions of limbs, exponentially multiplying the ways in which they can connect and interact. With each new thought or action, a burst of electricity more dazzling than the most extravagant fireworks display is discharged. And with this discharge, information is mobilised and transported across your brain circuits. The shifts in blood flow light up the images like a sparkly, starry night. The picture is utterly mesmerising.

Arranged largely by function, some brain circuits *perceive* information, others *retrieve* it, and still others *conceive* of what might be. Yet, separate though these functions may be, they come together when you are thinking—being creative, learning, doing many things at once, or problem-solving. These functions make the neuronal "arms" and "legs" reach out and intertwine with one another in acts of agile grace. Sometimes the dancers in your brain take turns to carry out their functions, conserving energy and relying on one another. Each new moment of sensing, responding and acting changes neuronal communications and connection, the choreography.

Whether you are focused (studying for a test) or unfocused (daydreaming or imagining how you would like to be graded) the rhythm of focus and unfocus determines how, where and when the dancers in your brain will rise or fall, rest or run, connect or pull away. And focus/unfocus determines which set of neurons will take centre stage.

In this mystical and magical brain dance, logic finds a home. Here you learn how to bake bread, deal with a lover's rejection, pursue an interest that has captured your imagination, believe in God, or build the business of your dreams. Mysteriously, we don't know how these processes are coordinated, but the brain has some control over the shunting of blood to and from different regions; in the end, *you* are the choreographer.

When you learn to switch back and forth from focus to unfocus, something profound will change in how you manage stress and risk and in how you understand life. You will find formidable parts of yourself that you never knew you had. You will even stop hating your unfocused mind. Learning how to do this will require you to be *purposeful* and *skilled* in how you unfocus and how you include it in your daily activities. You may already be doing it accidentally—stumbling upon a creative idea, perhaps when you don't mean to—but this book will teach you how to actively control or at least steer the process.

When people have tried out even a few of these methods in workshops, or in my private therapy and coaching practice, they often suddenly feel relieved, or they have the kind of ah-ha moment I mention above. There is hardly a single person in the world whose mind has not once in a while found itself floating out through a window in the middle of a day—if you knew how to harness this tendency for something positive, wouldn't it be amazing? Ah-ha indeed!

THE BEAT OF YOUR BRAIN

"Thought is the labour of the intellect, reverie its pleasure. To replace thought with reverie is to confound poison with nourishment."

Victor Hugo

In the years prior to my second year at medical school, I was an excellent student. During that year, however, in the context of an escalating workload, my grades suddenly slumped.

Even though I burned the midnight oil, I wasn't able to make headway. I sat for hours studying human anatomy, trying to memorise where muscles attached, and where in the body nerves and blood vessels travelled.

On more than one occasion, I ran myself ragged, only to wake up with my head buried in a pile of bones.

Nobody could have spent more time than I did studying and working, yet the harder I focused, the worse I seemed to do. Little did I know that I was operating my brain like a teenager driving a car for the first time, taking off at breakneck speed, then jerkily screeching to an abrupt halt. The result: too much wear and tear on the brake pads and gears!

I struggled to wrap my head around what was happening. And I didn't register that I was physically exhausted until the penny eventually dropped during the vacation between my second and third years. That's when I decided to make a few changes.

I was desperate and determined to start working smarter instead of just harder. I saw my failings as a code I had to crack, so I started to change my habits and lifestyle. Even though it went against my work ethic I took short breaks every 45 minutes while studying. I made an effort to spend more time away from work and with my friends. I committed to ensuring that I got enough sleep before any big stretches of studying I planned to do. And because I had always heard such great things about the restorative power of it, I started to meditate for 20 minutes, twice a day.

My grades improved. My energy levels rose. Eventually, I was at the top of my class again.

Looking back, I can see I was none the wiser about how exactly my lifestyle hacks had worked but I was certainly happy with the results, so I strove to include these strategies throughout the rest of medical school, with great results.

But I didn't really learn the lesson I should have from that episode. During my subsequent residency in psychiatry, I started off with a bang, burning the proverbial oil anew. Eager to immerse myself in my cases, I spent hours with patients in the hospital. And when I got home, I threw off my work clothes, ate my dinner, and started reading books and psychiatric journals voraciously. After my first clinical rotation, I looked forward to my feedback session with my supervisor. But the meeting went very differently to how I had expected.

"You are a really dedicated doctor," he said. "It must be a little frustrating that your knowledge base is far more developed than your peers'. You probably can't have the conversations that you want to, right?" I didn't really feel that way, but I thought I heard positive feedback and took it gladly. Then came a comment that I will never forget for the rest of my life.

"We're a little concerned that you spend so much time on the inpatient units. If you keep this up, I'm afraid you'll have a ton of information in your head but you won't receive a superior education. I presume that's why you wanted to come to Harvard in the first place?"

The question was ironic and chilling, to say the least. I realised I had gone back to my old bad habits. I was living my life trapped by the wrong assumptions about ambition, exhausting myself both physically and mentally all over again.

My supervisor continued to explain that taking breaks to allow thoughts to congeal was one of the most important aspects of a true education. He prescribed walking through the woods in the middle of the day, spending more time on the park benches with my colleagues, and even going into therapy to see if I could develop insights that could help me unpack my day.

Now, having studied how our brains manage focus and unfocus, I understand what my supervisor already knew: there was no nuance to what I call my *cognitive rhythm.*

When you think of great rhythm, you likely think first of music, say Michael Jackson, or Elvis Presley's dancing, or you conjure the amazing riffs of guitarists like Jimi Hendrix, Kurt Cobain or Keith Richards. In all of those instances, there is a run of notes or movement that repeats with regularity—a defining beat with "on" and "off" moments. Play "Voodoo Child", "Come as You Are" or "Jumpin' Jack Flash", and you'll connect instantly with their extraordinary rhythm.

But rhythm is not only a musical concept. It's essential in your body as well. Your heart has to expand and contract on time. You have to breathe in and out with great regularity. Then there is the circadian rhythm of sleep-wake cycles; while cognitive rhythm is the ability to intermingle focus and unfocus (the "on" and "off" moments) in the most effective way.

On any given day, you have to be prepared for and respond accordingly to the tumult of life: the constant starting, stopping, negotiating of "bumps" and changing direction. As I discovered in medical school, if the only tool that you have in your thinking toolkit is focus, you will quickly become fatigued. Your brain will shut down prematurely. That's far from optimal. It's better if you learn to proactively wind down your focus at times, to prevent the brain from crashing. Furthermore, even though you aren't aware of it, studies show that close to half of your day is spent in mini-mental journeys away from the task at hand. In other words, even when you are concentrating wholly on one task, it is impossible to remain 100 per cent focused; your mind needs downtime.

Like the difference between a light bulb blowing a fuse and dimming the lights to save energy, there's a huge difference between running out of power and putting your brain on one of its dimmer modes. In the latter case, you can metaphorically turn the light back on to bright again when you need or want it. In the former, you're finished for the time being!

Surfing Your Brainwaves

Although a brain cell's resting voltage is less than that of an AA battery, when electricity passes across the cell membrane, it generates a massive force—about 14 million volts per metre, more than four times the force required to produce lightning during a thunderstorm. Multiply that by 100 billion brain cells and that's the magnitude of your brainpower! It's impressive to say the least.

From the moment of birth, your brain is generating these electrical impulses across its complex landscape.

The impulses occur as waves, and every thought, feeling and behaviour corresponds with a different combination of waves in your brain. Attention is no exception. It's useful to think of the waves of attention as different musical notes—a combination of the low-pitched notes of a trombone, the high-pitched notes of a flute and everything in between. Even at baseline, your brain's attention fluctuates, aiming for a harmony between these different notes with astounding speed, power and accuracy. These "notes" can be detected with an EEG (electroencephalogram), in much the same way that the heart's rhythm can be captured with an ECG (electrocardiogram). When we observe all the waves that people can generate, we see them on a continuum from more to less frequent—in effect, faster to slower.

Beta waves are your "focus" waves. They would show up on an EEG when your eyes are glued to a task. Following beta, going down the "musical scale", you have alpha, theta and delta waves, each respectively slower than the last, generated during different states of unfocus from relaxation to meditation and deep sleep. Gamma waves are the odd ones out. They are faster than beta waves but come on both when you're focused *and* unfocused, indicating that focus and unfocus are not as separate in the brain as we might think they are.

Each of these brainwave "settings" correlates with different brain functions. Being a peak performer at anything—a parent, teacher, CEO, chess player, researcher—requires knowing when and how to switch between the different settings. And most importantly, it requires understanding that these waves work together to create the best brain states to perform the task at hand.

Your Circuits in Sync

There are those people who have astounding lucidity. They impress us with their seemingly tireless productivity and their clarity of mind. Georg Philipp Telemann, for example, composed 200 overtures in a two-year period, and Benjamin Franklin invented the lightning rod, a flexible catheter, bifocal eyeglasses and umpteen other things. These are the masters of the frontoparietal circuit, or what I call the focus circuit. Always on task, they have focus *on demand.*

Part of a larger "central executive network" (CEN), the focus circuit keeps you on task even when you are not as extreme as Telemann or Franklin. Whether you are following a recipe or complex procedure, filling out your tax forms, or listening carefully to your GPS as you make your way through unknown territory, your focus networks are like a flashlight, always lighting up the path just ahead.

Yet this faculty by itself is woefully insufficient, and, on its own, razor-sharp clarity can feel shallow. It's like a piano player playing all the right notes, without "heart". To be sure, if you have ever played or heard the music of Telemann, you would know that he relies on much more than "focus" to create his music. In so many areas of life, we see this shallowness manifest in those who, unlike Telemann, *only* stick to focus: the bureaucratic boss, the one-dimensional bottom-liner, the workhorse colleague whose reports are precise, yet lack depth—these are the people whose pronouncements are clear, yet leave you wanting more nuance. To extend the GPS metaphor—you want to know what awaits you further along your trip. You want to at least know the mid-term future, or be able to anticipate your next hour, rather than only focus on the immediate road ahead.

Nuance and depth require diffusing the beam of the focus flashlight so that you can see important objects and details in your periphery as well. There is a brain circuit that allows for this broadening of vision: the default mode network (DMN) or what I call the unfocus circuit. Before science understood its true function, the DMN was thought of as the "Do Mostly Nothing" circuit.

But over time, we have come to see that the DMN is one of the greatest consumers of energy in the brain, and it is extensively connected with the focus circuits so there is a kind of brainwave overflow and integration. Focus and unfocus are like a good bolognese: it's hard to tell if the meat is flavouring the sauce or if the sauce is flavouring the meat. They simply work together.

In the brain, a mix of brainwaves enters and leaves each circuit with a preponderance of one type of wave for any particular function. For instance, at the peak of unfocus, you might see the slower alpha waves in the

DMN, but they are not the only type of wave you see. You might also find other slow waves like delta waves in certain unfocus regions, and they may be mixed with the faster beta waves too, because focus and unfocus circuits are constantly "talking" to each other in the brain. Similarly, you may find more beta than delta waves in the focus circuit, to orient your focused attention. But it's rarely just one type of wave alone. Which is why talking about focused and unfocused circuits is a false dichotomy. They are both acting at the same time and designed to work together. It's we who stop this natural connection in our brains when we overfocus.

Take musicians, for example. When singers like Adele, Ed Sheeran or Sam Smith pull at your heartstrings, they are not just focusing on the lyrics and music. They are also connecting to an emotional memory, internally accessing past experiences of sadness, betrayal, joy or whatever they are singing about. When they do this, you feel connected to them, and you feel free to superimpose your own memories on the song too. Unfocus circuits bring on this rich complexity and authenticity. What's more, they can be nurtured and trained.

Fritz Reiner, born in Hungary in 1888, is known as one of the greatest conductors of all time. Many attribute the world-class ascent of the Chicago Symphony Orchestra (CSO) to his leadership. And it must have been entertaining to watch him at work: using his entire body, Reiner would usher in the strings with his hands, then puff out his cheeks when it was the brass section's turn, and when a section had to stop to his right while he was looking left, he would kick out a foot. As a testament to how great the CSO was under his direction, after a performance in Boston, Arthur Fiedler, the conductor of the Boston Symphony Orchestra, said to the CSO, "You're not men. You're gods."

As amazing a conductor as Reiner was, by most reports he was also tyrannical. He did not tolerate imperfections, and when he was rehearsing with the orchestra, nobody was allowed to be a slacker. When you were playing for Reiner, you had to play perfectly. You had to attend to all of him. One slip, and you were in trouble. And when you were silent, you had to listen without distraction.

A musician playing for Reiner or any exacting conductor, as you can imagine, faces the cognitive challenge of being internally connected enough to play deeply from the heart, while simultaneously being exquisitely sensitive to what the others are playing and what the conductor is asking of him or her. A musician who becomes lost in the playing risks missing cues and really hearing what others are playing. A musician who focuses too intently on what others are doing or on what the conductor is prompting is likely to play with less heart and emotion.

Somehow the brain has to manage the delicate balance between focus and unfocus.

But in our day-to-day lives, we sometimes forget this, and we might behave like a musician who is only paying attention to Reiner and not the other musicians: we might be so absorbed in a task, that we notice nothing else.

It's this same challenge that leaders, parents and team-sports players face as well—to be "in the zone", yet also to be aware of one's surroundings—to remember to focus and unfocus as well.

The Many Notes of Your Default Mode Network

When you understand the quality and extent of the DMN's connections in the brain, the cooperation of focus and unfocus becomes more apparent.

• *The DMN acts as a distraction filter:* paradoxically, unfocus circuits play an active and crucial role in keeping you focused; they act almost like sponges, absorbing distractions to keep you on a short-term task.

• *It builds mental flexibility:* unfocus circuits also act as a pivot, helping you switch your attention from one task to the next. Engage your unfocus circuits enough and your thinking becomes very flexible indeed.

• *It connects you more deeply with yourself and others:* unfocus circuits connect you with elements of your own story, stored in different parts of your

---

brain. They are the chief writers of your autobiography. Your personal traits and self-reflections can all become part of the moment because your unfocus circuits can activate them at the same time. Unfocus circuits reach far back into your stored memories, letting your history inform every moment of focus. In this sense, they transport you towards yourself.

Deep unfocus activates "social connection" circuits too. That's why leadership development coaches will tell you that the quintessential quality of being a leader is becoming yourself. It's why vocal coaches will tell you to find your own voice. And why any great educator will encourage you to discover your originality. Deep self-connection connects your brain to things far and wide beyond the moment and yourself.

• *It integrates the past, present and future:* past, present and future are all "happening" now in your brain. The "past" is stored as memories. The present is experienced through your five senses. And the future is represented by planning and imagination. Your DMN can bring them all together, and help you comprehend the story that is unfolding. It connects the dots on the timeline of your life.

• *It helps you express your unique self:* because unfocus circuits bridge such vast areas of your brain, they can also help you develop unique associations and originality. With this, you can also be more spontaneous.

• *It helps you dredge up intangible memories:* the DMN can also help you integrate memories that lie outside of the line of focus. Consider the experienced cook whose meals are inexplicably delicious because they embody more than just following a recipe to the letter. The chef who as a child watched her grandmother cook has taken in something that no book could ever teach. It may have to do with the rhythm of stirring the sauce—or the precise finger movements when sprinkling the cheese on the casserole or quesadilla. These are the kinds of emotions that the DMN can dredge up.

A case in point is my favourite Italian meatball recipe. Enter "Anthony's meatballs" into an online search and you'll see for yourself that it calls on a number of intangibles in the creation process. In addition to the ingredients list and the actual step-by-step instruction to measure, mix and cook, it includes the direction to put on some "Italian background music" to set the right mood. The result is a magically and exponentially more delicious dinner than a more literal recipe will yield.

Your Rhythm Busters

As helpful as unfocusing—or tapping into your DMN—will be to your brain and your life, there are systems and defaults already built into your life that may challenge the balance of your cognitive rhythm. Beware of these rhythm busters, and use them as signals to press your brain's "reset" button—a skill you will learn how to hone throughout this book.

Habits

Your brain likes to maintain the status quo—it's most comfortable cruising along in habitual, familiar behaviour. Trying to make a meaningful habit or attitudinal change causes a kind of stress in your mind or "cognitive dissonance", which is visible on brain scans. Your brain is trying to reconcile two things here: you want to change, but you can't change without psychological discomfort.

Take, for instance, the habit of focus itself. Although all the brain biology research points to the value of unfocus, if you're used to focusing for productivity your brain will reject or avoid making a change; unfocusing just doesn't compute to your rational, focus-habit brain.

Even after you start a few unfocus practices, your brain's default response will be to go back to what it was doing, to continue your habitual behaviour. That's what will settle it down. You have to recognise that there is a price you will be paying for change, and you have to be willing to pay it. It's called switch cost.

Switch cost comes in the form of fear, uncertainty and lack of familiarity. Your brain doesn't like these things; they are "expensive". You have to be certain that re-energising your brain is worth it to you, and convince your brain that your current structure in life is not working, as I eventually did when I changed my study habits.

One alternative is to stay stuck where you are (alternative A)—a shop-till-you-drop kind of mentality at Christmas, for example. The other is to change (alternative B)—to take a lunch or coffee break, or to spread your shopping out over several days instead. The more obvious the advantages of B over A, the more your brain is likely to comply. Also called "spreading of alternatives" (SOA), this obvious difference between A and B needs to be spelled out. When it is, SOA resolves cognitive dissonance. You can even see this resolution on brain scans. Blood flows away from the conflict centre and back to regions that will help you complete your daily tasks.

Uncertainty

Uncertainty is generally a negative to your brain; not just in itself, but because it also biases you to believe that the sky is falling.

When you're uncertain, all goals look like moving targets. Panicked, you may revert to focus, in the hope that you can detect the dangers coming your way, and hit the targets as you need to. But there's more to uncertainty than meets the eye.

In 2010, radiology professor Issidoros Sarinopoulos and colleagues examined how uncertainty affects your brain. In this experiment, people were shown emotional expressions—some neutral and some frightening. Just before the neutral pictures, they were shown an "O", and just before the negative pictures they were shown an "X". However, there were also trials in which they did not know what to expect and were shown a "?" When people saw the "?", they were more freaked out than when they saw the "X". Then everyone was asked, "What do you think the next face is going to be?" The people in the "?" group were completely off target. Seventy-five per cent of them said it was going to be threatening when it was not. Their uncertain brains simply kept expecting the worst. In these people, their conflict (anterior cingulate cortex) and disgust (insula) centres were in overdrive.

Bottom line—being uncertain shakes up your brain and skews the way you see the world. But once you recognise this, you will see that uncertainty's bark is worse than its bite. Unfocusing to correct this bias should be the first step in the order of things.

Focus addiction

Sometimes, focus casts a magic spell because you can just get so much done when you're in that zone. Plus, to come full circle to the idea of habits and avoiding cognitive dissonance, it's sometimes just a whole lot more psychologically comfortable to get through your day the way you always have and the only way you know how: through focus. But while it's desirable to have things go smoothly, you need to make sure you don't "flat-line" your way through life.

Instead, recognise that focus can impact your brain in much the same way as any addiction would. You'll get exhausted, have a one-track mind, feel depleted, and not be able to think clearly either. When you unfocus, on the other hand, your brain has time to recover and you can go back to focusing, rejuvenated and refreshed.

Focus relapses

Imagine you've just come back from a really restful, rejuvenating, mentally unfocused vacation. But now you face a huge pile of work and the associated stress about getting it all done. So you relapse into hyper-focus, relying on your pre-vacation habit of getting up early, working late, and not taking a lunch break.

This kind of U-turn into focus is common, and it's often very helpful (you'll certainly catch up on the work that's piled up). But after the necessary focused binge, you're depleted all over again. What good was the vacation?

Rather, even when you get back into the saddle, remember to unfocus as well as focus. That will take you to the finish line, and not exhaust you in the process.

Early Signs of a Jammed-Up Brain

Nobody stays in a healthy cognitive rhythm all the time. Like the rude awakening I had when my grades and energy dropped precipitously in medical school and again when my advisor pointed out my narrow-mindedness at the beginning of my residency, you eventually know when you have been operating completely out of rhythm. But if you know the early signs of a jammed-up brain, you can self-correct *before* you get totally off track.

- *Not having as much energy as you used to:* if you're feeling more drained than usual, you may be starting to lose your cognitive rhythm, and if you've had this thought for a few days in a month, then it might be time to see how you're utilising your day.

- *Not closing the deal:* there are a lot of people who work hard to get what they want, but they either choke or just can't close the deal. From the tennis player who surrenders several match points, to the negotiator who makes it to the final round but then can't bring about a settlement, or a politician whose campaign loses steam (and followers), closing the deal requires energy right to the end. You can't do this when you are on your last breath. If life starts to feel like you are repeatedly one number short of winning the lottery, it may be time to do a rhythm check.

- *Repeated mistakes:* everybody makes mistakes and many mistakes are helpful if we can learn from them. But making the same mistakes over and over again isn't efficient. When there are one too many repeated mistakes in your life, it may be time to reset your brain's rhythm.

• *Feeling easily overwhelmed:* in our fast-paced technologically stimulating world, being over-whelmed in an "I've had a very taxing day and need to shut the world out tonight" way is un-derstandable. But if you find that you are easily or quickly or repeatedly overwhelmed, it's time to take stock of your life. Your brain is a beautiful or-gan that you can use to advance your life and the lives of those you care about. Don't feed it trash or expect it to run on the neurological equivalent of junk food.

Settling: when we are younger, we are filled with dreams, hopes and ambitions. But when we get older, they seem to fade away. This is so common that some would say that settling is a sign of ma-ture behaviour. At times it may be, but most of the time, settling is a sign of emotional fatigue. You are not able to take on another challenge because you don't have the brain rhythm that you need to do so. But unfocus can help your brain get back in rhythm.

The Many Roads to Unfocus

Think of how you feel when you lie in a hammock on a hot summer's day. With your eyes half closed and mind adrift, your brain has the time and ability to bring back long-forgotten memories. In that state it can become a "memory fetcher", giving you a valuable glimpse of the past so that you don't make the same mistake twice.

Or recall how you sometimes have epiphanies while standing in the shower. Here, you're not necessarily in some dreamy state—just in a different place. Your mind is off the tasks that previously occupied your attention. All of a sudden, eureka! You've got it. Something you've been trying to figure out all week suddenly becomes crystal clear.

In other unfocused states, you may simply be doing something less demanding like knitting or gardening. Here, you're neither half asleep nor in the "shower" frame of mind. You're cruising along on autopilot, getting stuff done. When you do, your brain gets a much-deserved rest, but it also brings the puzzle pieces of memory together to increase the accuracy of future predictions.

Lying in a hammock, showering, knitting or gardening are all things that you can do to unfocus and relax. But there are more formal, useful and possibly surprising ways that you can unfocus too. These are the different methods you will learn to use in context throughout this book. And when you do, you will see how thinking less will help you, over time, learn much more effectively.

Reverie

When you speak to another person about your own uncensored thoughts as they arise, thoughts about something fanciful, imaginary or hypothetical, you're engaging in reverie. Reverie is a form of unfocus used extensively as a technique in psychoanalysis, but you can use it in your everyday life too. More seriously and practically, engineers or entrepreneurs use a form of it when they invite others (colleagues, investors, followers) into their strategic thinking at an early and low-impact stage of invention. As a group, you're just "thinking out loud", but generating ideas together and incorporating them into a project at an early stage can lead to more support and "buy-in" from those involved when it's time to act.

The same principle applies when you are trying to make a change in your relationship or even move furniture around your house. The more you invite someone else into your thinking at an early stage, the more ideas you'll generate and the more likely the others will be to agree with the "outcome", especially if you incorporate some of their suggestions into your plan. In a relationship, where there is usually a whole lot more at stake, you can use reverie as a way to imagine a better or different future together without getting entrenched in your respective agendas and going off in two different directions. That's when people grow apart. In either scenario, you are using a collective unfocus to find solutions you might not have landed on if you had focused on your own.

Imagination

When you imagine something, you are effectively suspending disbelief about the reality of its possibility. This is unfocus writ large. Trading increasingly zany "what ifs" about the future or about how you would deal with a scenario is a playful form of using your imagination and is often called prospection. Regardless of what you call it, though, this kind of projecting into the future (imagining) has been shown to activate the DMN and will spill over into your ability to imagine new outcomes for old problems or situations. In my practice, people who are stuck—either in a relationship or in their businesses—tend to use "reality" to escape their traps, when imagination is often a far better way to discover solutions.

Daydreaming

Then there's the all-important tool of daydreaming. Of course, one person's ideal environment for daydreaming could be a disaster zone for someone else. You, for instance, might be able to switch into autopilot and go daydreaming while doing DIY. I, however, would struggle—I need every ounce of focus I can muster on such a task. But you can choose whatever activity you find conducive to daydreaming. What are you likely to be able to do with little effort—painting by numbers, or reorganising the closet? The key is that it must not be stressful or effortful for you.

Self-talk

In many strategies that I suggest, I will be recommending

that you talk to your brain. At first glance, this may seem slightly deranged since when most of us see people talking to themselves we are quick to think they've lost their marbles. But recent research increasingly points to the usefulness of self-talk, especially as a stress reducing strategy. Speaking in the second person (addressing yourself as "you" or by your name) is more effective than simply talking aloud in the first person. You've probably seen professional athletes engage in this: Serena Williams sometimes shouts "C'mon, Serena!" instead of just "C'mon!" Basketball great, LeBron James, is famous for speaking to himself like this, too. It may sound implausible at first, but if you can tell your brain to lift up your right hand, why shouldn't you be able to tell it to approach a situation differently? In fact, you can. And it works!

A huge body of scientific study also points to the value of reframing your thoughts to yourself, even silently. These reframes can range from the overt (e.g. reframing "I'm useless" to "I need to acquire certain skills") to more subtly shifting our self-narratives.

For example, asking yourself "Why does this always happen to me?" will probably send your brain on a wild-goose chase to find the answer to this question—not a good use of your unconscious time. But shifting the query to "How do people with my disadvantages overcome them to get to their goal?" is a much more useful question to pose to your conscious and unconscious brain.

As long as you frame things in the positive, you're in the black. But talking in the negative, telling yourself *not* to do something, will cause you to lose ground. Psychologist Daniel Wegner has studied this phenomenon, and found that under stress, your brain will do the exact opposite of what you want if you give yourself a "do not" instruction. So ditch the self-admonitions.

Using your body

You can use your body to activate cognitive rhythm. As with daydreaming, different activities will activate focus or unfocus for different people. One person may want to go for a hike on an unknown path to activate unfocus. Another person may want to go on a very familiar hike (like a daily walk around a park in the same direction, along the same paths) since only in the familiar can they really get "lost". There are specific ways that you can use your body to get creative too.

Meditation

There are many forms of meditation: transcendental (using a mantra or word as your point of focus and re-turn); mindfulness (using your breath as a point of focus and return); walking meditation (using walking as a focus while you venture on a path); open monitoring meditation (no point of focus—just closed eyes); loving kindness meditation (generating loving and kind feelings with your eyes closed); devotion (e.g. to a God or field of interest); and simply self-inquiry (e.g. asking, "Who am I?" regularly). Regardless of the technique you use, and no matter how large or small the "dose", when you meditate you can make a shift, learn better, become more creative, multitask like a juggler and access a part of your greatness that is unavailable to your focused mind alone.

So now, the big question is *where to start?*

Rhythm-Building Training Wheels

When you first learn musical rhythm, you tap single beats, then two beats with an emphasis on the first, then three beats with an emphasis on the first, and so on. Gradually, you learn to break beats up into two or three, and when you are more advanced, the rhythmic complexity is much greater. Then, you learn how to improvise, ornament, almost imperceptibly robbing a beat and making up for this by prolonging another beat without losing step with the basic rhythm.

And so it goes with the rhythm of your thinking. You start with the basics, and eventually, you will march to the beat of your own drummer. Initially, though, you need to hold yourself to your promises, and you may need some help along the way.

Build in free periods

Almost by definition, timetables encourage you to book up every moment, every hour of your day, with focused work. How often have you said, "I'm booked back to back"? Don't stint on this; block off periods of time that are off-limits to your day-to-day work and chores.

Remember that studies show that close to half of your day is spent in mini mental journeys away from the task at hand. Why not take control of what your mind is intent on doing anyway? Why not harness your mental power by thinking less? It will give your brain time to allow the information that you are learning to sink in.

Since everyone's day is different, there is no set time of day when you should focus and unfocus, and how many periods of unfocused time you schedule in depends on you. There is no hard data on this, but from my own experience, it's most effective to take 15 minutes "off" for every 45 minutes you spend focusing. Your first focused period can be longer than the rest—you can go more like 75 minutes before breaking for some unfocus—but thereafter, strive for 15 minutes of unfocus for every 45 minutes of focus. Build these 15-minute segments into your daily calendar. You can still be at your desk when this is happening and in that case, maybe your unfocused time will find you listening to music, doing a crossword puzzle or playing a video game. The critical thing is that it has to be undemanding for *you*. Getting up and moving while unfocusing—going for a walk around the block or in nearby greenery *without your phone*—is even better since you can't cheat and get back to work before you are back at your desk!

I would also recommend creating a placeholder called "flexitime" in your weekly calendar. This is, say, two hours when you can decide on the spot what you want to do. You can work, or you can take a break. But you're in charge. For this period, no appointments or commitments to others occur. It's your time to do what you want with it.

Understanding that there is such a thing as cognitive rhythm is the first step to improving your own. Likewise, becoming aware of the moments in your life when you surely lack it—when you are exhausted, short-tempered, or failing to "close the deal"—will help you tune into your increased need for unfocus. And building in 15-minute free periods will be the tangible reminders to keep at your practice. But after you've internalised these concepts and strategies, you'll fundamentally need to get out of your own way! Rhythm is never achieved through rules.

To keep yourself on track and in rhythm, it's useful to approach challenges through the lenses of four identities as you course through this book: *The Jazz Musician, The Dancer, The Futurist* and *The Inventor*. There's at least one of each of these identities in you.

The Jazz Musician

To stay true to your best cognitive rhythm, you have to be able to trust yourself and be willing to step outside of, and back into, your rhythm.

Jazz musicians are masters of cognitive rhythm because they can follow written music and also invent and respond to the music along the way. The same brain regions that allow us to have a synchronised conversation with someone else also allow jazz musicians to anticipate what they will each next play. In 2014, brain researchers Ana Luisa Pinho and colleagues demonstrated that when this happens in the musician, the focus circuits in the brain are turned off, and the unfocus circuits are turned on so that quick associations can be computed by the brain, and subsequently probed for more accurate prediction of the next note.

We can take a page out of the jazz musician's book to implement cognitive rhythm. It all starts with self-trust and a conscious willingness to improvise.

If you think you are not an improviser, think again. As a toddler, you had to learn to crawl, then walk, then run. And now, not only can you walk without being consciously in charge of your movements, you can walk on a busy street and effortlessly avoid bumping into people coming the other way. If they look like they are coming towards you, you automatically move away. Or you might stagger your steps to avoid their path. That's improvisation at its most basic. Similarly, as you build up the capability for unfocused time, you can throw off the conscious triggers for it, the training wheels. You'll have internalised the need for unfocus and will tap into it more naturally.

The Dancer

In 2015, when clinical psychologist Anika Maraz and her colleagues questioned 447 salsa and/or ballroom dancers, they found that there are many motivations for their dancing: fitness, mood enhancement, intimacy, socialising, trance, mastery, self-confidence and escapism. When you learn to include unfocus in your daily life, you will experience these very same benefits. Your DMN, when active and honed, will improve your cognitive fitness, enhance your happiness, increase your sensitivity to yourself and others, give rise to useful daydreaming, and improve your learning and productivity while changing your consciousness state so that you are in the zone. You become a mental dancer!

That's why you should stop overthinking and practise letting go—all the while, thinking of yourself as dancing through life. Dancing is a highly demanding activity, and not only in the physical sense. It requires a balance of focus and unfocus, the ability to access emotions, detect rhythm, and express rhythm too. Dance integrates movement and thought, and involves controlling your posture, learning sequences and using your imagination. While dancing with skill requires focus, it also requires unfocus. Can you imagine someone dancing if all they did was focus on the right moves? Good dancing, like good cognitive rhythm, is when you stop overthinking, let go, find the beat and join it by anticipating the next beat too.

The Futurist

In 1900, Smithsonian Institution curator John Elfreth Watkins accurately predicted that we would one day have wireless phone networks, television, MRI machines, aerial warfare and food truck fads in cities throughout America. He also predicted some things that have yet to pass—like the letters "C", "X" and "Q" being removed from the English alphabet. When people like Watkins predict things correctly, they are using a form of thinking that is intelligent guessing. They may not always be correct, but when they dare to guess from time to time, they use the DMN and unfocus to look into the future.

If you were on vacation in Miami for the first time and heard the TV weather report forecasting intermittent thunder showers, you might be sceptical, when all you saw was the radiant sun in the sky. Yet, if you turned your beach-weary head and saw a pall of grey clouds slowly making its way towards you, you would likely put two and two together, pack up your stuff, and head for the hills (or back to your hotel). In this instance, you're an intelligent futurist—and your hazy, unfocused, sun-drenched mind may be just the thing you need to see the connection between the weather report and those clouds. And you don't even need explicit clues to be a good guesser.

In 2012, neuroscientist Julia Mossbridge and her colleagues reported on the findings of a meta-analysis of 26 studies on "guessing" from seven independent laboratories. They found that the human body can detect stimuli presented one to ten seconds in the future. For example, if I am about to show you a photograph of a violent scene or a neutral landscape, your actual physiology will accurately change—to anxiety when the image you are about to see is violent, or calmness when it is serene. In that sense, you're capable of guessing correctly, more often than not, what you are about to see before you do.

Called predictive anticipatory activity, this phenomenon may reflect your brain's unconscious ability to know the future. Part of the DMN, the frontopolar cortex, is thought to play an active role in this prediction ability, but the precise reasoning behind this surprising reality is not known. There may be some kind of unconscious mirroring at play—our brains' ability to sense what's about to come because brain circuits can act like mirrors, without us even knowing. And there are other theories based on quantum physics too. The point is— you don't always have to wait for perceptible knowledge. You know more than you might be willing to admit.

The paradox is that the more you unfocus and give yourself over to this anticipation, the more likely you are to get it right. Furthermore, taking that leap has a snowball effect. In study after study, we have seen a direct correlation between musical training and thinking abilities. Children who learn to play music have better verbal memory, second language pronunciation accuracy, reading ability and executive functions, not to mention fluency of speech.

Why does this happen in our brains? Well, focus alone brings the brain's attentional system to life, and activates the frontoparietal cortex (the brain's flashlight). But it also turns off the DMN. It is unfocus *together* with focus that connects us to rhythm, dance and music— and, more loosely, to walking, pausing before jumping into someone's arms, and having sex. Can you imagine if you thought your way all through an orgasm?

The Inventor

As useful as I believe the strategies in this book will be to you, I have to admit that I am always sceptical when authors or advice-givers compartmentalise things so neatly. It's important to remember that no two people are alike, and effective generalisations are hard to make. I don't offer policy! Let my recommendations be a map to help you navigate your own unique complexity. There is no "right" way to do anything except what feels right to you. The maximum value of the ideas I share can only be attained if you apply the science and adjust the findings to yourself. Take the ideas, strategies and information I offer and adapt them to your own brain.

~

Unfocus is an intelligent form of letting go. It allows our thinking to be flexible, allows us to surrender at crucial moments, provides a friction-free zone within which we can move to the next stage of thinking, and allows for a greater connection with the essence of who we are.

It may feel counterintuitive to rest, stop, daydream, turn your intensity down, or temporarily abandon a project just as things are heating up. You may feel like you are giving up or wasting time. But when you shift from FOCUS-FOCUS-FOCUS-FATIGUE to FOCUS-IMAGINE-FOCUS-REST-FOCUS-DAY-DREAM-WANDER, for example, you leave fatigue out of the equation and use unfocusing moments instead to re-energise your brain. Furthermore, FOCUS-KNIT-

FOCUS-REST-FOCUS-HAMMOCK is different from FOCUS-MEDITATE-FOCUS-SHOWER-FOCUS-SLEEP. Throughout the book, you will learn how to use these different forms of unfocus in context. And you will learn that thinking is not your only ally when solving problems.

Whether you want to become more creative, get unstuck from some difficult place you are in, learn more effectively, master multitasking or discover your own greater potential, cognitive rhythm will help you develop competencies that are relevant in a world where constant brain change is necessary if you want to thrive.

CONJURING CREATIVITY

"I began by tinkering around with some old tunes
I knew. Then, just to try something different, I set
to putting some music to the rhythm that I used in
jerking ice-cream sodas at the Poodle Dog. I fooled
around with the tune more and more until at last, lo
and behold, I had completed my first piece of finished
music."

Duke Ellington

If I gave you dirt, sugar, string and chocolate syrup in
one big bag, what would you do with them?

In all likelihood, this bag of odd-lot things would
lead you to the garbage, not inspire you to take pho-
tographs of them, let alone apply them in original and
evocative ways to a photographic canvas. Yet, this is the
kind of thing that the renowned Brazilian artist Vik Muniz thinks to do time and again. He also once daubed
peanut butter and jam in a painterly way on top of two

close-up shots of the *Mona Lisa*. In everyday life, peanut butter, jam and Da Vinci rarely go together. But Muniz suspends traditional thinking about how to pair ideas. When he does so, he brings potential conflicts between mind and matter to life (you wouldn't expect the *Mona Lisa* to be made of peanut butter and jam), showcasing the unexpected and bridging the mental gaps between concepts that would otherwise never be associated. This unexpected combination captures our attention and stimulates our imaginations to run a little wilder. That's why a lot of people take to his work. But whether his art is to your taste or not (I've heard some people joke that it inspires them to make artwork of their children's spilled food, or from the dirt that someone tracked onto their brand-new carpets), most people would agree that it is dramatic, provocative and stunningly creative.

If you don't consider yourself particularly creative at the Vik Muniz level, it's important to acknowledge that it takes creativity to manage conflicts diplomatically, cook a delicious meal from scratch, convince your stubborn teenager to see things from your perspective, or put together an outfit in an unusual but eye-catching way.

Even still, you might think of "creative types" as a breed apart; you think of creativity as something you either have or don't (and you don't have it). If you do think of yourself as creative, you might guard the secrets of your craft quite closely. More likely, you may not truly understand the ways in which your mind doodles its way to inspiration. And regardless of how creative you feel you are, most people would agree that creativity is elusive, not a capability that can be conjured or rushed.

There is a popular myth that creativity is a "right-brain" phenomenon, so some people declare that they are not "right-brained". Yet, recent studies indicate that creativity actually activates a widespread network in the brain, favouring neither hemisphere over the other.

For instance, when brain researcher Melissa Ellamil and her colleagues examined the brains of people who were designing book cover illustrations, they found that both sides of the brain pitched in to stimulate creativity. When the designers had to generate ideas, it was the medial temporal lobe on both sides of the brain that played a major role, known as it is for storing facts and memories that it can draw on. And when the designers had to evaluate their ideas, it was as if the brain called for a town hall meeting—a widespread network had to have a say. While there were two sides to this network, they were not left and right. Instead they were the focused and unfocused networks on both sides of the brain, each bringing analytical versus emotional or gut-level perspectives respectively.

In other words, when you are creative, you don't need to throw your logical brain away. Analysis, association and inference work hand in hand to ensure that the creative process flows smoothly for you. This chapter will show you how to activate unfocus to join focus so as to become creative—and it will help you to ignore your brain's assertions that you are not genetically endowed with creativity, a right brain, or the capacity to figure out the mysterious path to creativity. It's far less mysterious than you think. And more often than not, thinking less will serve you more.

The Implicit Association Test (IAT)

It feels good to have creative insights and we are often praised for having them. To wit: in 2014, Adobe hired Edelman Berland, a research company, to ask more than 1,000 college-educated professionals whether creative thinking was critical for problem-solving. Somewhat predictably, 85 per cent of them said "yes". In fact, nine out of ten people ranked creativity among the top factors that they believed drove salary increases. Yet, even as we laud creativity as a vital attribute, many of us are unconsciously uncomfortable with it.

You can measure this unconscious discomfort using a test known as the Implicit Association Test (IAT). It uncovers the hidden biases people have towards creativity in situations of uncertainty. That's exactly what management professor Jennifer Mueller and her colleagues explored in a recent study. In the IAT, with the quick press of a corresponding computer key, you have to match a positive word like "sunshine" or a negative word like "vomit" with a creativity-related word like "novel" or a practicality-related word like "useful". The speed of your response is factored into the calculation. Mueller's results showed that when they're uncertain, participants automatically associate creativity with negative words like vomit and agony. It seems that our unconscious aversion to novelty and uncertainty under these conditions is an instinctual reaction, in part because the unknown is a formidable obstacle to a mind that is set in its ways. That's why you may resist creativity, and why your creative abilities may seem to max out.

From Concrete to Fluid Thinking

Our society lauds the person who lives as an open book, as a straight shooter, behaving predictably. The slogan "What you see is what you get" is often applied as a badge of honour. And these concrete traits are indeed all good, especially when negotiating the price of a new car, or doing a complicated business deal. There's nothing wrong with concrete thinking when you need to impose order in your life.

But too much order can actually lead to disorder. In a sense, order implies stiffening up rather than allowing the fluid flow of thoughts. It suggests prematurely packing thoughts away rather than giving your brain the time to form new associations between them.

Concrete thinking is a kind of poison to creativity. It engages the brain's focus circuits, but when you focus exclusively—having only one "beat" in your cognitive rhythm—you necessarily switch off your DMN, the home of abstract thought. The result? Instead of finding a creative solution to a problem, you see only option A and option B. Instead of seeing the greys, you see only black and white. If you're a black-and-white thinker, learning to see grey will require challenging some of your habits of thought.

Embrace Chaos

Creative people recognise that disorder and chaos are precursors to a new order, a new burst of creative thought, a new solution to an old problem.

Creativity itself requires the fast and unconscious reorganisation of information in your brain. New associations have to be made to find novel solutions to the problems at hand. This can happen if your DMN is turned on—but to achieve it, you have to unfocus from the chaos and give your brain time to work things out. In effect, you have to surrender to the chaos. You don't bother with it—you let go. Instead of resisting the momentum, you join it.

Of course, you can't live in the la-la land of floating ideas for ever, but when you develop the temperament to progressively live on the edge of chaos for a longer and longer time, you allow a more creative brain to flourish. Indeed, the ability to surrender to chaos and yet not be overwhelmed by it is a hallmark of the creative mind. The study of the brain biology of creativity has shown that the creative brain is often in a state of tension between chaos and control—being less inhibited by orderliness but not so disinhibited that one falls off the deep end. In this state one's mind can make extensive connections, but not so many that one completely loses one's train of thought; one can dismiss linear solutions while staying true to a problem that needs to be solved. In general, one can tend towards a controlled chaos rather than towards order.

The scientific process is more chaotic than it is orderly. As Richard Feynman, winner of the 1965 Nobel Prize for physics, somewhat wryly pointed out, "Philosophy of science is about as useful to scientists as ornithology is to birds." There's no one way to do things. In fact, there are usually too many views—a chaos of facts that you have to navigate.

In support of this view, Kevin Dunbar's research is revealing. He is a researcher who studies how scientists work, and in the early 1990s, he observed four Stanford labs. He found that although scientists followed established techniques, atleast 50 to 75 per cent of their findings were unexpected, and their findings kept contradicting their elaborate theories. Scientific models pave the way for exploration—as I hope the models in this book do—but they often do not lead to the answer on their own.

When you are at a loss after your experiment fails, things feel up in the air. You ask, "What went wrong?" Was it the method? The middle stage? The way you analysed things? There are so many things that could have gone wrong, it would drive you up the wall trying to figure out the "right" thing. At this point of chaos, what you need is an insight, not prepared knowledge— focus and unfocus circuits need to chime in to generate ideas and evaluate them. That's not only what Vik Muniz does; it is also what free-form tattoo artists do, and what you do when you find an original combination of clothes, make up a joke or practise calligraphy. Learning to surrender to this process without anxiously tipping over into chaos is an art, a delicate balancing act. But we are wired for it.

Charles Limb is a doctor and musician who researches how creativity works in the brain. In 2008, he and another doctor-colleague, Allen Braun, studied six full-time musicians using functional magnetic resonance imaging while they either performed "overlearned" (memorised to the point that it is automatic) or improvised piano pieces.

They found that spontaneous improvisation was associated with widespread deactivation of the lateral prefrontal cortex (PFC), or "thinking brain". To be spontaneous, your conscious "thinking brain" had to be out of the way. Also, the more intuitive brain integrator, the medial PFC, was activated. In other words, unfocus was key for the improvisation.

At first, trying to embrace chaos may sound frustratingly glib and counterintuitive, akin to taking your foot off the prefrontal brake when things are out of control. However, if you think of being "out of control" as being analogous to driving on black ice, releasing the brake may make more sense. When you do, you avoid perpetuating skidding in chaos by trying to control it. On a day-to-day basis this would imply practising what I call "delay and deliver" thinking.

Imagine that on a given day you have set yourself a to-do list in a particular order. A kind of chaos ensues if someone or something puts a demand on your time unexpectedly that day: your to-do list is shot to hell or at least interrupted. In "delay and deliver" thinking you examine whether you can actually delay one or two of your to-do list items in order to accommodate the unexpected demand. If you find you can make this adjustment, you will still feel productive and in control of the day. Of course, you won't always be able to do so, but if you practise this kind of thinking, you will get used to not resisting the chaos that comes your way.

And embracing small chaotic time periods in your day can lead to mini-epiphanies. For example, in 2008 health behaviour expert Kenneth Resnicow, in conjunction with complexity expert Scott Page, looked at why people suddenly change their behaviour: stop using drugs, start exercising, or eat more healthily. He found that sudden changes are not the result of step-by-step escalations in the desire to change but rather of a creative process or sudden realisation in which motivation "arrives." The changes are not planned: rather, "resident chunks of knowledge or attitude may unexpectedly coalesce to form a perfect motivational storm." That's creative motivation—not "intention" as we know it. When you want to go to the gym, but just can't do it, you need creative motivation, in the form of a "motivational storm". When you need to cut back on sugar, but can't resist the apple pie, you need creative motivation. A few blessed people are able to resist temptation, but for the rest of us, creative motivation is often our only hope.

How you see chaos depends on you. You may see it as a thunderstorm or an invigorating fountain. Self-talk can help you choose between the two ("I'm going to treat this deluge of requests like a waterfall under which I'm standing on a hot summer's day."). Observing the chaos—pondering it even—is often far superior to escaping it.

Case in point: Arno Penzias and Robert Wilson were both astronomers. In 1964, they were using a radio telescope in suburban New Jersey to see what was going on in space. In order to map those vast tracts of the universe devoid of bright stars, they decided to make a detailed survey of radiation in the Milky Way. To do this, they needed a receiver that was exquisitely sensitive, able to pick up the slightest sounds in the vast emptiness. First in the order of things was to retrofit an old radio telescope, and then to install amplifiers and a calibration system so that the signals coming from space were a little bit louder.

To their dismay, whenever they pointed at the sky, they heard a persistent background noise that disturbed their observations— a kind of "static" sound. You can imagine how frustrating this was—like watching your favourite game on television, but having the commentary turn to static from time to time. No matter how much they conjectured, they couldn't find the source. It wasn't Manhattan or the pigeon droppings in the antenna either—although they thought of both and addressed them. Still unable to remove the noise, they decided to accept all this chaos and just try to get the data they wanted. But this too failed—they couldn't distinguish the faint radio echoes from the static. They scrapped the experiment, but continued to mull over the possible source of the sound interference.

In 1965, Penzias called Robert Dicke, a Princeton nuclear physicist, to ask what he thought about this sound. Dicke, who had been looking for evidence of the "Big Bang" and was building his own telescope, knew immediately what it was—radiation left over from the beginning of the universe.

This interpretation of the sound gave rise to investigations that allowed astronomers to confirm the Big Bang theory. Fast forward to 1978 when Penzias and Wilson win the Nobel Prize for physics for their astounding "accidental" discovery.

Many businesses recognise that controlled chaos is necessary for innovation. They pay close attention to the changing needs of people who use their products, initially avoiding detailed plans and remaining flexible. They don't mind entertaining many new ideas, especially when they can quickly and inexpensively test them. In this state, there's a certain chaos of new ideas coming in, most of them quickly failing, the promising ones going onto the next stage of development. But this high turnover and controlled chaos gives a company the momentum it needs to stay relevant and competitive.

To really grasp this, think of how airplanes can take advantage of a tailwind to move faster, or how a masterful sailor can manoeuvre a sailboat in a strong wind. Similarly, brain chaos offers you the opportunity to take advantage of it. Rather than defaulting to hunkering down and lowering your sails, you use the winds of change to give you the push you need; surrender.

Surrender to Ambiguity

A big part of creativity is practising the art of letting go. When you do, you detach from the external world as a guide for a time, and turn instead to your internal stream of attention.

When artists speak about their creations or the creative process, they will often point out that they are not guided exclusively by clarity and single-mindedness. Instead, periods of clarity are intermixed with significant ambiguity and even doubt. And often, this ambiguity may even be crucial and defining. Indeed, for creative people, the *expression* of conflict, ambiguity or vagueness frequently trumps the *resolution* of it.

In our relentless quest for meaning and understanding, we may inadvertently shut ourselves off from experiences by trying too quickly to analyse or make sense of them first. Worse, we sometimes deny ourselves experiences because we don't understand them or see them as relevant to our lives. In so doing, the creative process is compromised, to say the least.

Inspiration usually manifests like a mind pop—a spontaneous burst of creativity to which you can't quite attribute a starting point. Yet in fact, inspiration actually has an architecture, a three-part structure that we can discern, implement and allow.

Inspiration starts with an aesthetic appreciation of something through one of your five senses. For some people a sunrise is inspiring. For others it's a walk on the beach, as much for the feeling of sand between their toes as for the smell of salt and seaweed in the air. For others still, inspiration might be far more detailed and specific: watching the movie *Secretariat* to see the great horse win the Triple Crown.

After that appreciative, inspired feeling has been triggered, you need to allow your mind to wander in its presence. This is the phase known as "passive evocation". When you give yourself both the time and permission to bathe in the awe of your aesthetic appreciation, you will experience a swell of inspiration that grows inside you like the King Kong of all soap bubbles. It mesmerises you, entrances you, and is just the power you need to float into your creativity.

The third part of inspiration is simply the desire for something new to happen. Desire can also be difficult to generate spontaneously, but there are things you can do to foster it.

Find an online community that shares and breathes life into your passion. Look for a neighbourhood group that shares your interests. Why not even start a group, like Einstein and Picasso did? Think of how your creative desire connects to your wellbeing, and how it relates to your meaning and purpose in life. These groups and thoughts will help keep you motivated.

Two other pathways to desire are novelty and originality. Look for unusual things that pique your interest. They could be unusual and beautiful objects to place in your office. Or you may try to draw something (a friend of mine once decided to paint original patterns on the tiles in her hall.) Don't be self-conscious about getting it right. Picasso was famous for saying that he painted objects as he thought them and not as he saw them. Paint your thoughts. See what comes out.

Practise Abstraction

A natural way to prompt your brain to live in the "grey" and be more fluid is through what's known as symbolisation. Symbols convert concrete problems into forms of themselves that are easier to work with. They are representations of things.

They are also more prevalent in your life than you might initially think. We use mathematical symbols all the time: "+" or "=". And every word itself is a symbol—a shorthand way of describing something. Children often use symbolic thinking, playing in dirt as if they are making food, using towels as superhero capes, or using a stick as a sword.

As an adult, symbolic thinking can be helpful when you're struggling to let go of a relationship. One creative solution might be to place a picture of your former lover in a bottle, and then release the bottle into the ocean, symbolically letting go of the person, and using your emotional reaction as the trigger for resolving your grief.

You could use a symbol of something you know to model something that you don't know. For instance, you may not know how to foster cross-sector collaborations within an organisation, but if you're at an impasse, you might turn to symbols of successful cross-sector collaborations for guidance. Take, for example, the brain, where the right and left parts collaborate effectively. If they can work together, what's holding up your designers and programmers? Using such a symbol may help you identify the issue: that your brain stops its "cross-sector collaboration" when fear is the dominant emotion, or when there is no cognitive rhythm and it is stuck in focus rather than moving between focus and unfocus. So you know to address the same issues: the fears associated with interdepartmental collaboration and questions about how the teams communicate. You can encourage both teams to brainstorm more (unfocus) prior to executing a plan (focus).

Symbols are also helpful when something is unknown, yet needs to be dealt with. Say, for instance, you want to decide on where a desk should go in a room. Draw the desk fully into an architectural sketch, and you may have trouble even thinking about moving it. Depict it as an "X" instead, and you will see how suddenly, your ability to associate it with a wall or fireplace and then work out where it should go will speed up. You stop being caught up in the details, and your creative thought flow increases. Symbols or "simplified semantic structures" can help you accelerate your creativity.

Metaphors are also implicit comparisons that bring ideas to life: symbolisation in words. And their use can help tame chaos in your mind. For example, a "rollercoaster" experience is much easier to understand than "the edge of chaos". Thinking of life as a box of assorted chocolates—unpredictable, but not terrifying—might be the best metaphor of all.

Alternatively, you might think of a challenge as a wall you have encountered. When you think about your options for dealing with this challenge, extend the wall metaphor: drill right through, scale the wall, go around the wall, or dig underneath it. The creative process is necessarily abstract, but when you practise using metaphors like this, it helps your brain to work in a different way. It activates your DMN—and you are more likely to discover more creative solutions.

Higher-quality metaphors are more remote, novel and clever; they may require a bigger leap of understanding. It's a subjective call, but you can use these criteria to see if your metaphor works. The higher the quality of a metaphor, the more it will activate the same brain regions responsible for openness to experience. So keep reworking your metaphors as a creative exercise. Instead of obstacles to creativity being "a wall", you could compare them to "going uphill", but neither of these metaphors quite communicate the chaos of creativity.

So you might also try comparing the challenge to "controlling a bumper car", or "skiing down a black diamond slope", yet these may feel too frivolous or dangerous respectively. To strike the right balance, you might finally think of the challenge of creativity as "trying to concoct the perfect cocktail"— a few tastes, a few tests and mixers, and you're there. All you need to do is spread out the testing times so that you don't get too drunk, and to be experimental enough with the mixers that your creations are unique. Of course, different people may prefer different metaphors, but when you play with them this way, you stimulate your creative brain.

Switch Lenses

When you analyse situations, you engage in either "split thinking" or "bundling". Creative thinking involves exploring both perspectives.

Bundling takes in the big picture, grouping similar things together in order to understand them or to kill two birds with one stone. Say, for example, that you are an anthropologist studying the population of a remote island. If you're a bundler by nature, you look at the people as a whole, extrapolating or concluding things based on the bird's eye view of the inhabitants. If your thinking runs to splitting, on the other hand, you are more likely to focus on the differences between things. You delve into the individuals who make up this island nation—perhaps by age, gender or village. You either focus tightly on the specifics or you step back and consider the big picture.

Consider the usefulness of this exercise with the concepts of "mind" and "body". For many years, doctors and scientists saw these things as separate parts of the human makeup. The gut and its bacteria, for example, were entirely separate from the brain and a person's psychological health or moods. Seeing the gut and brain as separate is helpful when you specialise, but when you view them as connected within the body—as we have come to do— you develop fascinating new insights. Now, for instance, it is possible to map how signals from gut bacteria reach the brain and influence how depressed or anxious a person is. Also, new experiments suggest that Parkinson's disease—a disorder previously thought of as a "brain" disorder—may spread from the gut to the brain via the vagus nerve that connects them. People who have this nerve severed are 50 per cent less likely to develop the disease.

That said, splitting also has its own value. In 2012, psychologist Tony McCaffrey described "generic parts technique"— a split-thinking way to overcome blocks to your creative thinking. With this strategy, you ask two questions: can the object I am looking at be broken down further? Does my description of this object imply a use?

In a classic problem, McCaffrey gave people two steel rings, a box of matches and a candle and then asked them to create a figure of eight shape that stayed together. Most people try to melt the wax to hold the rings together, but the rings inevitably come apart. Anyone trained to use his generic parts technique, however, would ask the operative questions, and likely quickly make the leap that solves the problem: a candle is made up of a wick as well as wax, and the wick can be used as string to tie the rings together once you've melted the candle down.

People who use McCaffrey's generic parts technique solved these kinds of problems 67 per cent more often than those who did not.

Transcend Normal

"Openness to experience" is one of the personality traits extensively studied in creative people. When you have this trait, you have an active imagination, prefer variety, and are intellectually curious. You are also sensitive to beautiful things and attentive to your inner feelings. By contrast, a recent study showed that "normal" people define themselves as realistic, practical and task-focused. But paradoxically, these traits disrupt the smooth operation of your brain—you have less openness to experience.

It's been shown that when you have openness to experience, your DMN operates more efficiently, creating more order than disorder in the brain. In a sense you are going with the flow when you are open to experience, rather than swimming against the tide. Stay open to new experiences, and you are more likely to navigate your way creatively through the hustle and bustle of life.

But being open to experience doesn't mean you have to go sky-diving or swim with sharks! We're mostly talking about cognitive leaps of faith here, a willingness to loosen your need to control things and to control outcomes. By most reports, Vik Muniz has this temperament. A freak accident when he was 22 (he was shot in the leg trying to break up a street brawl) led to a bribe from the shooter that allowed him to finance a move to the US, something he had been chafing to do as a way to open up his creative future. He didn't know what he'd do or what he'd find, but he was open to discovering it. He leapt both literally and figuratively. Discovery consists of seeing new things not only as they are, but also as what they might soon be.

Listen to Your Gut

Intuition is your brain's ability to register subtle changes in your physiology that have not yet reached your consciousness. As such, hunches are body sensations that are yet to become thoughts. A number of different brain regions form an intuition network that pick up those subtle sensations to give you a "gut feeling", an understanding that hasn't been interpreted by your thinking brain. That gut feeling is vital information and you shouldn't ignore it just because its explanation is floating outside of your reach.

One productive way to manage your intuition (instead of dismissing it) is to step back and reflect with questions like, "What's making me feel this excited sensation in the pit of my stomach?" or "Why do I feel so nervous?" You may even conjecture a hypothesis or two. But if you're at a complete loss to explain your gut feelings, don't give up. When you remain curious, you turn your brain into a detective. It goes searching for evidence to string together to make a case for one of your hunches. Called "serial hypothesis testing", this is effectively your brain using intuition to surrender to an "internal" data search. Through this process, you are gradually accumulating bits of information. When you have gathered enough data, you have an insight. Often the insight will not occur when you are looking for it with your thinking brain, but when the data threshold for forming an insight is crossed. Progressive insights provide the orientation you need to navigate the edge of brain chaos in creativity.

Another way of managing intuition is called "predictive inference". Rather than looking for evidence, your brain leaps to a conclusion and *then* tests it out. This is akin to leaping before you look, or making a decision and then testing it. For example, if collating data about recent terrorist entry points leads to a dead end, an intelligence agency can't just give up trying. They've got to start somewhere—to at least infer when and where the next one might take place. If they just ignored their intuitions they might not act. Not knowing exactly why, and not at first justifying their hunches, they may name borders X, Y and Z as their top three suspicious points. Then, they will see if they can rationalise this with data. If the model does not work, at least they have new data—where the terrorists are likely not to be. Then they can reformulate the possibilities and keep working this out by nominating borders P, Q, and R, for instance, until their hunches and the data fit. When the data and the hunches fit, they execute a corresponding border safety plan. More often than not, this is exactly how intelligence agencies work—they engineer things backwards. Sometimes people make relationship choices this way too, first choosing someone based on gut feelings, and then inferring why they made their choices as the relationship progresses. If they collect enough evidence, they might get married. If they can't find any, they might end the relationship.

In this case, you've already concluded something, but you test the solution to see if it's correct. Then you reformulate your conclusion and test it again. After several reformulations, you arrive at a satisfying conclusion. This is also an effective and often time-saving way to create. Rather then spending endless time thinking, you learn more from "doing".

When you make both of these intuition management tools part of your mental toolkit, your conscious brain will turn its attention inward, with its roving searchlight looking for data.

Mind Pops

Unfocus helps you loosen yourself from your habits and stimulate new ideas. You won't be aware of the brain doing its work, but when it's ready, an idea or creative solution will surface to your conscious mind. Fragments of knowledge, words, images or melodies that suddenly appear to you as "mind pops" seem random. But researchers have seen that having a mind pop activates the same region of the brain that's engaged when you are open to experience. Unfocused and non-demanding activities like doing the dishes or mowing the lawn will often bring them to the fore. Even when the ideas and thoughts that emerge are muddled or conflicting, they are signs of your creative brain in action.

Dabbling Your Way to Eureka

Dabbling gets a bad rap. Too often we equate it with—or use it in a sentence to connote—something superficial, lacking in depth; people who dabble are dilettantes. There is also a prevailing sense that we are wasting our time when we are not deeply committed to a subject. But depth is relative, and there is a certain level and kind of dabbling that is clearly beneficial to your creativity, and to your life.

The late Apple founder and CEO, Steve Jobs, is dabbling's poster boy. In his famous Stanford commencement speech in 2005, Jobs told the story of dropping out of Reed College so that he could audit only the classes that interested him. One of those was a calligraphy and typography class. He had no idea at the time how he might make use of this knowledge but ten years later, when he was designing the first Macintosh computer, he used what he'd learned in that class. If he had not, the Mac might have had multiple typefaces and proportionally spaced fonts. Dabbling in a topic that interested him profoundly—even if it didn't immediately serve him—was tremendously useful in the long run.

And what of creative geniuses like Albert Einstein and Pablo Picasso? Although it may seem that they were creatively worlds apart, we do know that scientists and artists have brains that respond similarly, especially in regions where complex sensations, thoughts and emotions are integrated. Both groups display a high degree of DMN activity—demonstrating that it is not just depth of ideas, but connections between ideas that matter. That's why you dabble. You're giving yourself one more experience to draw on, one more thing to connect to—and it may be the missing link you were looking for.

Though Einstein and Picasso never met one another, they were both known to have been strongly influenced by Henri Poincaré, a mathematician, physicist and philosopher of their day. They discussed his theories in their respective "think tanks", Einstein with his study group, and Picasso with a group of avant-garde literati. Einstein extended Poincaré's brilliant mathematical and scientific theories a few steps further to come to his own theory of relativity. On hearing about Poincaré's thoughts on the existence of a fourth dimension where you could see everything at once, Picasso was inspired, too. In his painting *Les Demoiselles d'Avignon*, he depicted one of the faces simultaneously in front and side view—two perspectives at the same time—the fourth dimension!

Einstein and Picasso both dabbled in many other things as well. Einstein was strongly influenced by aesthetic theory and he was fascinated by Freud's work. Picasso was very interested in photography and X-ray technology. Neither man felt he had to become expert in these side interests. They indulged their curiosity, mulled over their responses, and discussed the resulting ideas with their respective think tanks. The results would change the world.

Choosing to dabble can be a profound decision. It means that you are willing to try something out and be a student again. In that respect, it is mind-opening and even though it is unfocused and away from your day-to-day routine, it is a way to take baby steps into "openness to experience"—the sine qua non of creativity. It's also a great way to get out of your comfort zone. Effective dabbling is a bit like taking a dive into the deep-end for a few seconds and then swimming away. It may be fleeting, but it can be profound, and often invigorating. For a brief life moment, you can lose yourself in it.

The Hobby-Creativity Link

Having a hobby is possibly the most socially acceptable way to dabble. Describing something you do as a "hobby"—i.e. a side interest—concedes that you know you shouldn't spend all your time with it. But if you've got one (or more), you shouldn't downplay it too much. Research suggests that engaging in hobbies for one or more hours every day may protect you against dementia later in life. Two studies by organisational psychologist Kevin Eschleman and colleagues show that dabbling helps you in the present, too.

In the first study, 341 people from different work backgrounds (including managerial positions, education, administration, and accounting) responded to questionnaires about creative activity outside of work as well as self-rating their at-work performance. People who engaged in more creative activities had a higher sense of their own work.

In the second study, 92 active duty captains from the US Air Force completed a similar questionnaire and others rated their work as well. Here too, whether based on their own assessment or that of others, being engaged in more creative activity outside of work was associated with higher work performance.

And then there is the important work of physiology professor Robert Root-Bernstein to bolster the value of hobbies. Between 1958 and 1978, Bernstein and his colleagues interviewed 40 male scientists four times concerning their work habits, use of time, hobbies, attitudes and related issues. They measured scientific impact by the number of citations of each scientist's work. The results were telling: hobbies that involved visual thinking, learning from doing rather than just thinking, and artistic and musical hobbies were particularly advantageous.

Interestingly, some of the least productive scientists in this study engaged in a variety of activities that did not have any great purpose to them. The difference was that the productive scientists all saw their hobbies or dabbling activities as having some beneficial outcome. They were working on the same thing from a different angle.

Blending Your Interests

Very often, we decide we want to live simpler lives. So we get rid of some possessions or we determine that we will live with fewer luxuries; we whittle things down to a simpler baseline—and there's nothing wrong with that. Yet, there is something terribly self-limiting about whittling your*self* down. What if you didn't have to choose between your love of one thing and your competencies in another field? What if you could more frequently find ways to marry your talents and interests?

Consider the positive example of Kirin Sinha. In 2012 she was an MIT senior majoring in theoretical maths, electrical engineering and computer science, and minoring in music. She was a scientist and a musician, and she didn't want to choose one over the other. So she didn't.

Sinha had studied Indian classical dance since she was a three-year-old, and she believed that learning dance builds confidence and grit, traits that are also necessary for doing well at maths. To marry her interests and her belief in their interaction, she launched SHINE, a free dance and maths programme aimed at sixth and seventh grade girls struggling with maths. Students enrolled in eight-week sessions led by MIT students with dance backgrounds. They learned hip-hop, jazz and other dance styles. The girls also learned to apply mathematical concepts from their dance by writing out their choreographies as formulae in which, say, x represents a turn and y represents a hip pop. Then, Sinha says, "They start to understand things like if you do 3x + 2x, you're doing the same move five times in a row…"

Saying Yes to Wandering

The ancient Greeks considered wandering to be a form of regression; it was the opposite of the stability and civilisation for which the Athenians were known. Odysseus, the king of Ithaca, said, "For mortals, nothing is more wretched than wandering." And famously, Oedipus, the mythical king of Thebes, was condemned to a life of wandering after being discovered as the murderer of his father and lover of his mother.

Now, some 2,500 years later, we may not use wandering as punishment, but we do tend to beat ourselves up for doing it in our heads. In 2008, psychologists Matthew Killingsworth and Daniel T. Gilbert conducted a survey to investigate how often people's minds wander and how they feel when this happens. They developed a smartphone technology to sample people's thoughts, feelings and actions throughout the day. They found that people spend 46.9 per cent of their time thinking about something other than what they are doing. This makes them significantly unhappy. We all know that feeling, right?

Involuntary mind wandering can make you feel out of control and unproductive. And you don't want your thoughts to be wandering while you're driving somewhere new or cooking Thanksgiving dinner either. Yet, many creative people vouch for the importance of mind wandering or daydreaming in their discoveries.

Orhan Pamuk, who was the 2006 recipient of the Nobel Prize for literature, put it this way: "...what is a novel but a story that ... answers and builds upon inspirations from unknown quarters, and seizes upon all the daydreams we've invented for our diversion, bringing them together into a meaningful whole?"

It's not that focus has no role at all in creativity. Clearly, whether you're Picasso painting *Les Demoiselles d'Avignon*, or an entrepreneur trying to make your company profitable, a certain amount of focus is necessary for your creative work. But focus exists on a spectrum. You can be intently focused, mindful (dedicated to your focus), or allow your mind to wander. The operative word here is "allow"—mind wandering and daydreaming are most productive when you are disciplined about using them.

Deliberate Daydreaming

As pleasant and preferable as simply staring out the window at work might be, it's not an ideal way to increase your creativity (or your productivity).

When you fall into daydreaming, it's a sign of cognitive failure or exhaustion—your brain needs a break and takes one without asking. It's like falling off the edge of a cliff. But when you plan your daydreaming, it's constructive and restorative. It's like diving off the edge of a cliff into a pool of water. In the first instance, you're not in control. In the second, the daydreaming is not only expected, it's planned too. Called "volitional daydreaming", this willful and scheduled flight away from the task at hand will help you become more open to experience; it's been shown to help you be more curious, sensitive, and more likely to explore your ideas, feelings and sensations.

Consider the findings of a 2012 study in which cog-

nitive psychologist Benjamin Baird and colleagues tested people's ability to find an unusual use for a number of
things, including bricks, toothpicks and clothes hangers.
The subjects had to be quick and creative, coming up
with as many uses as possible. Four groups of people
were tested several times in a two-minute period, and
then all but one of the groups were given a 12-minute
"break". During this break, one group engaged in a demanding task, another in an undemanding task (during
which they were not focused but allowed their minds to
wander), and a third group rested. The last group was
given no break at all. Guess who was most creative? The
people who were allowed the undemanding, mind-wandering time performed the best.

Writer's Block

If you're a writer, you have at some point probably experienced the dreaded phenomenon known as writer's
block. Sometimes writer's block results from feeling
fundamentally conflicted about expressing a thought in
writing. At other times, you are torn between plot options and stall for fear of making the "wrong" choice.
You might also be suffering from a kind of paralyt-
ic perfectionism—your inner editor won't let you put
something less than polished to the page. Sometimes,
you just draw a complete blank! A review of findings
from different brain studies suggests that writer's block
is in part a dysfunction of part of the frontal lobe (no

surprise, this is a key brain region involved in the generation and evaluation of creative ideas), the same region that is damaged when you can't produce speech after having a stroke, and when you're depressed or anxious.

To overcome writer's block, unfocusing from your thought loops is key. Some writers resort to starting in the middle of a sentence in order to liberate themselves from the tyranny of the complete thought. Others write the ending or conclusion they're sure of first, before the rest of the action or argument. All of these techniques are attempts to use a little chaos to jar the mind into action. There's nothing like discombobulation to jump-start the creative brain.

The Body Creative

It's not just a wandering mind that can trigger creative thought. A wandering body can help you become more creative as well.

In 2012, psychology professor Angela K. Leung and her colleagues explored "outside the box" thinking as it relates to literal, physical "outside-ness". They built a 5' x 5' box and asked 20 people to sit inside it. Another 20 sat outside of the box.

Both groups then took a creativity test called the Remote Associations Test (RAT). In this test, words like "measure", "worm" and "video" are presented, and the subject is asked to think of a fourth word that relates to the other three. The people sitting outside the box were significantly more likely than those sitting inside to come up with the word "tape" (measuring tape, tape-worm, videotape).

To confirm that the position of your body in space matters, Leung and her team asked another group of participants to complete divergent thinking tasks—also measures of creativity. These are tasks similar to what scientists call an unusual or "Alternative Uses" test. You have to think fast and call up relevant information at the same time.

Three groups of people were tested—one group walked around in rectangles while completing the mental test; one group walked around freely; and the last group sat down. The free-walking group outperformed the other two groups. Furthermore, walking outdoors seems to be the best creative trigger: another research group found that walking outdoors increased performance on Alternative Uses by 81 per cent and on the RAT by 23 per cent.

What your arms are doing matters too. Studying the creative impact of fluid arm movements (tracing a series of parallel and connected loops with your fingers) versus the effect of jerky arm movements (tracing a zigzag pattern), management professor Michael Slepian and social psychologist Nalini Ambady showed that fluid arm movements enhanced the ability to generate creative ideas, to be flexible in thinking and to make remote associations. Remote associations are an indication of creativity because they demonstrate that you can see connections.

For example, if I asked you what word is common to doll, paint and cat, one answer could be "house".

So, go for a walk outside, not necessarily following a path, and try to engage in whatever fluid movements you can to solve creative problems. This is useful not just for writing poetry or making music, but also for thinking about new business innovations, ways to solve your financial challenges, or even ways to get around seemingly unchangeable relationship challenges that are bugging you. A boss who annoys you by micro-managing, for example, may need to be addressed creatively. Coming up with a solution may be easier if you don't walk the beaten path—literally, from your office to hers. It sounds a little absurd, but walking on a winding path or just swinging your arms may yield incredible results.

"To Sleep, Perchance to Dream..."

Though exercise can get your creative juices flowing, almost nothing beats sleep for producing the juices in the first place.

For simplicity's sake, think of sleep as coming in two phases: non-REM (non-rapid eye movement) first, followed by REM (rapid eye movement). You cycle through these two phases over the course of your sleep, with the REM episodes gradually gaining in length. It's during REM sleep that you dream more and your muscles are more relaxed.

When you're asleep, your unconscious brain works its

magic in the dark. It puts new ideas together, recombines old ideas, and when the conditions are right, it will help you get to that "a-ha" moment that is the hallmark of the creative climax. Dreaming—the ultimate think-less-learn-more "activity"—is the brain's way of re-organising memories, shuttling them back and forth to cross the "dream bridge" that might not exist in your awake mind.

Clinical psychoanalysts have studied dreams extensively. Carl Jung argued that dreams allow for seemingly irreconcilable ideas of yourself to come together. If we take his point, it means that dreams not only recombine ideas creatively, but also allow for a more coherent *you* once you're awake. This, in turn, makes it easier to be creative because you're not battling with your contradictions. Paul McCartney reportedly composed the entire melody for his song "Yesterday" in a dream. It's a pretty melancholy song, so it's not hard to imagine that his brain might have put it aside during the course of his day.

Dreams also allow you to imagine the unimaginable. Just before articulating his theory of relativity, Albert Einstein famously dreamed that he was sledding down a steep mountainside, going so fast that he approached the speed of light. He also dreamed that time was circular, and also that time stood still so that lovers held onto each other for an eternity. When ideas like this come together, there is obviously no focused process. Instead, in dreams, your unfocused brain has the full licence to roam around and collect ideas at will. When you awaken, you might have a new insight.

In 2010, sleep expert Matthew Walker from the University of California and his colleague Robert Stickgold at the Beth Israel Deaconness Medical Center in Boston showed another benefit of sleep—the ability to solve anagrams more quickly and creatively. An anagram is a form of wordplay in which words or phrases are formed by rearranging the letters of another word. For example, the letters in "dormitory" can be rearranged to spell "dirty room" and "Jim Morrison" can be rewritten as "Mr. Mojo Risin'". (Incidentally, the latter is a phrase from one of his songs, though we don't know if Morrison was a good sleeper or not!) Walker and Stickgold compared flexibility of thinking in sixteen subjects using anagram word puzzles following REM and non-REM awakenings across the night. They found that people who were woken up after a period of REM sleep solved 32 per cent more anagrams than when woken after non-REM periods. As the night continued, though, problem solving after non-REM sleep got better.

Practically speaking, this means that if you have a shorter period to sleep and need to be creative, you should try and time your awakening for just after REM sleep, or about 90-100 minutes after you fall asleep.

The amount of sleep you "need" is debatable and personal, but common to many creatives is an occasional (or regular) nap. Napping is a great way to activate your unconscious to recombine thoughts in a unique way. It increases activity in the right brain which does some "housecleaning" to help creativity when you get up. Unlike proper sleep, napping is usually made up of a shorter period of non-REM followed by mostly REM sleep.

In a 2014 study led by researcher Felipe Beijamini, people were given a difficult video game problem to solve. Eventually, one group was allowed to nap for 90 minutes, while the other group had to stay awake. The people who napped were almost twice as likely to solve the problem when compared to the wakeful group. But when the investigators looked at brainwave patterns, dream sleep was not involved. Just dozing off was enough to recombine information in the brain and convert the gist of information into abstractions to allow problems to be solved.

On the other hand, psychiatrist Sara Mednick led a study in 2009 in which researchers used a word analogy test to see how well subjects did after a nap. For example, given "chips: salty: candy: _____" the answer participants were expected to give "sweet". Compared to non-REM nappers and no nappers, 90-minute REM nappers improved their performance by 40 per cent. They were able to make these associations at lightning speed!

While the jury is still out on whether short naps work to enhance creativity, they do appear to be better than no nap. In a 2002 study of sixteen healthy young adult sleepers, researchers created four conditions: no nap, 30-second nap, 90-second nap, and 10-minute nap. The clock was only started once the participants were actually asleep, as confirmed by EEG (electroencephalogram). The 10-minute nap was the only one that significantly improved alertness and cognitive performance.

How Much Sleep Is Enough Sleep?

In his book *Daily Rituals: How Artists Work*, Mason Currey reports that Japanese writer Haruki Murakami sleeps a solid seven hours from 9 pm to 4 am regularly. Benjamin Franklin and Maya Angelou also slept seven hours, but they slept from 10 pm to 5 am. Reportedly, Darwin slept less: from 12 am to 6 am, but then napped from 1-2 pm. If we stopped right there, it would seem that seven is the magic number.

But there are other creative people who did not sleep as much. Kafka slept in spurts—from 6 am to 8 am and then from 3 pm to 6 pm. Voltaire needed only four hours of sleep. He slept from 12 am to 4 am. And apparently, Thomas Edison did not need much sleep either: only three to four hours a night, plus power naps. More recently, Jack Dorsey, founder of both Square and Twitter, reported that he works approximately 20 hours every day, which obviously leaves little time for sleep.

From this range of sleep times, you can see that there is no ready formula for any one individual. You have to do what works for you.

PUTTING IT ALL TOGETHER TO TAP INTO CREATIVITY

Remember that in your relentless quest for understanding, you may inadvertently shut yourself off from experiences by trying too quickly to make sense of them. Worse, you could deny yourself experiences because you don't understand them or see them as relevant to your life. In so doing, the creative process is compromised, to say the least.

Creativity and creative surrender *emerge from* letting go. As I said earlier, when you let go, you detach from the external world as a guide for a time and turn to your internal stream of attention.

One of the major obstructions to creativity is a fixed identity. In the spirit of adopting an alternate identity to meet the challenge of conjuring creativity, consider wearing these two hats:

The Trainer
Muscular growth happens when you move against resistance. Similarly, to build your creative mind, you need to identify where your psychological resistance is and move against it. This is not simply about being oppositional; not everyone living in a counter-culture way is actually displaying creativity! Living against the grain is about training your mind to work against its psychological resistance to creativity.

Whether visible or discernible to you or not (conscious or unconscious), there are usually four reasons why your brain will put up a fight when you want to be creative: fear of the unknown, intolerance of uncertainty, being overwhelmed by the magnitude of the task at hand and trepidations about the task being too difficult. Think of these four factors as the wet blankets to creativity. Consider which wet blanket is holding you back. Knowing what is holding you back is half the battle. Unfocusing through the many strategies I offer in this chapter will help you periodically throw it off.

Creativity is as much perspiration as it is inspiration. In a sense, inspiration results from the automatic aspects of creative idea generation, whereas perspiration reflects the hard work of thought control that must "balance out" inspiration in order for you to reach the creative goal. This is the right and left brain, and the DMN and executive control network, working in synchrony.

The Trick-or-Treater

From time to time, I think it's helpful to engage in what I call "psychological Halloween-ism", a way to define and immerse yourself in a completely different identity as perhaps you did (or still do) on Halloween night. You don't have to notify anyone that you're doing this, and you don't have to wear a costume. Instead, simply change how you think about yourself by doing your best to think, feel and act like your "mask" identity for a period of time.

You could imagine yourself as anything you want: a

programmer, entrepreneur, baking aficionado, teacher, or librarian. As you immerse yourself in this identity, challenge the norms of "normal", think outside the box, expand on your self-concept. Of course, if you want to wear a costume, go for it! Whether you dress up or not, when you indulge your imagination in this way, you stimulate many of the brain regions involved in the creative process, including the DMN, the cognitive control network and the "doing" areas. As a result, you've warmed up your creative capacity, and with each new fantasy, this capacity will grow.

You don't have to keep the identity consistent or real. In 2016, psychologist Rosa Aurora Chavez described a specific type of imagery common in creative people, called primordial imagery. Think *Jurassic Park, Star Wars,* or *ET*—sort of science fiction. Human, yet obviously unrealistic—robotic, yet emotional—primordial images dare to bring fictional characters to life. When they do, they inspire you to think differently. They guide your mind into an alternate reality, which is how creative ideas are discovered in the first place.

~

You don't have to follow these tips step by step. Let them wash over your mind as you pick and choose the ones you can relate to. The table below summarises the major mindset shifts that are involved in becoming creative. Use this guide when you want to consider changes that you could make to your life.

Focused Mindset	Unfocused Mindset Shift
Focus on having enough energy to work through the day	Take 90-minute naps to increase your creativity
Have a one-track mind	Dabble in disparate disciplines to stimulate obscure but important connections
Avoid daydreaming	Build positive constructive daydreaming into your day
The best way to get to your goals is as the crow flies	Meandering paths on your daily walks or hikes stimulate creativity
All you can do is be yourself	Your "self" is subject to change. Surrender to your creative mind by challenging the norm, your biases about your creativity and your concreteness

DYNAMIC LEARNING IN A BRAVE NEW WORLD

"Our virtues and our failings are inseparable, like force and matter. When they separate, man is no more."
Nikola Tesla

"Fuckup Nights" is a phenomenon that began in Mexico in 2012, when a few friends gathered one evening to drink tequila and chat about their businesses. They realised that they had never really discussed their failures before, but found the discussion very helpful and stimulating. So they launched a monthly programme, to encourage discussion about failure publicly—to learn from others' mistakes rather than their successes. At each event, three to four entrepreneurs briefly share their stories of failure—the format is to tell the story in seven minutes using up to ten images. Following this, there is a question-and-answer session and then time for networking/mingling (when beer is served), so people can extend the conversation in a more informal learning environment. The programme has proved so appealing that it has now spread to more than 70 cities in 26 countries around the world.

You wouldn't expect talk of failure to be so open, let alone appealing. After all, failure is difficult to own up to, and often embarrassing. Yet it's so common— somewhere between 30 and 95 per cent of startups fail, depending on whether you're talking about complete liquidation or not meeting projected revenue goals— that people are relieved to learn that they're not alone. It's helpful to learn from the mistakes of others as well. This is one of the counterintuitive signatures of dynamic learning—to own up to, talk about, learn from and correct errors rather than follow a hypothetical "right" way—for which there are many methods, but none that seem to work too well for more than just a few people. In fact, some experts might even have you believe that there is a "right" way to learn, despite the fact that no two brains are alike. "Fuckup nights" helped to dispel that myth.

With all that talk of failure, you might expect people to feel down in the dumps. But that's not necessarily the case. They might be sad or frustrated (or broke) at the time of the disaster, but American entrepreneurs especially seem to bounce right back.

The current trend of thinking is that, rather than failure being a signal to drop everything and run, it's really a learning opportunity—as long as you "fail forward", "fail fast", and recognise that "done is better than perfect".

When you do, you avoid intellectual stagnation and overcome fear of failure.

Put more simply, talk is cheap, so get on and do what you need to do—and keep doing it until you get it right. If you fail, tomorrow is another day. Indeed, ask any software developer and they will likely tell you they would prefer to produce a quick prototype rather than endlessly discussing an ideal finished product. Spend too long researching the next new product for your company without actually getting to the development stage, and you run the risk of competitors beating you to market. That's why, if you fail in a relationship, for example, people will tell you "there are plenty of fish in the sea" or "if at first you don't succeed, try, try again". You have tried to make something work, and that's better than doing nothing. Prepare yourself to think in a new and dynamic way about failure.

In the past, people spent a lot of time learning about their craft or skill before they applied it. But now, it is becoming increasingly obvious that quick and dynamic application of learning is the new way to succeed. Those who are ahead are beginning to train their brains in this new way already. And in this chapter, you will learn how to do just that.

Dynamic Learning

Brightworks School—and its summer camp corollary called Tinkering School—is in San Francisco's Mission

District. It is an exemplar of a think-less-learn-more school. Housed in a 9,000-square-foot warehouse, it was founded and is run by a writer, computer scientist and brilliant educator, Gever Tully. Brightworks now has schools in Chicago, Los Angeles, Austin and Buffalo. All this from a self-described "lousy student". No doubt in reaction to his own experience in a traditional school setting, Tully has created a different kind of school, an atypical one to say the least. And it's not one my parents would ever have sent me to. That's my loss.

Brightworks students do not work by grade—instead, they work in "bands" so they can interact with students of different ages. There are no formal reading or writing classes and all learning is facilitated by "doing" and interacting. Students are invited to delve into the questions posed in conjunction with a topic, then make something from the answers and present the findings to the group. If, for example, the theme for the month is "nails", one person might write a screenplay that in some way has something to do with the word (or one of the word's meanings) while another might make a chair, using a hammer and nails in the construction, and still another might drop paint-filled balloons onto nails stuck to a canvas to create Jackson Pollock style art. They form teams, set deadlines, and manage the projects with varying degrees of supervision. They are masters of their own universes—by all counts they love it and by both objective and subjective standards, it's a success. Brightworks students are, on average, two full grades above the national reading and writing levels. All parents of children who are trying the school out want them to stay on. And to visit the school—as I did—you see happy learners and team players. These children are part of a new revolution in learning. They are anti-authority, but pro-team, pro being guided and pro-learning.

This is not to say that there is no place for traditional education or that the yardsticks by which we measure it aren't meaningful. After all, it's hard not to be in awe of the spelling-bee winner, the maths whizz, people with steel-trap memories for dates and data, or the person who has scored highest across the board throughout their academic career? These people seem to have mastered learning processes that mark them as special and successful.

But are high test scores and grades the be-all and end-all? Do spelling, maths, rote memory learning and even good writing skills truly imply higher intelligence? Certainly most top academic scholars have tremendous intellectual capabilities, and clearly even a place like Brightworks cares about comparisons with mainstream schools for test results, but just as surely, there have always been people who don't score or test well who have extremely valuable talents and deep intellects.

Thankfully, modern cultures and economies have started to acknowledge this. In schools there is a trend (on view at Brightworks to be sure) to test mastery of a topic through means other than test scores—project-based learning, performances, presentations, portfolio assessments and team (as opposed to solely individual) accomplishments. At the university level, too, there are changes afoot: Harvard professor of the history of science and physics, Peter Gallison, asks his students to create films instead of just writing papers—in this way, he feels, science comes alive and isn't just theory to be rote-learned. At MIT, there is a "Hobby Shop" in which students are encouraged to tinker; they have produced an intelligent toothbrush that knows when you are brushing too hard, a foldable ukulele, and a spherical robot that rolls uphill and ascends stairs.

And in all kinds of work environments, employers are looking to hire or promote people with skill sets that can't be totally measured empirically—life experience, team-building prowess, the capacity to motivate others, a head for juggling lots of tasks, the ability to learn from mistakes, and "emotional intelligence". Google's hiring practice, for instance, excludes test scores and grade averages from consideration—it's less about what you have learned, and more about your interest in continuing to learn; less about what you know, and more about how you are willing to use what you know adaptively.

In simplest terms, learning used to be centred on a period of study (our education) at which point we mostly switched to "cruise control"—applying recalled specialised and specific information to different tasks and challenges in a timely way. In contrast, the new approach is dynamic, encouraging people to be nimble thinkers and creative problem-solvers, to use their critical thinking skills to figure out what they don't yet know but need to know. Ever more so given that most people switch jobs multiple times, it's important to learn skills that transfer across disciplines, to think of themselves as capable thinkers and learners regardless of career. We have to say goodbye to fixed labels (A+, B-, pass/fail), narrow definitions of work identity ("I am a marketing manager for consumer products") and, most of all, our obsessive focus on specialisation ("I am a marketing manager for health and beauty consumer products"). We must also embrace the idea that learning takes place all the time outside of a traditional (or even non-traditional) classroom, including learning to *not* date the same kind of jerk over and over, or *not* repeat counterproductive habits. Any time you are engaged in better understanding yourself, other people or things, you are learning.

Imagine the old learning style like a fork that targets and spears specific information. A fork operates through focus—its work is decisive and linear. And it is an essential part of the plate setting. But when you learn dynamically, you use a spoon too. Spoons get you to the mélange of flavourful juices and bits at the bottom of your bowl, the ingredients that are every bit as important to the meal, even if they aren't clearly distinguishable. Anything that the direct piercing of focus misses is a spooning (unfocusing) endeavour: creative problem-solving (lateral thinking), making inferences through associations, predicting the future, and course correcting. (No wonder, then, that the default mode network is one of the biggest consumers of metabolic energy in the brain.)

To extend the silverware metaphor, consider the power behind a fork and a spoon working together. In 2009, a psychologist named Jackie Andrade asked two groups of 20 people to listen to a 2½-minute tape. Beforehand, they were told the tape would be "rather dull".

Actually, the tape was unbelievably boring. Although framed as a birthday party invitation, the message rambled on and on, with the host talking about someone's sick cat, her redecorated kitchen, the weather, someone's new house and a vacation in Edinburgh, Scotland, that involved museums and rain. In total, she mentioned eight place names and eight people who were definitely coming to the party.

Before the tape began, one group had been asked to shade in some little squares and circles on a piece of paper while they listened. They were told not to worry about being neat or quick; the other group were not asked to doodle at all. But all the participants had been asked to write down the place names, as well as the names of those coming to the party, while the tape played, which meant the doodlers had to switch between their doodles and their lists.

Afterwards, the papers were collected and both groups were asked if they could remember the places mentioned and the names of the people coming to the party. When tallied, the results were revealing. It turns out doodling (unfocused "spoon" work) can help you remember specifics (focused, fork targets): those who doodled during the tape recalled 29 per cent more than the average recalled by the control group. Another way of looking at these findings? Your focused brain is like a stiff sponge, while a doodling brain is looser and more absorbent.

For anyone educated only in the old linear way, the kind of dynamic learning that will get you hired at a place like Google first requires mastery of a dynamic learning-friendly cognitive rhythm: a deliberate mixture of high and low-beam flashlight pointing, of taking control of challenges and circumstances (focus) while also letting go of the need to have all the answers (unfocus). Fortunately, we have the brain bandwidth to make this adjustment.

After all, we now live in a world in which our phones—portable little brains that they are—have relieved us of our duties to remember and execute on facts, figures, translations, computations and memories (the latter in the form of our stored photos, conversations and contact information). Also, modern sensor technology is, in many cases, outperforming our biological capabilities: sensor chips detect food spoilage before your nose can; IBM's Watson trumps human data processing abilities; and machines are increasingly doing diagnostic work for doctors—an echocardiogram can pick up heart valve abnormalities more accurately than the doctor's stethoscope. In the not-so-distant-future, you may not even need to teach your children to tie their shoelaces: Nike's self-lacing sneakers sense your foot, and automatically tighten or loosen to fit. At the time of writing, self-driving cars are hitting the market and household robots are on the horizon.

Keeping up with all this technology—including

adapting to each new evolution of it, and integrating it into your daily or work life (or even competing with it on the job)—can be a challenge. It can make your head spin. But while machines may have taken over old brain functions, their existence has given you the opportunity to reconnect with yourself and your own learning capacity—to re-employ your newly unemployed brain tissue. All this mind-blowing change means that when we off-load whole categories of tasks to technology, we literally and figuratively free up brain space to learn new things, in new ways. We've got more available grey and white matter. Once you recognise that you've got brand-new brain space to develop, you can start the new learning journey.

Rediscover the Original You

Before anyone knew that there was a standard way to do things, someone had to invent it. That's the character you want to invite back into your life, the kind of person who takes the first chance. Think of whoever programmed computers before "computer programming" became a course you take in school or college. Think of the singer who sang before voice lessons were invented. Their brilliance was not created by knowledge at schools. There was no knowledge in the first place. All they had was the thoughts in their heads. This is the part of you that has been lost to education.

You come into this world with the power to make a difference with your originality. But somewhere along the way, you lose this originality to the knowledge that is given to you at schools. This "knowledge" takes over your thinking. It becomes your "go-to" whenever you need to know anything. As helpful as this can be, without your originality, it is far less powerful. Education is best when it helps your originality emerge—not when it suppresses it.

I once introduced new software to a group of educated and very smart executive coaches. I gave them an hour to figure out how it worked. Most of them were lost and didn't get very much past the sign-in. Their preconceptions held them back from thinking that they could get started without an instruction manual. We have come to live our lives with instruction manuals, forgetting that we are wired to figure things out on our own.

Consider the "One Laptop Per Child" (OLPC) project. In 2012, OLPC gave children in rural Ethiopia sealed boxes containing tablet computers that were preloaded with educational software and a memory card that tracked how they managed the new technology. Thinking at first that the children would simply play with the boxes since they probably had no idea of what computers were capable of doing, the project managers were shocked to see the actual results.

Within four minutes, one child opened the box and found the on/off switch and powered up the tablet. Within *five* days, each child was comfortable with the apps; within two weeks they were singing ABC songs. And within five months, the children had hacked into the Android operating system. OLPC had tried to freeze the desktop settings, but the children worked around this even though software had been inserted to prevent any changes. Somehow, through their own ingenuity, they customised their desktops so that each one looked different.

We are capable of incredible things if we stop behaving like automatons and start trusting ourselves more. OLPC may not have increased standardised test scores, but its example demonstrates the innate ingenuity that each of us has.

Quick on the Draw, Strong to the Core

In the same way that you have a physical balance point—a centre of gravity (COG)—that keeps you upright and prevents you from falling, you have a psychological balance point, a psychological COG. This is the place that originality (your own true voice) grows from, as well as the mechanism for emotional self-control. In real-life contexts, this is the inner compass you tap into when you are unsure about where you should go, how you should respond, what you need to do next in any given situation. It's noticeable in the form of self-pep talks that keep you buoyed in the face of overwhelming emotional or intellectual "input": commentary from well-meaning advisors and teachers, anxious investors, or vocal critics. In other words, your psychological COG keeps you grounded and true to yourself as you make your way through the learning journey called life.

A case in point from a sampling of those of my clients who are stockbrokers. Some investors do really well when the market is volatile, and just as many tank in a tumultuous economy. Given my proximity to their inner thoughts (what they tell me in therapy, anyway), I have noticed a discernible pattern: investors who perform superiorly choose stocks that they understand well. They also stick to their own investing style, and the more volatile the market gets, the more deeply they connect with themselves and stick to that style. This activation of their psychological COG gives them the stability they need to avoid making bad decisions in the midst of stock-market change. (In his bestselling book, *One Up On Wall Street*, the hugely successful Fidelity fund manager, Peter Lynch, recommended a very similar strategy to non-professionals: stick with investing in companies whose products you use and think are great, he advised. The operative word here is *you*.)

Investors who do poorly tend to be overwhelmed by market volatility. When the going gets tough—or at least when it gets blurry—they are unduly influenced by the opinions of others. They go whichever way the wind is blowing, following the latest investing trend in the new, new thing. Sometimes they get lucky and the investment they make pays off. But more often than not—and certainly over the long run—their lack of self-connection to the idea, to the trend, yields lower returns.

In brief, great investors do not lose their connection with reality when they go deep inside themselves for gut guidance. On the contrary, they find a compass in themselves to navigate the sea of change. And everything they learn is incorporated and integrated deeply, giving them that crucial extra bit of understanding and confidence in the face of the next rough patch too.

The lesson here, of course, is that the more you are in focused, old-school learning mode—follow the leader, study the facts—the less you'll hear what your COG has to say. The best way to tap into it, to hear it, is to activate your DMN. Meditation, listening to music, and, perhaps not surprisingly, going on holiday have all been shown to improve your brain's ability for COG-connected original thinking ("self-circuits") and emotional control. And exercise too, which is both a great way to activate the DMN, and an example unto itself. Almost all exercise requires engaging your abdominal muscles. Warming up this key area by lying on your back and lowering your legs from 90 degrees to the ground or doing some planks engages these muscles—your core. In the same way, you invoke unfocus to get your psychological COG firing.

Though many people have grown to connect with their psychological COG automatically and unthinkingly, you have to commit to cultivating this sense of self, and catch yourself whenever you are operating outside of it. Simply wondering to yourself if you are or are not connected to your COG is a sure-fire way to locate it. Try this when you're lost in an argument, or when you find yourself arguing yourself into a corner. Or when you're at a fork in the proverbial road, at a decision point in your career or personal life, ask yourself—literally, and using the second-person self-talk I have described before: "Are you operating from your COG or are you being swayed by someone else's opinion or needs?" It's quite amazing what this deliberate pause and self-questioning will do to build confidence and optimism in whichever path you choose. And remember that it'll reduce your stress too.

Psychological Centre of Gravity Manoeuvres: Reflecting and Relating

In 2016, psychiatrist and brain researcher Christopher Davey and his colleagues looked at which circuits in the brain are active when we self-reflect, the first step towards self-understanding and being able to really hear our psychological centre of gravity (COG). They asked 96 study participants to say whether an adjective applied to them or not. They gave them words that were not particularly favourable or unfavourable and that would elicit self-reflection rather than an immediate response: e.g. "sceptical", "perfectionist", "lucky".

When participants reflected on themselves, it was activation in the DMN that showed up on the brain scans. Science can actually tell us which specific DMN regions are responsible for different parts of the self-reflection process, but the big picture take-away is that this process stems from the ability to unfocus.

Connect to your psychological COG through unfocus, and all of a sudden you may have an increased understanding of not only yourself, but others too. Studies show that three discrete circuits within your DMN "light up" when you are trying to think through three corresponding social intelligence puzzles: understanding how someone else feels, how you are different from them, and how they see the world. In other words, you are using the same parts of your brain when you listen to your COG as when you are negotiating, forming teams or anticipating another person's next move.

The Bounce Back: Talking (to) Yourself Out of Failure

When you fail at something, you've got to pick yourself by the bootstraps and keep going, proceeding with the valuable lessons from the failure itself. This is easier said than done, especially when your brain is largely conditioned to hear and remember the negative, to respond to the crisis and not the lesson within it. Indeed, for every successful dynamic learner who has been able to learn and move on from his mistakes, there are far more people who have made a mistake or failed at something and been beaten down by it—they discontinue their effort and settle for something else. Whether it is a small issue like an office project or cooking a new dish or a larger issue like a career choice or relationship, only a blessed few are able to truly feel inspired when they fail. Psychologist Martin Seligman has referred to the deflation we feel with repeated failures as "learned helplessness".

In 1988, psychologist Carol Dweck explained that it's not so much the magnitude of the failure that matters, as the mindset we have about it. If we think we're doomed and forever stymied by our failure—if we have a fixed mindset—we won't try again to succeed. But if we believe that intelligence is malleable—if we have a growth mindset—we will rebound much faster.

To demonstrate that our brain is in fact wired to rebound from failure, David Franklin and Daniel Wolpert, engineering professors who use computers to model how the brain makes decisions, pinpointed the five basic mechanisms on display in the brain when a person bounces back. Outlined below, these are ways to help your failure-defeated brain regain the specific spring coils it needs to recover. Self-talk is the activating agent for each of these mechanisms and more energy and enthusiasm are the result. Because scientists know which brain regions correspond to each mechanism, they know what you need to ask yourself to make the spring coils come back online again.

This five-step system of brain "spring coil regeneration" (my own phrase, not a scientific one) gets you switching from the low beams of focusing on your failure to the high beams of attention and wondering. When you're learning under stress (e.g. after failure, slowing down, confusion, or hitting a wall), one of these might get overstretched. By asking yourself the right questions, you can put the spring back into every step of your brain's learning process.

1. Fighting the Feedback

We get feedback all the time and from all kinds of sources: responses from people, beeps and screeches from machines, new mail piling up in our inboxes. The feedback we get (or give ourselves) from having failed can be particularly overwhelming and stressful. Unfortunately, when you are stressed out, your brain has trouble deciding what's important; the stressed brain thinks *everything* is important, negative (unhelpful) feedback included. This is when you need to help it out—to manually tag information as relevant (helpful) or dramatic (unhelpful). Dynamic learners are experts at this kind of feedback control.

For every obstruction you encounter, ask yourself, "Is this relevant or dramatic?" It'll help you separate the wheat from the chaff when your brain has too much to handle. Often, you won't even recognise what's making you feel bad. But when you realise that your brain is unconsciously dramatising recent feedback, you can tag it appropriately and put it aside.

One thing that can be especially helpful if you're trying to create something is to keep a re-routing journal—a notebook or computer file in which you document changes to your thought processes. Review the journal regularly to discern the progress you are making as it will help you remember each point of change. It also helps you see the feedback traps before you fall into them again.

The question to ask yourself: what dramatic feedback am I mistakenly considering relevant right now?

Believers Bounce Back

In 2006, Columbia psychologist Jennifer Mangels and her colleagues studied what happens in the brain when people with fixed versus growth mindsets receive feedback. They found that when you have a fixed mindset, your brain tends to dwell on negative feedback, expected or unexpected. But perhaps even worse, it ignores the corrective suggestions that will arise as you try to figure out what to do.

In this study, the researchers first determined the mindset—fixed or growth—of 47 participants. They then asked a slew of general knowledge questions. The test-takers typed in their answers, and then rated their confidence about being correct. Next they were told whether they were correct or not, and afterwards, the correct answer—all this while their brains were hooked up to machines that could detect and record their brainwaves. After eight minutes, they were asked to return for a surprise re-test on all the questions they had answered incorrectly. They were only informed about this stage just before they started again.

Despite similar performances on the initial tests, people with a growth mindset performed much better on the second test. They believed they could bounce back, so they did! In the fixed group, the brainwave responses to negative feedback were correspondingly greater, indicating that they had wiped out these mistakes faster, without giving themselves a chance for correction.

2. The Resistance Rebuttal

Do you know that feeling when you just can't seem to get ahead? No matter what you do, something is stopping you, but you can't tell what. The universe of possible impediments to your progress can be divided into three categories: people, places and things. Once you understand which category you're dealing with, you can institute the "resistance rebuttal" (more formally known as impedance control), the second mechanism that Franklin and Wolpert described. By working out what's in your way, over time, roadblocks in your life become surmountable because they lose their power to silently terrorise you.

Say you're trying to learn how to use a new team-building software platform at work, a technology that will allow you and others to report on what you're doing. But you just can't get your head around it. What's the real issue here? Is the technology itself really difficult (the thing), is your office too loud or busy to allow you to concentrate (the place), or are you intimidated and distracted by how quickly everyone else seems to be picking up when and how to log in and navigate through the programme (people)? Let's imagine that you decide it's the people, so now you've recognised the issue. Having done so, your stress and negative chatter will start to dissipate. You know the real problem here. Now, pivot to the solution.

For starters, consciously designate a longer period of time to learn your way around the new software. Now go a step further and divide the designated learning time into phases: perhaps before your morning staff meeting you will try to learn the basics of logging in and navigating the main tabs. Before lunch, you decide you want to learn how to enter your own information quickly and send it to specific others. After lunch you decide you'll try to actually send a message to the group. In between each phase, build in an unfocus period to let your mind synthesise and consolidate the information you've mastered in the last phase. Fifteen minutes of consolidation time is enough to go out and get a coffee or read the front page of the newspaper or play solitaire on your computer. It's in this unfocused "down time" that your resistance will drop and you'll regain the needed energy and optimism to tackle the software. If you're a procrastinator, it may sound counter intuitive to spend even more time-away from the next task—yet, it's exactly this kind of deliberate unfocus that will give you the time you need to overcome the resistance that is in the way of your learning to act.

The question to ask yourself: What's stopping me? (People, places, or things?)

3. Your Predicting Power

Your ability to predict the future is probably better than you think. Some people refer to this as "systematic forecasting"—an ability to estimate the greatest likelihood of things happening by collecting data in the present and applying it to the future. Even if you are using the prediction algorithms of machine learning in a business, at some point being able to predict where to apply this, or where new markets exist, is a valuable skill. Researchers call this prediction control. It's like learning how to jump the gun intelligently. Paradoxically, being "intelligent" here implies thinking less.

Neuroscientist Moshe Bar wrote a helpful paper in 2009, explaining how the proactive brain works. Even if you have done something very similar many times over, every moment is actually a brand-new experience in life, he reminds us. For example, every time you get into your car, you see a driver's seat, and even though you've seen the seat before, this new moment has never existed previously.

Your brain is constantly engaged in making analogies, then associations and predictions. But when you're learning something totally new to you (or difficult, especially in a nonlinear, fact-based way), or when you're uncertain about something and need to clarify things, hypervigilance and overfocus use your brain resources to pay attention only to what you are seeing. This shuts down the process of prediction, and so you become stalled or stumped.

If you think about it, we unfocus to predict all the time. For example, satellite images can be used to predict weather patterns, volcanic eruptions, rains that trigger mudslides, or even infectious disease outbreaks. In these instances, we are literally unfocusing to view patterns from above earth.

But you can unfocus to look into the future too.

When you turn your brain's predictive capacity on, you can predict bad investments, the consequences of going into a mosh pit, or even relationship success when you simply ask yourself what the future will be like, and then look around in your head to find evidence to support that view.

By first predicting the future, you set up a signpost for your brain—a target for it to hit. Entrepreneurs, for instance, will often have a BHAG (bold, hairy, audacious goal). It acts as a signpost for your brain to start devising conscious and unconscious plans. Initially, that target doesn't have to be a reasonable one. Sometimes, when you're stuck, you unfocus to go for the big goal. Your brain will figure out the rest.

Life is a series of successful experiments that can be tweaked as each new finding sheds light on prior ones. Your brain is wired to do this if you dare to be the principal investigator—the "Futurist"—of your life. So go ahead and set up hypotheses and test them after you predict what will happen—it'll shake things up in your brain and allow you to jump right over the obstacles in front of you.

The question to ask yourself: what can I infer from the information I have so far?

4. Balancing Brain Equations

We like to think that we are aware of the pros and cons of our decisions, but our brains are in fact not wired to judge if our efforts are fruitless; we will only see the futility of our efforts if we consciously ask "What am I getting for what I am putting out?" When you're focused and determined to make a situation work, you assume that your determination justifies the effort, when it may be obscuring the fact that you're doing a lot for close to nothing in return. Often, we forget to ask this question overtly. That's why we might stick around in relationships or organisations despite them having been on the decline for years. Even a glimpse of possible hope can keep you stuck in a familiar situation when you should be cutting your losses and moving on. Of course, there are other instances when your brain does abandon ship, like when you're not that psychologically invested in something. But that kind of overreaction can be a misstep too.

Whether you are trying to come up with a new idea, or make a relationship or business work, you are always learning. Every so often, while following your initial strategy, ask yourself what is working and what is not. You'll be surprised by how wasteful you are about personal energy, often doing things for which you get nothing in return. When you think overtly about the pros and cons of your behaviour, you will keep yourself out of mind-traps like "I already bought the unhealthy food—I should just eat it" or "I might as well stay for this entire horrible movie because I've watched half of it already". Understanding the pros and cons of continued actions can help you make more fruitful decisions.

The question to ask yourself: if I keep on doing what I am doing, is my effort worth it or not?

5. "Feel and Do" Learning

Learning from touching prototypes and doing things is called sensori-motor learning. Every time you act, you advance by learning in real time through real experience rather than through thinking. At medical school, for example, when we were understaffed and needed to learn new surgical procedures, the common aphorism was "see one, do one, teach one". There was no time wasted in learning through endless reading, observation or thinking. Thinking could only get you so far. Doing was the pathway to learning. It was the only way to ensure improvement too.

Learning from doing replaces learning from over-thinking. Even your mistakes can help you discover new things. It's also more practical, because you learn to envision the future from multiple concrete iterations rather than thought iterations.

The question to ask yourself: what one action can jump-start my brain?

PUTTING IT ALL TOGETHER FOR THE LOVE
OF LEARNING

Here's the shorthand for dynamic learning: the 4 Cs: Change direction, Be Curious, Curate advice wisely, and, lastly Co-Construct your learning.

Change Direction

In your brain, attention exists on a metaphorical pivot. When you are focused on learning within a traditional classroom or when you have set your sights on specific goals, you are externally focused. You are using your "fork". There's certainly a time and place for that. But don't forget the "spoon". Being able to pivot inward—as you would do when listening to your intuition and your psychological COG—reconnects you to your original self and expands your learning beyond the facts on the page. This switch of focus allows you to bathe in the sea of memories, aspirations, values, meaning and purpose that make up the complexity of you. And that's where the magic lies.

Pivoting inward happens when your mind wanders spontaneously; there are known psychological vehicles that can help you make this switch.

Mental simulation is one such "unfocus" vehicle. It involves imagining what it *might* be like to do or be something. And it uses your predicting power too. You can simulate what it would feel like to be in your ideal job, with an ideal partner, or in an ideal life.

This should not be brief or casual fantasising. You set aside time for it. First, think of what you want to learn as you did in the Resistance Rebuttal. Say it's the ability to use the new software programme as in that example. One way to prepare yourself for your Rebuttal is to simulate what you actually want by taking yourself through a series of steps in visualising how you would get there: calling a colleague to find out how to do it, setting an hour twice a week to do it, and imagining what you might want to truly collaborate about. You don't just think out the steps; you simulate it in your mind as if it is actually happening.

You might want to do some or all of this mental simulation out loud—to yourself or to someone willing to listen. You can also pick a time when you're alone to walk through your learning goal mentally: in the shower, walking the dog, or when you're feeling bored, or have nothing to do. Every opportunity to actively simulate a situation will give you a chance to activate your psychological COG.

Studies on what happens in the brain when you mentally simulate situations show that you are activating the DMN. Also, the more specific the visualisation, the more meaning you'll get out of it and the more you will activate your psychological COG.

So, whenever you get lost while learning, whether you are following an instruction manual to build a cabinet or developing an email list for your business, simulate the result you want in your mind. Be as specific as you can be (visualise the finished cabinet or the audience that is responding), and this will pivot your attention to engage your COG and predicting power, and will help motivate you to get to the finish line.

Curiosity

We are all born curious—we explore by putting all kinds of things in our mouths as babies, we play make-believe as children, we ask challenging and often counter-culture questions as teenagers. Over the course of our maturation, however, our innate curiosity takes a back seat to a view of the world that is more concrete.

But learning clearly improves when we are curious. And when we're curious, we often follow our instincts and interests without thinking too much about them. In 2014, neuroscientist Matthias Gruber and colleagues asked nineteen students to examine more than 100 trivia questions. Unsurprisingly, the students recalled 71 per cent of the answers that really piqued their curiosity, compared to 54 per cent of the answers that didn't. Curiosity about the trivia questions activated their brains' reward centre, and in this manner, probably facilitated learning. When the questions did not elicit curiosity, they were easily forgotten.

But the more surprising finding was that the students were able to identify even incidental facts more when they were curious than when they were not. This effect persisted a day later. Their brain scans showed that long-term memory (the hippocampus) was more engaged when students were curious, thereby helping them to remember the incidental facts. The mere sense of anticipation was enough to get their memory jazzed.

When something interests us, we are more likely to

remember it. When we are curious, our brain rallies to make sure that we remember, not just what we are curious about, but anything else that we come across around the same time. This is a fringe benefit that many innovators take advantage of—they remember and connect surprising parts of their discoveries because they are fuelled by curiosity. And they can handle the tension and surprises that come with curiosity because they are connected to their psychological COG.

Curating Advice

We live in a world of advice-givers. Parents, teachers, self-help experts, financial gurus, personal shoppers and spouses are all willing to offer their view and opinions. You probably offer it to others as well—it's human to opine and advise. Giving and getting advice is, however, less benign than you might think.

First, giving advice: in 2015, Dean Mobbs, a psychology professor at Columbia University, and his colleagues looked at the brains of advice-givers. They found that we seem to be wired to want our own advice to lead to the success of others. Even though it's often unconscious, we care more about our own advice being accepted than people winning as a result of it. Well-meaning though it may be, we should take advice from others with a large pinch of salt.

How about responding to advice? In 2009, Emory University neuroeconomist Jan Engelmann and his colleagues used brain imaging to examine what happens in the brains of people making financial decisions.

Participants had to choose between financial puzzles, where the chances of winning were clear, and lotteries, with different probabilities of winning. They had to figure out the probability of success prior to making a choice. In half the trials, an expert economist gave them his economic advice. When the subjects got that advice, the regions of the brain involved in the valuation process were inactive. But when the expert did not give his advice, the "valuation" regions of their brains actively were involved as they tried to figure it out themselves.

Lo and behold, expert advice replaces active valuation by the brain! When you give advice to someone, the person passively listens but does not actively process or absorb your advice. In other words, blindly accepting advice does little to stimulate thinking. It is the opposite of discovery. So by all means listen to advice, but make sure you tinker with it. Put your own discovery process first.

Co-construct Your Skin

Machines are gaining traction in the workplace. And it's not just mobile devices and faster computers that I'm talking about. As we speak, robots are being made to take over countless jobs, probably even your own. This impacts how and what you choose to learn, and how you define yourself professionally too.

Oxford University researchers estimate that 47 per cent of jobs in the US will be automated in the next two decades. The World Economic Forum has predicted that robots will replace 5 million jobs by 2020, many of these in the "office and administration" category, although others sectors will be affected as well. So what will you do when there is no "administrative assistant" position, and how else might you apply your organisational skills?

You are more likely to be able to switch jobs and invent a new one if you keep your work identity looser and your learning more flexible—if you connect with your ingenuity and psychological COG.

Other service jobs will be impacted too. For instance, Tech-No-Logic has made a robot cook that can pick up ingredients from separate containers and whip up a meal by following recipe instructions from an app. And Momentum Machines has made a multitasker bot that can make and flip hamburgers in ten seconds and soon will be able to replace an entire McDonald's crew. That's why there is so much talk about the need to "upskill"— as the easier jobs are taken over by machines, dynamic learning for new roles using all of your brain's spring coils will be key.

Learning to live with and develop alongside machines will require a new learning frame of mind—one that will compete with them where relevant, and also cooperate with them. That's where your ingenuity—your original intelligence rather than your learned skills—will be crucial. But your own ingenuity will have to be applied in the context of the community of machines that is becoming increasingly interconnected and connected to you.

British entrepreneur Kevin Ashton coined the phrase "the internet of things" to describe how machines are increasingly connected to us in our brave new world: you can control your garage door from a remote location, and watch your kids at home while you're at work. What was once an obstruction to connection—distance—is no longer relevant in our wireless world.

More than ever, it is important to realise that your brain is part of this "internet of things". After all, it's wired with electrical circuits like any other device. It can be activated or made to rest. With its buzzing electrical circuits and information systems, it is set up to connect with the world of devices and external information storage. And this development is changing our brains and how we think and act.

In 2010, one of Google's co-founders, Sergey Brin, said, "We want Google to be the third half of your brain." What he meant was that he wanted humans to start thinking of Google as a way to relieve the stress of having to store so much in our brains. He was suggesting that we can offload the storage of information to the sites that Google will take us to, and free up our own thinking machines—our brains—for other things. In other words, use our newly freed-up head space to help our brain's spring coils work more effectively, or connect with our psychological COG and ingenuity.

When you apply the principles of dynamic learning, you will adapt to the speed of change, course-correct when necessary by using your brain's spring coils, and most of all, use your internal compass to activate the ingenuity that is inherent in you.

While it's true that machines will always be better at being machines, you have the edge when it comes to being human.

Learning in a Focused Mindset	Learning in an Unfocused Mindset Shift
If lost while learning, focus on external cues to get back on track	When lost, remember to turn to your inner compass from time to time. Ask "Who am I?" Your own ingenuity should be your primary guide
Respond to feedback—positive and negative	Carefully consider feedback with a growth mindset; challenge its relevance
To be agile, fail fast, and fail forward	You can't fail forward or fail fast without reactivating your brain's spring coils—so build in self-talk to stay agile

Base your next action on evidence and data	You are as much a creator as a follower of data—so simulate and imagine solutions as well
Machines are separate from you	Your brain is part of the "internet of things"

–4–

SUPERTASKING

> "Simultaneity . . . is the property of all great poetry."
> LeRoy C. Breunig

When you're doing two or more things at the same time—reading email and speaking on the telephone, for example—you are multitasking. When you are trying to accomplish multiple tasks on the same day—like trying to finish a report while tending to the needs of a sick spouse—you are also multitasking. You could even describe multitasking as doing two things over an extended period of time, such as working at your current job while starting another business on the side. Both might demand your attention equally, requiring you to constantly split your attention between the two.

Though many people wear their multitasking "ability" like a productivity badge of honour, the short-term accomplishments are often dubious. Even if you actually finish the multiple tasks you start, more often than not, multitasking leaves you frazzled and spent; your brain's attentional flashlight sort of runs out of batteries and as a result, the path ahead can seem confusing or dimly lit. This is what I call "wobbly brain syndrome", the point at which you become effectively disconnected from access to the calming influence of your default mode network (DMN). Doctoral student Kep Kee Loh and cognitive neuroscientist Ryota Kanai recently described this phenomenon when they studied media multitaskers—like people who text while watching TV and browse the internet at the same time. They saw that the conflict detector in the multitasking brain (the anterior cingulate cortex, or ACC) had less grey-matter density compared to people who used just one device at a time. It was as if multitasking had gobbled up brain tissue in this region. To make matters worse, the more people multitasked, the less the DMN was connected to the ACC. As a result, a big task load created unbearable conflicts. In lay terms: a resulting confusion, discomfort, forgetfulness, and, as much as they tried to stay focused, less attentiveness.

For real-life context, consider the example of a nurse who calmly prioritises patients in a chaotic emergency room. Or in a totally different environment, the director or producer who is required to direct live, multi-camera television: managing many monitors at the same time, making sure the teleprompter is working, deciding which angle to highlight in any given moment, when to add graphics or information at the bottom of the screen, all the while listening to feedback in an earpiece and giving directions through a microphone!

So what's the difference between a nurse or director who is drained and depleted at the end of the shift and one who might even whistle his or her way to bed at the crack of dawn? The former is a classic multitasker—they may get things done, but they do it all with their "hair on fire". The latter, on the other hand, is what I refer to as a supertasker—the neurological juggling here is more fluid and, as a result, the action is more productive.

Some people seem to be in some way born wired to supertask. Psychologists Jason Watson and David Strayer studied 200 people while they were in a driving simulator. In the experiment, participants had to drive behind a car that was constantly braking, so they had to be on high alert to avoid a collision. It was like being in stop-and-go motorway traffic.

In the multitasking portion of the study, participants had to solve simple arithmetic problems while driving. And in between problems, they were asked to remember two to five words they were shown. Imagine actually doing this while you are driving in motorway traffic—it certainly requires more attention than speaking mindlessly on your cellphone.

No great surprise, this research showed that doing two things at once was close to impossible for most people. However, 2.5 per cent of the group separated themselves from the pack. Not only was their driving unaffected when multitasking, but some of them even drove better.

Whether or not one is born with the neurological connections, however, it's clear that a certain amount of practice breeds supertasking ability. You know this in your own life—the more you have to juggle the same two (or more) responsibilities, the better you tend to get at keeping those particular balls in the air; or not. In which case, you (and the nurse or director) realise a career change might be in order. But what if you didn't necessarily have to put in the hours or months or years of practice to become so neurologically facile?

Just as we can see what's breaking down in the brain when a person multitasks inefficiently, we know what is working *right* in the supertasker's brain. In essence, the nurse or director has learned to "staff" their brain with just the right capacity to remember, filter and manage conflicting information. They exhibit a variety of strategies for "brain training", making neurological connections where at first there are none, and finding ways of avoiding redundancies of thought and action, thus becoming more efficient and less exhausted multitaskers: supertaskers. In other words, we know the cognitive rhythm that provides the best conditions for supertasking regardless of the specific tasks that need to be juggled. The common strategic denominator? All involve invoking the power of unfocus.

Dissolving Stress

Stress isn't always a bad thing. A little stress—called eustress—is always going to be necessary to motivate you to get any kind of job done. But after a certain point, eustress becomes distress, creating chaos in the brain, disrupting the functioning of the DMN, and throwing you out of cognitive rhythm.

One recent study compared two groups of medical students—a group applying for residency, which is a particularly high-stress juncture in a medical career, and a group who were not yet at that point, and therefore were less stressed (though no doubt tired; that's par for the course). Compared to the less-stressed medical students, those applying for residency had a DMN that was not well connected to the rest of the brain. It was out of the loop. Furthermore, their brains' conflict centres perpetuated the internal chaos. When you're always "on"—waiting, nervous, anticipating, wondering—chaos and fatigue are the end result. That's the classic pattern for a multitasking brain, quite different from that of a supertasker.

There are numerous things you can do to reduce your stress—exercise and meditation are popular and effective. They have both been shown to normalise DMN function so that your brain can get back into gear. Alternatively, you can use self-talk to reframe your tasks as "a more intense period that will soon be over" or "an intense period and time to practise being a supertasker". This is similar to what you did with the possibility mindset—deactivating your amygdala and reviving your DMN, which is the recipe for getting back into cognitive rhythm.

But one counterintuitive thing you might not think of doing when you have a million things to juggle is to add another task to your day. Here's the (happy) rub: this added task should be playful and joyful; it should take your mind off the growing to-do list that you have. When you give yourself this joyful or playful "task", your brain will respond with a metaphoric sigh of relief. (This is why companies like Google provide games, sport and workout equipment to their ambitious and supertasking employees. The management knows that having unfocused time can help their employees manage their days much more effectively.)

If video games are your thing, consider research by cognitive neuroscientist E.L. Maclin. He and his colleagues trained people to multitask while using a video game called Space Fortress, and found that playing the game increased the participants' alpha wave power, one of the unfocus frequencies. Once in alpha, the multitasking they were asked to do became easier. It's like trying to swim in calm water rather than stormy waves. Being more in alpha mode replenishes your brain, and from that refreshed baseline you are better able to switch your attention, a hallmark of supertasking.

To be clear, I am not suggesting that you abandon your patients when you are a nurse or drift off into a stupor in the middle of a work day. But before you arrive, and in the course of a multitasking day, add an unrelated task requiring little effort. It will help to warm up your DMN and make you more relaxed. With your brain relaxed, you then take your cruise control to a completely different level.

The Advantage of Age

If you're thinking that supertasking training is for the young and nimble, you're in for a nice surprise. Your age does *not* necessarily limit the effects. Kinesiologist Joaquin Anguera and his colleagues demonstrated this in a 2013 study. They used a three-dimensional video game, NeuroRacer, to train people at supertasking. Results showed that men and women between the ages of 60 and 85 became better in supertasking than 20-year olds who were untrained in the game. Sure, training a 20-year-old would probably place them at an advantage too, but the point is that you can reverse age-related multitasking deficits with training.

Calling on Your Silent Partner— the Unconscious

Your unconscious brain is a silent but powerful partner to your conscious brain in dealing with the world. People were aware of this alliance of the conscious and unconscious mind long before the current era of information-processing psychology. For example, in the late nineteenth century, educated public figures were fascinated by a phenomenon known as "automatic writing", during which people could allegedly write prose while carrying out other tasks. Such people, who included

Georgie Hyde-Lees, the wife of famous poet William Butler Yeats, claimed that they felt as if they were owned by something else, and in this state of what is now known as "dissociation", they would be compelled to write by this "outside" force. Even Sir Arthur Conan Doyle—creator and author of "Sherlock Holmes"—thought this spiritualism was genuine. But as explained in a recent review paper by psychologist Wilma Koutstaal, this very real phenomenon is probably related to automatic brain processes that cause the individual to switch from conscious intention to a state of awareness in which memories and understanding are automatically activated in the brain.

The idea that you could voluntarily switch your state of mind so that something automatic could be activated may sound challenging, to say the least, yet you actually do this all the time, even if you aren't aware of it. When your eye sees a colleague's hand outstretched so that you can shake it, your brain registers this image but it also guides your hand to do the actual shaking—you don't merely stare at the hand. There is a conscious process that allows you to see your colleague's hand and an unconscious process that guides your hand so that you don't have to actually look at its destination—your colleague's grip.

The "seeing" and "guiding" in this scenario are handled by different visual wiring systems. "Seeing" is a conscious act involving the ventral visual stream (a bunch of neurons that go from your eye to your brain). "Guiding" is an unconscious act handled by the dorsal visual stream (a bunch of neurons that also connect your eye and brain behind the ventral stream). These wiring systems go to different parts of your brain to help you see and guide at the same time. Too much seeing and no guiding would make you stare at your colleague's hand the whole time. (That would look strange, to say the least!) Too much guiding and no seeing would make you miss the hand.

When people are unable to supertask, it is because they do not have the right balance between seeing and guiding—specifically, they do not trust their guiding neurons. They get caught up in the detail of a task (metaphorically staring at the outstretched hand) instead of loosening up enough to let the unconscious do its job.

Fear of the Unknown

Your unconscious brain contains a mixed bag of intimidating emotions and experiences. Anger, fear, sexual impulses, loneliness, neediness, feelings of abandonment—things you don't really want to be too visible—live in your unconscious. They are neighbours of your unconscious guide system, the "less controversial" part of your unconscious mind. Knowing that these things sit next to each other tends to makes us reticent to let go of focus. If we let go by stirring the unconscious mind, we fear that we may inadvertently open that mixed bag of emotions. Yet, if you don't take that chance, only the "conscious you" will try to supertask. That's like braking around a corner rather than putting your foot on the gas. Not only will it wear down your brakes, but it could also cause you to skid off the road. You absolutely have to dare to dabble in your whole unconscious pool—good AND bad—as it will help make supertasking more fluent.

One way to activate your unconscious brain and release yourself from the clutches of focus is to doodle. It's a fun way to think less and learn more. As we have previously seen, it activates the DMN and gets your focused, conscious brain out of the way.

When you set aside time to doodle, you will find yourself drawing seemingly random things that are probably not as random as they seem. In a 2002 paper, psychoanalyst Marion Milner explains that doodling overrides conscious obstructions and allows your unconscious self to kick in. The symbols that you draw reflect the goings-on in your subterranean brain.

Psychologist Robert Burns has also studied doodles for much of his life. In an interview published on "The Register"—a British technology, news and opinion website—he said that doodles reveal much of the inner workings of the mind. He pointed out that in the same way that an EEG pattern (electroencephalogram) can record brain activity with a stylus when connected to your brain by electrodes, so can a doodle because it is connected to your brain by your hands.

If you hesitate to doodle on the job in order to supertask, consider the fact that by 2007, 26 of 44 US presidents were self-confessed doodlers. If there's any job where you need to be a supertasker, that's the one, right? Other notable figures like the painter, print-maker and theorist of the German Renaissance, Albrecht Dürer, also doodled, as did the prolific Russian writer, Fyodor Dostoyevsky.

In fact, it was Dostoyevsky who noted how the conscious mind can get in the way when he wrote in *Winter Notes on Summer Impressions*, "Try to pose for yourself this task: not to think of a polar bear, and you will see that the cursed thing will come to mind every minute." As long ago as 1863, he recognised how conscious, focused thinking could fail us. More than a century later, social psychologist Daniel Wegner's research has proven that if you think "do not drop the ball" when you're juggling and stressed, you are more than likely to drop it. Your conscious brain gets in the way, takes up energy, leaving none for the unconscious brain to guide you.

The Power of Music

Studies show that even in older adults, just four months of musical training can help improve focused and unfocused attention. It can also increase your overall IQ, and improve your ability to spell. When we examine brain images to find out what's changing with music training, we see that regions that make your fingers move, and regions involved in listening, are beefed up. That's no surprise. But of interest to us, and the concept of unfocusing, is the beefing-up of the brain bridge that connects both hemispheres. When you add more lanes to the brain bridge, thought traffic flows more easily.

When you play the piano, you learn to play parts for the left and right hand, and the patterns of movements for each hand often differ. When you're playing a piece that uses both hands, you can't focus on one hand at a time. You have to focus on both. To do this, your brain unfocuses—deactivates—and your attention deepens as you let go of your focus on each individual hand, especially if you're playing a concerto as opposed to something simple like musical scales.

Focusing on one task at a time is called serial processing. Serial processing makes bottlenecks worse. Instead, you should unfocus. By activating parallel brain circuits and deactivating focus, you allow your brain to share the energy it has to attend to both hands, making supertasking possible.

Getting Through Brain Bottlenecks

When you need to respond to an email while you are on the telephone, you have to read, write and listen at the same time. But your brain can often only do one task at a time properly. It's as if there's one checkpoint and

145

tasks that need to be done have to arrange themselves in a single file in your brain.

When many tasks try to squeeze through to attention via a bottleneck, the results can be disastrous. Think of trying to join a jam-packed motorway when driving. That's what every new thought is faced with—it slows down, and eventually your brain becomes a parking lot for thoughts. Your immediate reaction is to drop the multitasking, when instead you should see this as a signal to switch to supertasking mode.

In 2015, neuroscientist Omar Al-Hashimi and his colleagues looked at how certain people's brains overcome bottlenecks—how they manage to deftly switch brain lanes and somehow find a way through. They used the video game NeuroRacer to see how this happens.

The game is designed to have people follow single- and then multi-component tasks, such as keeping a car within a target box versus doing this while responding to various road signals that increase in number as the game gets harder. As the number of things that the participants had to pay attention to increased, an information bottleneck was created in their brains.

When the researchers looked at the brains of people with superior multitasking performance (those with faster response time, fewer errors and greater accuracy), they noted that the superior parietal lobe (SPL) was a key player. This brain region helps you quickly switch between tasks by loosening the grip of focus. It also efficiently manages brain resources by keeping things for a longer time in your short-term memory cup so that you can, effectively, more easily "start where you left off".

Another way to reduce bottlenecks is through "re-dundancy reduction"—the ability to combine one or more tasks so that you save time. Even though stopping to consciously think through the ways to reduce redundancies might take you more time at first, taking the step of unfocusing on your separate goals and tinkering with them to see which ones can be combined is what will decongest your bottleneck. And, with practice, this becomes much more automatic.

Getting Physical

You aren't conscious of it necessarily, but your body supertasks all the time. Walking is supertasking 101; it uses many leg and abdominal muscle groups and requires you to look where you're going, too.

There are certain physical exercises that enhance neurological supertasking as well. At your local gym, for example, you can probably find a piece of equipment called a ViPR. This is a rubber cylinder about belly-button high on a six-foot person. There are spaces cut into the cylinder like a jack-o'-lantern so that you can put your hands through to get a grip on it. To practise multitasking, get down on one knee and rotate your upper body to the left. Then place the cylinder vertically on the ground with two hands inserted into the jack-o'-lantern holes. This is the first move. Next, lift up the cylinder with both hands, swing it to the horizontal position, and take it with you as you rotate your upper body all the way to the right, keeping your lumbar spine stationary and only moving your thoracic spine as you extend your arm at the elbow to lift the ViPR up horizontally. This simple lift and twist requires you to think of multiple things at the same time. It warms up your supertasking brain and helps you train your brain to overcome bottlenecks. Called embodied cognition, this technique of brain development relies on the fact that changes that you make with your body can translate into cognitive improvements as well.

You can also use your cognitive flexibility (rather than hunkering down with focus) to integrate the tasks on your "list". When you cut yourself some slack mentally, it allows your brain to conserve energy so that you're less tightly wound up, and there is enough energy for the various unconscious unfocus processes. Your brain will start, pause, switch and restart tasks all the way. It's believing in unfocus that will allow you to do this.

Fine-Tuning Feedback

Without feedback, your brain loses track of its own results. This only makes multitasking more difficult. But it turns out that the "scope" of feedback that you allow yourself to consider is meaningful.

Cognitive science researcher Hansjörg Neth and his

colleagues compared local and global feedback in the context of multitasking. They used a computer program called Tardast, aptly named after the Persian term for "juggler," to investigate multitasking behaviour, complex system management and constant supervision.

During the experiment, the researchers presented the participants with ten trials via a computer screen. For each five-¬minute trial, the participants had to manage six tasks.

Performing a "task" meant pressing buttons below a series of vertical white bars so as to fill the bars up with black. When you pressed a button, the level of black in that bar rose. When you released the button, the level fell. The goal was to get the black to rise to the highest level within each vertical bar. And you could only press buttons one at a time and in quick sequence.

The challenge, however, was that some bars were more difficult to fill than others. The more difficult bars had a higher value that increased the total score. For example, each bar increased and decreased at a different speed. After each five-minute trial, participants received feedback on how they had done.

The upshot was that any kind of feedback improved multitasking. However, local feedback (how the person did on the last trial) was superior to global feedback (how they had done all day) for multitasking.

Without feedback, your brain gets overwhelmed. Dipping into conscious feedback is a way of taking stock if you feel like you have a billion things to do in the course of a day. But don't just take it for granted that your brain is updating information as you go along. Give it local feedback instead. Stop and think about what you just did and how it relates to what you have to do next. It is this momentary period of unfocus from your task that will allow you to adjust your approach to make it better.

Seeking Interconnections

When you are in supertasking mode, your brain remembers half-completed tasks while you move on so that you can return to them. In this mode you remember not to leave on the stove when the phone rings. The brain also constantly re-strategises about pending goals as you go along.

The brain region that enables you to do both of these tasks is your frontopolar cortex (FPC); it acts as your "personal shopper". Think of your shopper standing by with a bag containing clothes you are considering buying as you try on new things. It seems to specifically become active when you need to keep recently completed tasks in mind as you do other things.

Say, for example, you had just opened an email as you picked up the ringing phone, but as you did, your boss came in and dropped a note asking you to complete an urgent task. You might take the call, and then complete the urgent task while still remembering to come back to the email. Your brain's personal shopper stands by, holding the message from the email while you complete the urgent task. Studies show that damage to your FPC makes multitasking much more difficult.

Many other studies show that your brain's personal shopper is also a great connector. It likes to match the similarities between things and makes leaps of connection even between things that have what's called "semantic distance", or a distance in meaning.

For example, a bird and airplane may have a medium semantic distance. They are different enough, but they both have wings. On the other hand, an airplane and a fox have a greater semantic distance. Your personal shopper looks for connections between concepts. The greater the semantic distance, the more innovative it will make you in connecting two things. It might, for example, suggest that an airplane and a fox could both be on a mission. It might also suggest that pilots should learn from the attentiveness of foxes to know how to navigate difficult terrains. The more you think about it, the more similarities you will find. Your brain's personal shopper will use its extraordinary matching abilities to help you achieve this.

This type of thinking is called analogical reasoning, and although it can happen spontaneously, it helps to make a conscious habit of it. People who perform analogical reasoning well have greater fluid intelligence—they are more flexible thinkers. This kind of mental flexibility is what allows you to connect with your cognitive rhythm. Rather than thinking more, you think flexibly.

To train this region, you must set aside time to make different kinds of connections. Start with fifteen minutes a week at first. Then incorporate it into your day, in the shower, when you're bored, or when you can't find something to do. It's a great replacement for crossword puzzles or Sudoku. Start by comparing items in your bedroom, and then in every other room. It's not a focused mental journey. Rather, it is a journey of discovery as you realise what the connections are.

Your personal shopper is part of the DMN. It turns on with unfocus as you search for connections, wait to see them, or tinker with the objects so that you can see them another way. Plod right through your day, and there'll barely be any time to make connections.

Filtering Distractions and Eliminating Interruptions

When you supertask, you have to manage distractions. If you don't, they have the potential to tap you on the shoulder on the dance floor, stopping the flow of your focus/unfocus choreography, and bringing about cognitive mayhem rather than cognitive rhythm. The key is to develop a filter—a way to identify the distractions and lose them.

In 2010, brain researchers Todd Kelley and Steven Yantis found that it is possible to train your attention to filter out distractions. Stuff still comes at you, but once you've learned Kelley and Yantis' techniques, you can filter out what does not belong and allow in what does.

In their experiment, they showed people a square, but rather than the square being made of four lines, each side was a series of dots, and the space within the square was filled by dots as well. Some of these dots were red and others green. Participants had to quickly determine if there were more red than green dots or vice versa. And while they were trying to figure this out, they had to contend with distracting images surrounding the square which made it more difficult to concentrate. However, when trained to concentrate by practising attending only to the square over and over again, they did much better in their red- or green-dominant determinations.

The middle frontal gyrus, a chunk of tissue on the left and right side of your frontal lobe, midway between the top and the bottom, is the part of the brain that you can train to be a filter.

There are two ways to filter distractions: proactively and reactively. With proactive filtering you prepare to ignore anticipated distractions. This is what Kelley and Yantis taught their subjects to do. With reactive filtering, you swat unexpected distractions as you encounter them. You need energy and brain resources for both. So rather than tensely completing each task on your multitasking list, you limit the intensity of focus so that you have the energy to flexibly deal with unanticipated distractions.

When we try to inhibit irrelevant information, there is greater brain synchrony of alpha and beta waves. Both focus and unfocus waves become more aligned. Filtering out distractions quite literally activates cognitive rhythm. That's why it's useful to consciously label the distractions in your day. If you're kept from your work by the regular ding of your Facebook feed—a modern-day distraction, to be sure—you can anticipate and react to the noise: remind yourself that the ding is a distraction that will keep you from your work. Or better yet, turn the sound off your phone so you are not aware of the update notification. In so doing, you free up attentional resources to be able to supertask.

Not all distractions are created equal. Some might be better described as interruptions that can't be filtered out in the same way. In 2010, neuroscientist Wesley Clapp and colleagues found that distraction occurs when you are presented with irrelevant stimuli. For example, your sister sends you a funny cat video while you are reviewing an important email at work—that's just a distraction and irrelevant to the current email. Interruption, on the other hand, occurs when something requires your attention. If your boss sends you an urgent email about a new deadline, you need to take care of it (as opposed to the cat video which you can either save for later or ignore).

Distractions and interruptions have unique impacts on your brain. While they can both shake up your short-term memory cup, making you forget what just happened, interruptions are far worse than distractions. Distractions disrupt but don't obliterate the connection between the middle frontal gyrus and seeing brain (visual cortex)—so whatever you were doing is still remembered by your brain. You can come back to it more easily. When you're interrupted, however, switching tasks derails you, and this connection falls apart. Although distractions can reduce your productivity if you do not tag and filter them, interruptions can be even more disruptive.

Nobody can stop all interruptions to their day, but sometimes you have to make it a priority to eliminate interruptions that are not part of your supertasking list. To do this, label tasks as "interruption-free" if they need to be, and engage in them in places and ways that reduce the likelihood of distraction and interruption (i.e. not only turn off the volume, but turn the dinging phone off for a little while). As a doctor, I protect the time I allot to filling out medication prescriptions. Same thing for when I'm driving somewhere new. For me (and my patients, in the first example), answering the phone or talking to others in these instances could be disastrous.

PUTTING IT ALL TOGETHER FOR EASY BREEZY SUPERTASKING

As with any area in which you want to improve, it helps to dedicate some time every day to supertasking techniques. If you set time aside each morning, for instance, to get yourself in a supertasking frame of mind, the collective practice of each of the techniques I have outlined above might take about half an hour. You don't have to do all of them at once, of course, and you might not want to do one or two of them at all. But whatever amount of time you give over to unfocusing will repay your efforts in your ability to supertask.

As you explore your supertasking capabilities, it will be helpful to keep the two following ideals in mind.

The Happy, Playful Juggler

When you're used to being methodical and sequential, juggling may seem like a nightmare. Just the thought of it may make you break into a sweat. Yet, your brain is wired for juggling tasks, so why not think of every day as a day to find and train that part of yourself?

It all starts with being playful. Metaphorically, you should not be the juggler who looks to your juggling with dread. Rather, you should be the one who juggles on the street corner with a smile on his face and a hat at his feet, expecting that people will reward him for his efforts. It's all about dissolving the stress in alpha!

Contrary to what we think, play helps the brain become less distracted. In fact, in animals, play helps the frontal lobe of the brain mature. Also, when (human) children play, it helps them become less impulsive and inhibits random behaviour.

In 2009, neuroscientist Jaak Panksepp suggested that ADHD might occur as a result of children not playing enough. He explained that play—of the rough-and-tumble or fantasy variety, not play dates and organised sports—has a vital role in regulating the brain and allowing us to focus. You could also call this an attitude of inventiveness. He pointed out that in our "no child left behind" curricula, we emphasise regimented functions like arithmetic, writing and reading, at the expense of natural play. Play is to education what unfocus is to cognitive rhythm. You may be thinking less, but you are in fact learning much, much more.

Pretend or forced play does not help. Instead, play should satisfy a basic need to survive and grow. If it doesn't, studies show that you will become more obsessive and distressed. On the other hand, when you have a passion for your chosen "game", it improves your well-being.

Some people feel that life is serious and there is no time for play. Life can certainly feel that way when you have work to do and bills to pay. But in this context, seriousness amounts to worry. And worry is rarely as necessary as we think it is. In fact, a recent study indicated that people who worry do so in order to create a buffer whenever something negative happens. It helps them make a smaller emotional switch from worry to sadness or loss, than the more precipitous one that comes from falling from playful/happy to sad. If that's the case, why not learn to manage the switch, rather than prevent yourself from enjoying the playfulness and happiness that you can?

Somewhat paradoxically, it was the serious philosopher, Plato, who offered one of the most well-known definitions of play. (Even Plato subscribed to the thinking-less philosophy at times!) He described play as "those natural modes of amusement which children find out for themselves when they meet." In that sense, play is discovered, invented, enjoyed, and then made into a pattern until children run out of steam. Run out of steam though they may, children are still more likely to stay engaged in play than the drudgery of homework. This kind of play is constantly reinvented with local feedback until the game is exactly what they want it to be.

If you're a leader, you can infuse the mentality of play at work. If you're a homemaker, you can add this mentality to chores. Either way, finding a path to playfulness can lighten the burden of the tasks at hand. You don't have to fake a playful attitude. Find the right fit for you, the way children might try out a few different games before they settle on one.

The Optimistic Cruiser

Hunches can be like tailwinds that propel you forward fast. Once you learn how to fly in them, supertasking will be that much easier. Initially, a hunch may be vague and unclear. But it doesn't have to stay that way. Examine it more closely, mull over it—this will shake off the dust, reduce the vagueness, and give you more data to consider.

In 2011, psychologist Arie Kruglanski explained that learning to examine your hunches is an art. Your unconscious brain has a set of rules that it follows anyway. These rules are mental tools, formally called inferential devices, which you can mimic consciously when you don't know what to do. And you could estimate the consequences. In the worst-case scenario, you'd lose a year of school, but probably also learn a lot about yourself and about life. When your brain registers, "This is important—I will regret not trying—there's not much to lose", it will quickly make a decision that you're not even aware of, and it will start planning your path forward and look for ways to reach your goal faster.

Of course, there are lots of other rules like associations, or comparisons with the past. But Kruglanski points out that rational and intuitive thinking use the same rule systems, and they work hand in hand in the brain too. The key is to have an "optimising" attitude that drives your intuition to find the right rational rules. You aim for the finish line with grit and determination, learning all along the way. When you do this with a positive mood—it will make your intuition that much more accurate too.

To further understand this concept of "optimisation", think of a ball player in baseball or cricket who has to run to catch a flying ball. As he chases the ball, he has to adjust his speed, keep looking at the ball, and prepare to catch it, all at the same time. When he does catch it, it's because he and the ball were always connected despite its changing speed and his changing speed and position. He's not calculating the trajectory or running ahead to where he thinks the ball will land. (That would be a mental distraction, which, even if he tried it once in practice, he could tag and ignore subsequently.) He follows it until he catches it. No book could guarantee that he would catch the ball. Only repeated practice could help him know how fast to run, how much to slow down, and how to connect his gaze with the catch. As he runs, his brain calculates he might miss the ball—so he slows down—but if he slows down too much, his brain would have him speed up again. Each little adjustment is a part of the optimisation strategy.

We marvel at these moments because they involve rational actions like a cupped hand, and intuitive actions like speeding up or slowing down. They happen at the same time. This is cognitive rhythm in action. And it's supertasking too. Learning to make quick adjustments to fine-tune your hunches may even become your primary strategy when learning to thrive in a supertasking world. When you apply unconscious rules and optimisation strategies, you also know full well that you could drop the ball. But you will eventually learn to become comfortable with the course correction and focused execution without feeling sick to your stomach, due to your supertasking speed.

The supertasking mindset is one that requires many steps, yet you have to be careful not to overwhelm yourself. As with other chapters, let the information wash over you, and then come back to institute one or two things at a time. The table below summarises the major mindset shifts that are involved in supertasking. Use this guide when you want to consider changes that you could make to your life.

Focused Mindset	Unfocused Mindset Shift
Take a serious and focused attitude when supertasking	Be more playful and self-forgiving as you start to supertask
It matters most to stay alert, conscious and focused on the tasks at hand	Practise relaxing into your automaticity from time to time—explore your unconscious by doodling
Be super-rational as you plan	Practise being intuitive and see if tasks can be joined to be done at the same time
Complete tasks as you initially planned	Do tasks when they best fit into your day and provide local feedback as you do this
You can only learn to supertask by thinking more clearly	Movement, functional exercises and video games can all help to develop your supertasking brain

GETTING UNSTUCK

"...what we usually consider impossible are nothing but engineering problems...there's no law of physics preventing them."

Michio Kaku

February in Boston can be quite depressing. The promise of the New Year has worn off and the cold has taken its toll. The roads are an ugly mix of sand and slush and you can't really get anywhere without having to negotiate snow banks, black ice and crawling motorway traffic. If you've lived here a while, February gives you an excuse to kvetch about something—if not the weather, then just life in general. Yet, as I sat across from Jackie during her therapy hour, the tone in her voice signalled more than the customary winter blues.

"I feel exasperated," she protested. "I don't know how I ended up here, working like a dog, lugging around groceries, and endlessly driving the kids to their activities.

My life feels like a stuck record. My husband is a good man, but our relationship has reached an all-time low. We're just stagnating. I don't even do things that I really love—playing the piano, gardening or just walking on the beach. And to cap it all, I think I've hit the glass ceiling at work. How did I become a prisoner in my own life?" she asked.

Jackie's story was familiar to me. I had heard many different versions of it over the years. Regardless of the context, routines—once comforting and safe—can gradually become a rut. Stability in your relationship, once a prized goal, can become a thrill-killer. The monotony of even a secure and fulfilling job can start to wear you down (and not just in February!). As a result, you start to procrastinate more than usual. You tend to feel ambivalent, and therefore have a hard time making decisions. And a general lack of motivation often leads to unhealthy lifestyle choices—eating junk, sleeping less, stressing more—which only makes you feel worse, more stuck. It's a vicious cycle. Nobody is totally immune.

Regardless of how we're stuck, when we hit that breaking point, we try to jolt ourselves out of our doldrums to varying constructive and destructive degrees. In a marriage, that might mean introducing romantic date nights or having an affair. When you're feeling generally stymied, you make an effort to find "me time" or "work–life balance" without knowing what the best "me time" or "balance" actually is. At work, you might try to avoid contentious situations and just try to get your job done well, or you might quit. Some of these strategies may work for a while, but because they are static solutions—singularly focused on prioritisation, recalibration of your duties, or hunkering down—you get mentally exhausted quickly.

Furthermore, these attempts at steadfast focus usually don't last. In every case, you're trying to change using conscious strategies against a far stronger unconscious pull. There's no point in Jackie having a date night when her intuition has given her the sinking feeling that her relationship is going downhill. Work–life balance lasts until the next hurricane of tasks sweeps you off your feet. And hunkering down to get the job done is useless if you take two steps back for every step that you take forward.

In all of these scenarios, a focused mind rarely brings lasting and authentic solutions. Eventually your stuck mind returns to its conveyor-belt mode, with your psychological baggage going around and around; the more you focus on the problems you are facing, the more stuck you might actually get.

Of course, stuckness isn't always about big, life-altering shifts or dead ends. It can also manifest in small ways. Take, for instance, the mundane scenario of not being able to conjure up a specific word when you are mid-sentence or a name when you run into someone. It's at the tip of your tongue, you might say, but it just won't come. Your mind seems frozen.

Putting early Alzheimer's or a minor stroke aside, neurologically, what's happening when you can't—for the life of you—remember a word or a name is the same thing that is happening when you feel malaise or stagnation about your life. Intense focus on trying to re-member it rarely does the trick (instead you often end up feeling more at a loss for the word or name). Like a fly furiously and repeatedly butting against a closed win-dowpane, your mind is stuck. Searching for a way out is futile. As your angst escalates, your brain's cacophony reaches an all-time high. (This is also a hallmark of writ-er's block.)

Though it may seem miraculous when, minutes or hours later, the word or name pops into your head, there are actually known psychological and neurologi-cal processes at work that have brought it to the fore. And what's more, the processes—the cascade of small psychological and neurological shifts—are reproducible. The fly needs you to open the window for it. Figurative-ly, you can do this for yourself as well.

The Possibility Mindset

Empowering your mind to get unstuck begins with a shift in perspective. Instead of thinking about your predicament—which will only incite anger, anxiety, or sadness—you need to get more emotionally neutral (unfocused) about your situation. I call this shifting to the possibility mindset. When you can't find a word or a name, sometimes just releasing yourself from a focus on coming up with it (the need to find it) and allowing yourself the belief that it'll come to you any minute is enough to jog the word or name into your view. That's the possibility mindset in action.

Possibility is the proverbial key in the ignition of your mind; you can't drive to your destination (unstuckness) without it. When you have a possibility mindset, you actually increase your brain opioids, relax the brain, reward the brain, and make it possible to get moving. You can't move against the resistance of a belief in impossibility.

When I recommended this to Jackie, she rolled her eyes. "I don't want some super-optimistic nonsense that's all inspiration, no destination," she said, doubting me. The vice president of human resources at a large corporation, she felt some urgency to get back on track or get on another one—she didn't have the time or patience for platitudes.

Steer your brain towards possibility

Manufactured optimism is, by definition, false. False optimism would have you tell yourself to "look on the bright side" or to reassure yourself that "things are going to get better". Generating authentic optimism comes from a subtle shift in your self-messaging: simply tell yourself, "getting unstuck is *possible*". With that small tweak of phrasing, you have significantly altered the message and you will have begun to galvanise your brain towards change. Just as you might suddenly start seeing white cars after buying one, when you "buy" this message, your brain will start to look for things consistent with the possibility of a solution. Called attention shifting, this is simply steering your brain in another direction.

So say it out loud, say it to yourself. But send this message somehow. Let this new message capture your brain's attentional network and begin to work its magic.

Your ability to stay in the possibility mindset will not be uninterrupted, of course. You'll have moments of doubt and what I describe as foggy patches—times when relaxing your brain into the idea of possibility seems to be too structure-less and free floating. When you're feeling that way, you'll revert to focusing on what is right in front of you. But your earlier efforts to imagine possibility will not have been for nothing: you'll find that when the fog clears, you may be better able to look even further ahead; your ability to relax into possibility will also be incrementally improved and useful to you when you encounter the next foggy patch.

"Buying" into this idea is a process; it doesn't happen overnight. Once possibility steers you in a new direction, you may still need to take steps to calm and neutralise the anger, anxiety or sadness you've been feeling.

To get your feelings under control, you can try "affect labelling", a fancy term for naming your feelings. Look at your anger, your frustration or your sadness from as many angles as you can, and try to describe it accurately. For example, rather than stewing when she was mad, Jackie learned to say out loud, "I'm really angry." And rather than sighing in frustration, a process that fed on itself and just made her more anxious, she learned to catch her anxiety just prior, and call it out. Naming your feelings may seem like a child's strategy, but it serves a very sophisticated purpose: it is effective at putting up a barrier between your brain's anxiety centre, the amygdala, and your thinking brain, the prefrontal cortex (PFC). This barrier acts as ballast in a way; in setting the course for possibility, you give yourself some protection and your undefined emotions won't feel like a tidal wave about to consume you.

Change Your Brain Lens

Renaming things can also help to *reframe* your emotions, applying less judgmental descriptions to them. Whereas you might feel flat-out angry at how stuck you're feeling, the reframed, less negative way to put it would be that you are feeling "emotional intensity gone awry". And rather than being annoyed by your frustration, you can see it as "a signal to change". This isn't only semantics. And importantly, this is different from being urged to take a deep breath before acting or responding—common advice for calming your emotions. Taking the proverbial deep breath is an act of suppression. Introducing the idea of possibility—simply saying *getting unstuck is possible*—is *pro*gression—forward thinking—so to speak. And it is an all-important first step. Many studies have demonstrated that reframing your emotions also calms down your amygdala, your brain's anxiety processor; reframing trumps suppressing them when you're trying to reduce stress.

Ask solution-based questions

Armed with a new mental calmness and simply stated sense of possibility, you are ready to start asking yourself productive, solution-oriented questions. The operative phrase here is *solution-oriented*. That is, don't ask open-ended "What should I do?" questions of yourself, but shift to a "How can I make this happen? What specific things can I begin to do?" line of questioning. Instead of asking, "How do I change my life?" which is the kind of daunting self-questioning that might actually make you feel *more stuck*, ask instead, "How have others successfully navigated this impasse?" By being solution-oriented, you are also using focused techniques to navigate the very unfocused sense of possibility. In your brain, focus and unfocus are working together in a more productive cognitive rhythm. You don't default to either extreme.

Jackie started to look around at other marriages—those she admired as well as those she thought were problematic—and she also started to look more neutrally at how others had broken through the glass ceiling at work. Seeing how others had navigated these waters before her gave her a starting template to work from and to tailor to her own situation.

Think of being solution-oriented as "playing to win" rather than "playing not to lose". Consider the example of my tennis hero, Serena Williams: in the 2012 US Open, she was tied with Victoria Azarenka, one set each. In the third set, Serena found herself down by two games at 3-5. Azarenka was looking strong, but Serena did not prepare to lose.

Slowly but surely, and rather amazingly, Serena marched back from her deficit and won the last set at 7-5. In a post-match interview, she said that rather than focusing on the high probability of losing the tournament, she shifted her mind to consider a different question: what will it take to *win*? Calculating that all she needed was twelve more points to do so, she used possibility thinking to guide her point by point to the trophy. In other words, she switched from *probability* thinking (what are my chances here?) to *possibility* thinking (twelve more points and I'm there!).

Really?

Reality, as you see and experience it, is not written in stone. To the visionary, in fact, "realism" is a blindfold. It is an unnecessary and limiting distraction to a mind working on becoming unstuck. Your aim is to construct a vision of what you want—unrestricted, unedited and unrestrained. You can shape it to fit reality later on. Stretching your mind outside the life that is facing you can be lifesaving. Yet even the best of us may be tempted by the reassuring lure of apparent pragmatism.

This is reflected in experiences of people who have succumbed to that temptation. In 1929, Irving Fisher, a Yale economist, was quoted in the *New York Times* as saying that stock prices had reached "what looks like a permanently high plateau". This was three days before the stock market crash that triggered the Great Depression. In 1957, the editor in charge of business books for Prentice Hall said, "I have travelled the length and breadth of this country and talked with the best people, and I can assure you that data processing is a fad that won't last out the year." Following an audition by the Beatles in 1962, a Decca Records executive said to their manager, Brian Epstein, that they had no future in show business. Epstein recalled that the executive didn't like their sound, and that he believed that guitar groups were on the way out. Fast-forward to recent years and this pattern of "expert" and "measure" predictions remains questionable too. In 2016, the majority of Brexit polls were wrong—the United Kingdom ended up voting to separate from the European Union despite widespread predictions to the contrary. And in that same year, Donald Trump's victory over Hillary Clinton in the race for the US presidency was missed by the Upshot section of the *New York Times* and the Princeton Election Consortium, which put Mrs Clinton's chances of winning in the 70-99 per cent range.

It's tempting to believe authoritative people who are certain. Their clarity may be reassuring. But they *can* certainly be wrong!

Stay true to yourself

A crucial ingredient in adopting the possibility mindset

is being true to yourself. Being persistent is important but persistence for the sake of it—relentless focus because you believe that focus will get you to your goal—is about as effective as false optimism.

In 2010, psychologist Charles S. Carver and a colleague asked students from the University of Miami to fill out multiple questionnaires related to pride, response to missed goals and self-control. Two kinds of pride were measured: authentic pride—where a person feels a genuine sense of accomplishment or a heartfelt desire for something—and hubristic pride, which is pride that comes from arrogance or self-importance ("pouty" pride).

People with greater authentic pride reported a sense of energised happiness when they achieved a goal, and their responses also revealed that they had greater self-control and control of their attention. People with hubristic pride were angrier and impulsive.

When you get what you want, your brain feels rewarded and its reward system activates. But this reward system has two parts—one for registering rewards from within, called intrinsic reward, and the other for registering the rewards that come from others, which is called extrinsic reward.

When you have "authentic" pride, you get an intrinsic reward. You stop focusing entirely on external benchmarks and other people for pats on the back, and instead turn more frequently to your own sense of accomplishment and pleasure as your beacon. When you hanker after external rewards (compliments, money, promotions, gifts), your brain's intrinsic reward system can be undermined—it activates less and the good feelings you get from the extrinsic reward are not as long-lasting.

When you are in possibility mode—moving forward bit by bit as your goal becomes clearer—you have to find a way to stay committed to your path despite great uncertainty. In that case, it's the intrinsic reward system—feeling good and true to yourself—that will keep you on track. Intrinsic rewards are your brain's compass under conditions of uncertainty. But you can't be in uncertain mode the whole time. From time to time, you will necessarily revert to and rely on old behavioural and psychological habits. That's where extrinsic rewards play a role—it can feel very good indeed, and even advantageous, to get praise or a raise. Yet, the moment things become less certain, praise and the raise lose their power, and may even turn your intrinsic motivation off. You can focus on external rewards, and then be guided by internal rewards. Switching back and forth between both reward systems is cognitive rhythm in action.

It's a little like going for a jog. You may like the extrinsic reward of appearing healthy, but the jog needs to help you feel healthier today for the goal of "health" to be motivating long term. Intrinsic and extrinsic rewards can both orient and motivate you to get to your goals. The key is to strike a rhythm between the two and to check in with yourself from time to time to assess your real level of satisfaction.

Understanding this was an important component for

Jackie in getting unstuck. She started to speak from her heart. She suspended the need to convince her husband and her boss to help her, and shifted instead to a heart-felt understanding of what she truly wanted.

In therapy, Jackie allowed herself—in fits and starts—to look away from the fact of her stuckness and instead embrace the idea that things could be different. Freed up to imagine and invent a future in her mind, her zig-zag train of thought led to unexpected realisations and convictions. She would have missed memories and feelings that were tucked away if she had only focused on what was obvious. In one session, she talked about how she wanted her husband to be more engaged in their marriage but then she reflected on the fact that her life in general felt increasingly devoid of passion. And in seemingly unrelated nostalgia, she recollected how she had climbed the ladder at work much faster than she had anticipated. And it wasn't because of some kind of strategy or external goal. It was because she was driven from within.

As she talked, she began to realise that her relationship, money, or job position were really not her primary concerns. The thing she most cared about was reigniting that spark within herself. Your spark is your greatest ally when you can find it. It is the best guiding light that you could have. As in the Carver study above, it gives you more self-control.

Fully in the possibility mindset, Jackie had transcended the distraction of specific unhappiness. Instead, she started to get inspired—filled with purpose and autonomy. Her mind was no longer stuck. It was intent on wandering, ready to explore the field of possibilities that unfocusing had ushered into her life.

Your Mind Aglow

To imagine what is happening in your brain when your mind wanders, think of the default mode network (DMN) we discussed in Chapter 1. Imagine that it is an octopus curled up into a ball. Releasing focus makes it "glow", a phenomenon we can actually see in functional brain-imaging studies.

With the DMN aglow, it reaches out its "tentacles" to connect with the tentacles in the past (your memory bank brain circuits) and future (your visionary brain) as well. These tentacles are nerve fibres that connect brain cells in different regions. The more you unfocus, the brighter the glow, the better your recollection of the past and imagination of the future.

When the past, present, and future join tentacles, your life makes more sense because your identity—your internal story about yourself— is less disjointed. And information starts to flow spontaneously too. This flow of information is called autonoetic consciousness—think of it as spontaneous thoughts or automatic knowledge.

When you are stuck, spontaneous thoughts are such a welcome intrusion. They are a sign that you have activated your unconscious brain. And that's a good thing.

Your conscious brain processes information at 60 bits

---

per second at best. Your unconscious brain crunches information much, much faster—some have said at 11 million bits per second. Despite the debate on the actual number, most experts would agree that your unconscious brain is a much, much faster processor. It works under the radar, but it forages for data that your conscious, focused brain won't find.

Fifty Shades of Cognitive Grey

The downside to having such a turbo-boosted unconscious is that, at this rate, your brain is prone to jumping ahead of the logic of your conscious brain. In these instances, your unconscious brain can be less accurate too. As determined, passionate and possibility-oriented as Jackie was, the big leaps that she made sometimes spooked her. (Nobody said that thinking less is always easy!)

Especially after developing confidence with her initial progress, an "all or nothing" attitude was alluring, yet intimidating to Jackie. It's fine to want to "go big or go home" and confront situations head on. There's a time and place for that. But black and white thinking can sometimes be all show and no substance—and it can be too much, too fast. When you are stuck, the answers often lie in the many shades of grey—minor tweaks in your thinking rather than a complete overhaul. You don't have to pursue every possibility that your wandering mind produces either. You can revise the options, mull over them, modify them. That's a spirit, as well as a process of doing things.

As journalist Alec Foege writes, "Contrary to popular opinion, most great American innovations have been happy accidents made by serial dilettantes and dreamers, not trained engineers or professionals." He points to Benjamin Franklin—who invented the lightning rod and bifocals, as already mentioned, as well as the Franklin stove, the odometer and the US Postal Service—and Thomas Edison, who is known to have spent enormous amounts of time trying to find the right combination of materials to make a light bulb. And he posits that perhaps their tinkering mentality came from the rich soil of the pioneering American *spirit* of their era.

This switch from a focus on your problem to seeding the idea of possibility involves many complex processes, but unfocus is necessary to help your brain remain in the possibility mindset. Rather than thinking there is no solution in sight, you replace "not knowing" with a new hypothesis: a solution *is* possible! You activate your *imagination* to design possible experiments to discover a solution.

In 2013, brain researcher Luigi F. Agnati and his colleagues explained that imagination is a result of tinkering with old ideas and thoughts based on your unique experiences to create newly recombined ideas. This kind of switching tracks between one experiment and another, or going back and forth to old ideas before you find the right ones, is an unfocused process.

Think of it this way: every skyscraper was first an idea, then a sketch, and then a formal design. At each of those essential stages, there were redrafts and adjustments along the way. To reach the heights of your own life—to become unstuck—learning how to think less is an indispensable competency. When you think less to learn more it is not wild meandering; it's well-considered freedom.

Tinkering with possibility—with a number of ideas for the future—is like "thought sketching" until you get the picture right. When you're afraid to take big leaps, you can and should examine the fear that the big leaps inspire. A big leap will feel more manageable if you tinker with ideas for smaller, incremental steps.

It's not just about taking small steps, though—it's also about looking at things from as many angles as possible and indulging your curiosity. Curiosity activates your cognitive rhythm. It takes you out of focused "goal-targeting" into unfocused "goal discovery".

When you are in a state of curiosity, blood flows to the brain regions that process arousal and conflict. Resolving that curiosity activates the ventral striatum—an intrinsic reward centre. When your tinkering is fuelled by curiosity, you are in an unfocused, activated search mode, and when it is resolved by discovery, you feel good again.

There is no "one size fits all" solution for your stuckness. The possibility mindset will empower your wandering mind, but tinkering with the ideas and feelings it stirs up is the most productive way to consider your options.

Strategic Mental Meandering

Figuratively and literally, unfocus best works its magic on your mental patterns when you strategically set aside time to let your mind wander. Many successful people have built what I call strategic mental breaks or meanderings into their lives at times when they are lost or stuck.

Steve Jobs, founder of Apple and Pixar, never completed college. He said that he "…decided to drop out and trust that it would all work out okay". Notice that he trusted. He had a sense of possibility. In 1974, he spent time at an Ashram in India, meditating, ruminating and walking around local villages. In 1976, he founded Apple.

Bill Gates still takes a secluded "think week" twice a year to ponder the future of technology. In one week in 1995, he was inspired to write a paper, "The Internet Tidal Wave", that led Microsoft to develop its internet browser and fend off their competitor, Netscape.

Successful visionaries understand the benefit of taking a break to chew on ideas. When you let go of focus, amazing things happen in your brain. Your wandering mind becomes a detective in search of more elusive thoughts. It helps you put two and two together, when prior to that, you were stuck. A wandering mind in a state of inspired possibility is actively in search of something. You don't get in its way. But you don't have to be a capital V visionary, drop out of school or go to exotic destinations to muse on things. You can activate your visionary capabilities, and you can do this right where you are.

Understanding Your Personal Nooks and Crannies

As energising as it can be to tinker with your thoughts and explore them from many angles, you might start to lose steam after the initial burst of excitement. Especially if you feel like you are going nowhere fast, you may want to give up believing and simply do something more "realistic" or "concrete". This is understandable—nobody wants a brain that is aroused and conflicted 24/7. It's not that pleasant. You need some intrinsic reward so that you can feel energised to pursue your goals even when the solution is not obvious. You have to refuel your brain so that more of *you* is present.

A brilliant paper about how the mind works by philosophers Bryce Huebner and Robert D. Rupert explains how people motivate themselves to get from point A to point B. They explain that goals may be what you aim for, but they do not by themselves motivate you. Jackie, for instance, could not actually maintain a motivating picture in her head of what her relationship and work life would look like. The goal was too vague to motivate her.

In order for *you* to pursue *your* goals, *you* have to

show up to life—to be present as fully as you can be. And I'm not referring to the level of your attention, when I say "present". I am referring to the number of "self" circuits that are activated in your brain. There has to be a critical number for you to have enough motivation to keep going.

Goals activate your beliefs and past—metaphorically, they hang up pictures in the gallery of your brain's memory centres, bringing as much of you "online" as possible. When there are enough of the right pictures, you feel juiced. When there aren't enough or the pictures are a mixed bag of things you like and dislike about yourself, you may feel uninspired.

Regardless of your age, race, job and family situation, there is only one you. The small puzzle pieces of your past matter. The devil is in the details. And tinkering is the only mental tool small enough to get into the nooks and crannies that make up all of you.

The smell of your grandmother, that crisp fall day when you played ball with your dad, the shame that you felt when you brought home your school report, the joy of a cue stick in your hand, and the thrill of being lost in a game of Power Rangers are all memories that are stored in your brain, but not accessible to a focused mind. Tinkering unearths this nostalgia. It allows your predictive brain to use your memories to fill in the gaps in your mental picture of yourself so that it can construct a different picture of your future. It also makes you feel more complete and whole. This authenticity fuels your path forward.

Lau Tzu once said, "When I let go of what I am, I become what I might be." Possibility is simply about "being" and letting go. Tinkering is the process of "becoming".

Making Lemonade from Lemons— Neurologically

Most people—and certainly most corporations—prepare for errors by trying to prevent them. When we do this, however, we miss the potential upside of errors, the things we can learn from them and the way we can use them to transform our lives.

Have you ever forgotten a piece of cheese in the fridge that subsequently went mouldy? Well, thank goodness that Scottish biologist Alexander Fleming was not squeamish or eager to dispose of smelly things. One August, Fleming returned from his holiday to find a strange fungus growing in the staphylococci cultures he had been investigating in his lab. Rather than automatically tossing the petri dishes out, he noticed with interest that the fungus had killed off the surrounding staphylococci. This led to the discovery of penicillin. If he had seen the fungus, blocked his nose, closed his eyes and thrown it out, we might have seen much slower progress in the treatment of infectious diseases.

A focused mind regards unintended consequences as irrelevant. An unfocused mind stops to think and ponder the possible opportunities. Like Alexander Fleming in the lab, the possibility mindset in action is not just reactive, but responsive; not just error aware, but opportunity seeking—and willing to unfocus from what is right in front of one's eyes.

Think of all the things that you have chalked up to a "bad day" and ask yourself, "What if I *didn't* throw the baby out with the bathwater?" What if we had the inclination to metaphorically doodle while sitting with our errors? We prefer to forget our mistakes and obliterate any trace of them. Yet, they may offer a fruitful opportunity.

Laugh a Little

In 2015, cognitive psychology professor Henk van Steenbergen and colleagues conducted an experiment to examine the impact of humour on the brain. They wondered if humour actually affected the brain by softening the impact of stressful situations.

Participants were asked to complete a task that put stressful demands on their thinking. In the "arrow-flanker conflict task", an arrow symbol appears on the screen, pointing left or right. The participants have to press the corresponding arrow key on a keyboard as quickly as possible. However, on either side of the target arrow, there are other arrows pointing in the same or in a different direction.

If the arrows on either side point in the same direction as the central arrow, it's easier for your brain to respond. If they are incongruous, most people need to pause to take in and sort the options, and then press the key.

Prior to each set of challenges, participants saw neutral or funny cartoons. The investigators were trying to see if seeing something funny helps your brain out.

It does. The participants who saw the humorous cartoon had to use less mental effort to get the arrows right. In their brains, the positive emotion of humour helped out the brain's conflict detector in the frontal cortex. It dampened the demands on this brain region and allowed the brain to be more flexible.

Errors do, however, create stress, and in the process of getting unstuck, humour plays a huge role in "moving on". It can be our greatest asset when we are faced with what we think is a horrible mistake, because it allows us to think differently and often more clearly.

PUTTING IT ALL TOGETHER TO EASE THE FRICTION OF LIFE

Most people listen to advice and try to make the corresponding changes to little or no avail. That's because they change their thoughts and actions without changing their fundamental philosophies or belief systems.

Think of your mind as an aquarium. Your thoughts and actions are the fish; your philosophies are the "mental medium", the water, oxygen and food that feed those fish. You need to work on changes to your mental medium before you try to change your thoughts and actions. From now on, every time you hit a wall in your life, make mental-medium changes first.

Silence the Excuse-Making Machine

In 1956, psychologist Jack Brehm conducted an experiment in which he asked people to rate the attractiveness of household appliances such as an electric sandwich press, desk lamp, stopwatch and transistor radio. In many instances, people rated two things equally. When that happened, he asked them to choose one of the two things they had rated equally to take home with them. Twenty minutes later they were asked to re-evaluate the appliances.

Somewhat surprisingly, they rated the gifts they had chosen to take home more highly, even though they had previously rated them the same. For example, if they had chosen to take the sandwich press home instead of a stopwatch, they downgraded the rating of the stopwatch. They convinced themselves that they had made the right choice.

In 1968, psychologist Robert E. Knox and colleagues asked people to rate the chances of a horse winning a race. When they had not yet betted, on average people rated the chance as 3.48. After a $2 bet, the average rating for the chance of winning was 4.81. Again, when we're invested in something, our brain considers it more important. The same principles apply to how we rate a holiday choice before and after we make it. And research actually shows that this bias can remain even two to three years later; we tend to remember what we value and value what we remember.

In other words, the brain is wired to rationalise or excuse our choices and this will work against our best efforts to get unstuck. Even the thought of changing course or the slightest unfocus will cause brain chaos. The technical term for this is "cognitive dissonance". The brain rebels against change, even if it is good for us, and irrationally tries to stay stuck. Stuckness can feel safer than change.

The first step towards silencing this excuse-making machine is to simply recognise that this could be happening to you. Of course, sometimes your excuses resonate with the core of your being. You might say, "This is just not for me." You defer to your "insight" about yourself. You might rationalise the choice to accept the status quo with the idea that you're not a born adventurer. Thoughts like this are signs that your brain's excuse-making machine is starting to interfere, so give yourself a pep-talk.

(Much research has been done to isolate and identify an "adventure" gene. While several studies have reported that a dopamine D4 receptor gene—DRD4—may be associated with novelty-seeking, a slew of other studies have been unable to replicate this finding. Even when your genes contribute to this behaviour, they account for only 4-6 per cent of the total picture. Suffice it to say, if you are currently not much of an adventurer, this is not a death sentence. You are not a prisoner of your genes or your habits. You have the ability to change your mental philosophies if you so choose.)

Live a Belief-Driven Life

Beliefs are a biological gateway to incoming sensory information. They tend to direct your senses. Change your beliefs, and you change the things you see and hear as well.

Medical literature is replete with examples of illnesses appearing and disappearing based on belief. In 1988, psychologist Nicholas Spanos and colleagues did a study in which people with warts underwent hypnosis to make their warts go away. The effect of this intervention was compared with receiving a placebo as well as with no treatment. Hypnosis was associated with wart regression, especially if it was imagined vividly.

There's still a debate about how this works. Like most interventions, it probably doesn't work for every kind of wart or in every situation. But more than 20 studies, some controlled and some anecdotal, have shown this effect. People who have seen this effect theorise that belief activates "biochemical battle strategies". Chemical messengers help immune cells kill microbe-induced warts or they cause small arteries to be selectively constricted, cutting off the vital nutrient supply to warts. Belief has an underlying biochemistry. That's also why it may help when you're feeling stuck.

Don't be afraid to rationalise this to your brain—to

explain (out loud or just by thinking) that you need belief to reward your brain. Remind yourself of the pain relief and placebo studies that I mentioned earlier.

If there is one person who has done what you want to do, it's doable. At least one person who was dirt-poor has found financial freedom. Many people in the world who were single into their later years have found love at last. Remember, we're not concerned with how likely this is, but whether it is possible. When you recognise this deeply, you are on your way to being unstuck.

Look to the Horizon

Think of limits as horizons. Rather than letting them paralyse or deter you, keep going and tinker on the way. When you do, you'll see that just like horizons, limits can shift. What often seems like an end is not so if you keep exploring.

With this concept in mind, try to think of your ideas and even your roadblocks as dots on the horizon. Know that they will shift—perhaps they'll get bigger, perhaps they'll recede—as you approach them; turn them over, consider each as an option. Take this principle to heart—one small step a week for the first month; then one small step twice a week for the next month. The steps don't have to be progressive or connected.

Say, for instance, you want to switch jobs but can't for practical reasons. Rather than ignoring the possibility of this, start looking for another job, knowing full well that you are flying in the face of practicality. Spend 30 minutes browsing the internet for job offers. This will expand your idea of what is possible and potentially stimulate your brain to consider new possibilities.

Open the Daydreaming Door

Living a "whole brain" life means that you make time and space for your unconscious, which works in very unfocused ways under the radar. To do this, you really have to build waiting and wandering times into your day and life so that you don't keep metaphorically banging your head against the wall of stuckness.

In the 1950s, Yale psychologist Jerome Singer conducted a series of groundbreaking experiments on daydreaming. He identified three kinds of daydreaming: positive constructive daydreaming, a process relatively free of psychological conflict, in which you imagine things playfully, vividly and wishfully; guilty dysphoric daydreaming, driven by a combination of ambitiousness, failure and aggression, or an obsessive reliving of trauma; and the kind of daydreaming you might call poor attentional control, which is typical of the anxious and those having difficulties concentrating. It's the first kind of daydreaming you want to shoot for—positive and constructive.

When you allow yourself to daydream, your reflections help you to plan better for the future, and to pay attention to the multiple things that your brain is processing. In addition, the daydreaming breaks give you a chance to detach from habit, a great way to start becoming unstuck.

A Visit with Your Heart

Your brain's emotional centres are connected to your thinking brain. This is not as esoteric as it sounds. Think about it: if you saw a wolf on a hike, your anxiety would make you think to avoid it, right? If you saw your best friend at a shopping mall at the top of an escalator, your excitement would make you think to rush to the top. When I put it this way, can you see how thinking and feeling are intricately connected? In fact, neurologist Antonio Damasio wrote an entire book on the subject called *Descartes' Error*. He asserted that it's neurologically incorrect to say, "I think, therefore I am." Instead, thinking and feeling circuits are interwoven in the brain.

Operating from your heart when your head is stuck makes good sense. (Of course, your brain is very much involved in what we call "heart" as well—it processes intuition, love and instinct—but I'm speaking metaphorically here.)

When you are lost, it is important to go back to what you truly want and believe, a place where you don't need to convince yourself of what truly elevates you.

John Cassavetes, the Greek-American actor and director, was regarded as one of the most influential film-makers of our time. When asked how he decided which movies he wanted to make (often on a shoestring budget or loans), he replied that he had a one-track mind. All he cared about was love. So he only made movies about love. Exploring love was his passion. What makes *you* feel in your element? Admit it. Embrace it.

To incorporate this into your life, once a week, schedule a "heart visit" to do the thing you love by yourself or with someone close to you. This doesn't have to take much time but is an important piece of the puzzle, a way to keep you on track. If your element is cooking, then set aside one evening a week to prepare something masterful or that makes you feel nostalgic. The point is to do something emotional. More studies than I could ever mention now point to your emotions as guiding lights when you are lost.

During this check-in time, ask yourself, "What is my guiding philosophy? What do I truly care about? How has it changed?" When you do, you will activate strong feelings that will help you fit the puzzle pieces of your life together.

When focus holds you captive, you are stuck. When possibility is your compass, you can't possibly be stuck! By adding new unfocused philosophies and principles to your focused day, you can tap into your cognitive rhythm. You will no longer be in a stalemate with life. In fact, life will feel less like a chore, and more like an adventurous game.

The table below summarises the differences that focus and unfocus will bring to your mindset. Use it to guide your thinking; it's always helpful to have a bird's eye view.

Focused Mindset	Unfocused Mindset Shift
Let external reality guide you	Let your beliefs shape external reality
Create strategies and execute on them	Wait within and between strategies
Accept that life is stressful	Make "stress-less" periods a rule during the day. Set aside time to do something you love
If you can't reach your goals, think about a foolproof strategy before acting	If you can't reach your goals, think of every new action as chipping away at the sculpture that you eventually desire
A solid thinker is rational and goal-directed	A solid thinker always connects with the heart as well

FROM DISENCHANTMENT TO GREATNESS

"I think it is possible for ordinary people to choose to be extraordinary."

Elon Musk

In January 1964, a son was born to a newlywed teenage mother in Albuquerque, New Mexico. Barely a year and a half later, the mother decided she could not stand her inattentive and alcoholic husband, so she filed for divorce. When her son was four years old, she married a Cuban immigrant and they moved to Houston, Texas, and when he was a teenager, to Miami, Florida. The boy never saw his biological father again.

Despite the disruptions to his childhood, the young boy was curious and driven. As a toddler, he felt he was too old to sleep in a crib, so he took it apart with a screwdriver. As a boy, he rigged an electric alarm to keep his younger siblings out of his room. He made an automatic gate-closer out of cement-filled tyres. And from an umbrella and tin foil, he made a rudimentary solar cooker. Eventually, his parents made him move the clutter of his invention and experimentation to the garage, which became his laboratory. When he was twelve, he was featured in a book on "bright minds", but although he was described as "friendly" and "serious", he was also referred to as "not particularly gifted at leadership".

As a teenager, the boy became preoccupied with computers, and while still in high school, started an educational summer camp with his girlfriend. Called "The Dream Institute" (not the "Think" Institute, note), the camp promoted creative thinking for primary school children. So much for not being a leader! He graduated as valedictorian of his class and went on to do an undergraduate degree in computer science and electrical engineering at Princeton University. Then he held jobs at Fitel, Bankers Trust and the investment firm D.E. Shaw, where he became the company's youngest vice president.

But the financial promise of working on Wall Street was not enough for him. The real "Dream Institute" was in his head. It had to emerge. So in 1994, despite his extremely lucrative career, secure job and the promise of a big bonus, he quit his job and moved to Seattle. There, in his garage, he started to develop software.

In July 1995, he started the online bookstore now known as an online everything store: Amazon.

That boy was Jeff Bezos, a man who would become a great devotee of books, education, and people. In 1999, he was voted *Time* magazine's person of the year. In 2008, *US News and World Report* selected him as one of America's best leaders. In 2012, Fortune named him businessperson of the year. In 2016, Forbes listed him as the fourth-wealthiest person in the world, and *Harvard Business Review* named him the second-best CEO in the world.

When you think of all that Bezos has achieved, it's easy to confuse "greatness" with accolades or money. But the kind of greatness Bezos embodies is about things other than just accumulated wealth and power. What makes him remarkable is his faithfulness to his own vision—and his willingness to act upon it and even change his mind if the results start to go south. In fact, Bezos is noted for saying that consistency of thought is not a particularly positive state of mind; rather, he believes that people who get things right may even have ideas the following day that contradict their prior opinions altogether. His example teaches us that greatness is not only an exceptional state of mind—it is a translation and constant iteration of that state of mind into an act of profound meaning.

Given that such profundity is often abstract or difficult to achieve, many might think that "greatness" is an artificial goal. Just the thought of aspiring to greatness may turn you off. But it's less off-putting if you think about it as rearranging your brain's cells and circuits so that you can be the best that you can be— a capacity that every human being possesses. Your brain can change— and the beautiful thing is that *you* can change it.

Focus is undoubtedly part of the formula for greatness. Yet, more importantly, it is the origin of this focus that will determine your success. In this chapter, you will learn how greatness is only as far from you as your willingness to build unfocus into your daily thinking.

When it comes to unfocus, it's not just "rest" and "time away" that are important. Instead, in the context of greatness, unfocus will help you express different sides of yourself, immerse yourself in a sense of purpose, examine past experience from different angles, think outside of logical sequences, and imagine and then express your vision of the future. In every instance, you have to finesse your relationship with rational thought so that it is not a burdensome obstruction.

Your Two-Sided Self

The very essence of human nature is paradoxical, and therefore, greatness is paradoxical too. In many instances, you have to be cruel to be kind, naïve to be smart and curious, and vulnerable enough to explore the strengths that lie alongside your weaknesses. Yet, the conventional habit of defining your identity one way or another forces you to focus on only one aspect of yourself. It's the same with defining yourself by your professional title. When you express only one side of yourself, being "great" is like trying to catch a ball with one hand tied behind your back. Focus amputates the other side of you, and your greatness.

196

There are also at least two sides to every story. For instance, on the one hand, the uniqueness of original art is cheapened by reproductions that anyone could hang on a wall; on the other, these replicas allow people access to what might otherwise be unaffordable. Then there are genetically modified foods that may be toxic to the body, yet they also require fewer insecticides and provide a sustainable alternative to feed the world. Capitalism is another example of contradictions. For all its associated excesses and exploitation, it provides an opportunity for economic and political freedom. And even though we complain about the distraction caused by gadgets during conversations, we revel in the connectedness that technology affords us.

More often than not, we form opinions about one or the other side of the argument, swayed as we are by a focus on our own preferences. Sometimes, this focus leads to us take strong positions. We may even join social causes— political rallies, veganism, anti-GMO establishments, or "Occupy Wall Street". There's nothing wrong with taking a position. Yet, when you only focus on one side of an argument, you run the risk of being narrow-minded. Also, you lose the galvanising advantage of the tension inherent in conflicts, paradox and contradiction. Oversimplification frequently breeds disenchantment. You have to learn to unfocus to see the big picture from time to time, and you have to be a dynamic tinkerer to diffuse disenchantment.

Take Jeff Bezos, for example. Although he is known as one of the more generous CEOs of our time, he is also notoriously temperamental and harsh with his employees. And even though he comes across as being very serious at heart, he is reportedly also quite playful. Jeff Bezos's advice is to be stubborn and flexible—stubborn so that you don't give up on experiments too soon, and flexible so that you're open to different solutions. Being able to be different people at different times is a licence that great people grant themselves. You don't have to focus on being one thing only.

It's the same kind of thinking when it comes to making decisions. Although Bezos loves data to help him assess his options, he will sometimes sell something that research "proves" customers won't buy, because he believes that short-term research is not a great predictor of long-term viability or popularity. There's no point in thinking about this. He unfocuses from the data in front of him to look at the longer-term ramifications. His high beams are back on!

Complexities, and not sterilised personality traits and opinions, are what great leaders are made of. And for you to reach your own greatness, it will help to unfocus from your supposed identity—to look at the other side of who you are. When you do, unfocus will help you feel more integrated and give you the power you need to activate your greatness.

Embracing Paradox

In your brain, pain can lead to "pleasure" chemicals being released. Stress can direct your attention in a timely manner, but if you don't manage it, it can throttle you. Parallel brain circuits of love and hatred can run at the same time. The default mode network (DMN), when it activates to allow great self-connection, also connects you with others more profoundly. You are wired for paradox—so why not acknowledge this?

One unfocused way to understand your paradoxical nature is to think of any self-defining attribute that you have as being on a spectrum rather than a fixed quantity. Then, on any given day, or in a conversation, reflect on this spectrum. For example, rather than calling yourself an introvert, reflect on situations in which you behave more like one, and those in which you prefer to let your hair down. You might also write out three things that are true about you. Then, look for one example for each characteristic where you did not stick to this rule. Do this every week and soon you will see that there are many colours to your personality and beliefs that focus could never capture.

The think-less mindset challenges you to explore uncomfortable assumptions, and to manage paradoxes: to focus, but also to unfocus; to supertask, yet not multitask; to be so intensely engaged that you can surrender. These apparent contradictions reflect the actual complexity of who you are. The think-less mindset acknowledges this, and is supported by it.

Life is not about *finding* the time to do what you love.

It's about making the time because your life matters. If you manage your contradictions and show up to your life as "you", you increase your engagement and productivity because you can be all that you are, and not a sterilised and limited version of yourself.

Fuel for the Dream

Greatness requires being the most empowered version of yourself. And this empowerment often comes from a sense of purpose, even when the going is tough.

When you have a sense of purpose, it is neither a thought nor a feeling. Rather, it is an often imperceptible, spontaneous and recognisable drive that fuels your ambition. And it confers an intelligence—a way of making things happen—that frequently defies purely rational explanations. Your brain's reward centre is activated every time it makes an appearance.

People who have a sense of purpose are "on a mission". They are driven and inspired by the continuous reward that it provides. The key thing is that they must "feel moved", *after* which they may consider their impact on the world or their legacies. If you look at *Time* magazine's 100 most influential people of 2016, they range from the singer Adele to reality TV star, Olympic athlete and transgender activist Caitlyn Jenner to NBA star Stephen Curry. You may balk at the idea that these people could be in a group that also includes the Pope, Aung San Suu Kyi and Angela Merkel. But they are there for a reason. These are the people who made it to "centre stage" with unforgettable and influential "performances" because they are plugged into their sense of purpose and drive, not because they all started out trying to change the world. Their journeys will, of course, afford them a global platform to be able to change the world if they so desire, but it all started with their own sense of purpose. In my practice, people who try to hitch themselves to social goals upfront rarely connect with a sense of purpose, although they do experience a temporary reprieve from a social conscience. Also, soapboxes, rather than being effective vehicles to express a sense of purpose, frequently just provide a platform for those who are disenchanted.

For example, a doctor who loves her job is not usually driven by wanting to save lives, although this is often the enjoyed and desirable outcome. Instead, she is fuelled by the sense of living as her highest self. That is an abstract feeling. The goal—to save lives—is a way of reaching that feeling state. But it's the feeling that drives her, not the goal. If you've ever tried to connect with your sense of purpose (rather than your goals), you'll know that it's like trying to catch a butterfly with your hands. It's elusive and won't land until it really wants to. Focus won't get you very far, no matter what great cause it connects you to. Instead, unfocus, like waiting for the butterfly to land on your hand, is what will get you there.

If you asked the luminaries I've mentioned about their sense of purpose, most would be unlikely to say that they wanted to serve humanity. More likely, they would say that they wanted to be their best and as true to themselves as they could be. That's your first priority in the order of operations. The problem with this direction is that it's vague and you can't really focus on being your best or "most true"—you have to discover it, and it's an ongoing process. Moreover, embarking on an unchartered journey of self-discovery can be anxiety-inducing. Yet it is precisely this discomfort that will help you become self-actualised.

Many of us, when faced with this tension, run out of fuel. When we do, we are tempted to lower the bar of our ambitions to reduce our anxiety. Called self-handicapping, this decreased effort may allow us to avoid our fear of failure, but as tempting as this may be, it is the last thing we should do. Make self-handicapping a habit, and you may well develop more grey matter in a brain region that suppresses negative emotions—the conflict detector. But while protecting your self-esteem, this prevents your access to a sense of purpose and greatness too. On the contrary, when you're anxious, you should consider upping your game. And upping your game requires unfocus—exploring yourself and spontaneously responding to what you find.

Kazimierz Dabrowski, a Polish psychiatrist and psychologist, developed the "theory of positive disintegration" to explain why anxiety and tension are necessary for self-actualisation. According to Dabrowski, anxiety and tension shape your personality, but more importantly, without them, you cannot grow. They light a fire under you. As tennis great Billie Jean King has famously said, "Pressure is a privilege". You simply have to know what to do when you come apart. Changing your brain for greatness is all about reconstruction.

As the name implies, "positive disintegration" results in coming apart in a good way. You come apart, only to build a bigger and stronger version of yourself and your life. This is not a one-time process; it's a lifelong labour of self-love, rebuilding yourself to progressively higher and higher forms of greatness.

The Dynamic Drummer

The development to your full potential depends on three factors—your ability to thrive in the extremes of life, your current talents and ability, and a drive towards growth and autonomy. There is no "right" path to greatness, and it is anything but focused and well demarcated. Gifted students often experience positive disintegration. Given their emotional sensitivity and propensity to march to their own drummers, they are often misdiagnosed with ADHD. But they are not inattentive—they've simply shifted their attention to a better version of themselves and are adjusting to this new and emerging mental state. Despite frequent disintegrations as a result of their emotional sensitivity, they subsequently reintegrate.

The disintegrations are frequently referred to as "dynamisms", so called because they are states of emotional flux in which these students intermittently take themselves apart with self-questioning, and on every occasion, put themselves together in an altogether different way until they reach a version of themselves that is acceptable to them. People will tell them to focus, choose or settle down. But gifted students will sacrifice the peacefulness of never coming apart because for them, the suffering of stagnation is far worse.

In every human, this "gift" awaits. Your greatness relies heavily on your willingness to unwrap it.

To achieve this state of positive disintegration, Dabrowski explains that you have to first address (not *resolve*) conflicts within yourself, and then between your current self and desired higher self. He calls the conflicts *within* yourself "horizontal conflicts" as they are conflicts that arise at your current level of self. However, the conflicts between your current level of self and your higher self are "vertical"—they call for an upward movement into a higher or greater version of the current you, your greatness.

When you have horizontal conflicts, you are trying to figure out whether you should stay at your current job or change, or stay in your current relationship or move on to another one. The choices are not clear. You can't make up your mind easily. The conflict tears you apart, but you don't panic. Instead, you learn to tolerate the tension welling up within you, much like you might hold a dumbbell up to feel the burn before you bring it back down again. Each anxious moment, like a heavy lift, gives rise to pause. When it becomes too much, you let it go.

You might at first wonder what good this will do. After all, why not just end the discomfort and make a quick decision, right? You don't, because that would be like not working out, and mistaking your lack of emotional exercise for productive relaxation. They're not the same.

Also, as you are practising this anxiety tolerance, tinkering with the different levels of anxiety (like increasing weights as you get stronger), you enter the vertical conflict phase. Here, you simply ask, "Am I living as the highest version of myself?" Most of us are not. And when we think of the time we've wasted, we might freak out. Here again, rather than running away from this anxiety, it's advisable to welcome it, little by little, letting go of it to breathe when it feels like too much. Over time, this anxiety becomes the fuel that allows us to take off to our higher selves, propelling us to our greatness.

Anxiety and tension may tear us apart, but if we're patient with them, if we let them activate our greatest fury, determination and strength, we are more likely to activate our greatness.

It's difficult to resolve our horizontal and vertical conflicts because we fear that we might inadvertently make the wrong choices. Our brains are super-sensitive to error, and this is not just an adult fear—it's present from birth. In 2006, psychologist Andrea Berger showed showed six- to nine-month-olds an arithmetic equation (e.g. 1 + 1 = 2 or 1 + 1 = 1.) Alongside each number, she also showed them one or two puppets depending on the equation on a TV monitor. When the answer options of "one" or "two" (together with the corresponding number of puppets) were offered, the child stared longer at the wrong answer than the correct one.

As adults, this sensitivity only grows. When you do something wrong, your brain's conflict and anxiety alarms go off. Ideally, you'd want them to light a fire under you, but if you're not in a "positive disintegration" frame of mind, you freeze or flee. In some cases, that's the right reaction, but when regret freezes you and you ruminate on it rather than examining your mistakes and correcting them, you can quickly become stuck in self-flagellation.

You can see this in action in competitive sports when a person is under pressure, off their game, defensive and losing. They start to come apart! But then all of a sudden, they realise that they are choosing between defensive options—stuck in horizontal conflicts— and not being the truly aggressive competitor that they can be. All the prior practice they have put in justifies the fact that they should be playing at a higher level—that they should also be thinking of their vertical conflicts. They make new conscious choices, leaving the defensive ambivalence behind and reaching a whole new level of play instead.

In everyday life, it helps to navigate career choices this way. For example, if you are a doctor who really wants to be at the nexus of technology and medicine, you might give up your regular practice and academic medicine, and take time to reintegrate a new career in medical technology. The time for rearrangement is often the most distressing, disintegrating. You know you're on the right track when you start to feel in charge of your own destiny.

Spontaneity

Spontaneity is a gateway through which your purpose can emerge—a moment of relaxation when the truth will show itself. When you're spontaneous, you don't overthink things, so your sense of purpose is likely to feel more authentic and less contrived to you.

Being spontaneous is easier said than done, yet it is of immense value in discovering and expressing your sense of purpose. When you are spontaneous, it's as though your brain's control regions relax the door of the memory vault, and allow memories to come out and mix with the rest of the brain activity. Spontaneity also activates the improvisation circuit—your willingness to make mistakes and "not know" because you will explore and create a solution in the moment. Jazz musicians, for example, do not focus in the traditional sense; rather, they submit to the unpredictability of the musical information coursing through their brains.

The Past That Never Happened

Experience informs us. If you've done a certain something before, you have gained the experience to help you do that same task the next time with greater ease. Even when trying to do something new, you can draw on a similar experience to help you find your way. But past experience can also turn out to be a trap. For example, in 2009, when business consultant Andrew Campbell and his colleagues studied why good leaders make bad decisions in the moment, they found two culprits: emotions were incorrectly tagged due to past experiences, and prior patterns were incorrectly imposed on current ones. Your very own past could be your prison too!

Our memories are like a house of mirrors. Your brain, by randomly inserting information, can fictionalise the stories that we "remember". Our brains can also invent things that didn't happen at all, in so-called memory illusions. Your mood can strongly influence what you remember.

When researchers study this phenomenon, they use lists of related words (e.g. nurse, sick, medicine) and ask people to later recall these words. Among the actual words shown later are distractors called "lures" (e.g. doctor.)

Funnily enough, when you're in a negative mood but not so down that you're depressed, you'd be able to remember that doctor was not part of the original list. That's the one upside of being in a funk! But when you're in a positive mood, you are more likely to "recall" the word "doctor" even if it was never presented to you. Your stress level as well as your level of arousal or excitability can also distort memory recall.

And it's not just the actual memories, but timelines that can be distorted too. In 2014, psychologists Youssef

Ezzyat and Lila Davachi described how very shifty and inaccurate our recollection of timelines could be. We regularly miscalculate the timeline of seeing the faces of people on any particular day, depending on the emotions and memories that are intruding.

The long and short is that your memories are not reliable. They may be a broken compass when you are remembering breaking up with someone, reflecting on a job interview, or thinking about a big leap in your life. So why focus on them? Instead, break up your coherent narratives—re-examine them and make them whole again in a different way. Playfully retell yourself a different version of your life. Of course, memory has a place in day-to-day activities, but over-investment in memory does not.

The Future of Your Life Is Written in Sand, Not Stone

Logic, like memory, is both helpful and misleading. We couldn't do much without it, yet there are reasons to temper our blind faith in it. Great thinkers always question the apparently inevitable. They are sceptical of logic alone, even when the focus that it provides is comforting.

For example, many years ago, doctors believed that stomach ulcers occurred when hydrochloric acid (HCl) ate into the very lining that secreted it. They also believed that eating spicy foods would cause more HCl to be secreted. Based on this information, they advised people who had stomach ulcers that they should avoid spicy foods. This kind of logic seemed to make sense at the time. Besides, who would believe the opposite—that eating non-spicy foods might actually put you at risk of ulcers?

In 1995, led by gastroenterologist Jin-Yong Kang, researchers in Singapore questioned 103 Chinese patients with stomach ulcers about their chilli-eating habits. Compared to people with ulcers, the group without ulcers ate chili three times *more frequently* every month, and also ate close to three times *the amount* of chilli. It seemed that chilli had a protective effect against ulcers!

Subsequent studies explained that the active ingredient in chilli, capsaicin, inhibits acid secretion, stimulates alkali and mucus secretion, and promotes gastric mucosal blood flow, all of which help in the prevention and healing of stomach ulcers. Capsaicin also protects you against the current "real" cause of ulcers, which is the bacterium called *Helicobacter pylori*.

Great minds like Dr. Kang's refuse to accept apparently obvious things. They realise that when someone says that something is inevitable, they may simply be tired of trying to change it. They frequently pause, unfocus, and look at things from another angle.

Part of the problem when trying to change an old belief system is that we use focus to justify our biases. In 2012, brain researcher Martijn Mulder and his colleagues found that people tend to believe in choices that they think are more probable and have a larger payoff for them. When they do, it's the frontoparietal cortex—the brain's focused flashlight—that's to blame. Focus keeps the eye on one line of logic only, but great minds know that this is a trap because logic and truth are not synonymous.

We also regularly take shortcuts when thinking in order to avoid mental effort. Stereotypes are one such shortcut. They can be helpful when they are conscious and true, and when they describe rather than evaluate people. But there are times when stereotypes make us think inflexibly, and frequently they are inaccurate. They compromise our greatness.

Take "age" for example. Most people would say that "age" is the number of years you have been alive. But what is a year? It is the time it takes for the earth to revolve around the sun, right? So someone, at some time in the distant past, decided that the age of the human body is somehow linked to the movement of the earth around the sun. Doesn't that sound a little random?

Until recently, we just accepted this system of thinking. As sure as the earth keeps moving around the sun, we expect that we will keep on aging until we die. But progressively, this connection between our bodies and the earth's movement around the sun has come into serious question.

Even though the earth keeps on moving around the sun, we can make it seem, cosmetically at least (plastic surgery, Botox), as if our skin is resisting aging.

Now, we've advanced even further. In 2011, PhD researcher Mariela Jaskelioff and her colleagues were able to reverse aging in mice by reactivating an enzyme responsible for keeping tissues young. The results were very dramatic—the aging process reversed. In December 2013, David Sinclair and his colleagues discovered a naturally produced compound called NAD that rewinds aging-related death in mice. When mice are younger, NAD helps their cells stay young and energetic. But as they age, levels of NAD drop.

One researcher found that giving mice a substance that could be converted into NAD could reverse aging. The result was astounding. In human terms, it was as if specific cell functions in a 60-year-old person were like those in a 20-year-old. By exploring more deeply than the skin, Sinclair and his colleagues were able to further disrupt our assumptions about age. Studies with humans are now also in progress. Renowned Harvard geneticist George Church has explained that aging is just a programme that can be rewritten. Soon, our bodies will likely be able to resist the passage of time even more.

You don't need to change genes to change the effects of aging either. In 2015, psychology doctoral student Daniela Aisenberg and her colleagues studied two groups of elderly people. One group believed that 82-year-old people still had strong cognitive skills, whereas the other group thought the opposite. They found that when you think of the elderly as being sharp, and you are elderly, you are able to perform a task that challenges flexibility in thinking more effectively than if you carry a bias about the elderly that is negative. Similarly, in 2015, doctoral student Deirdre Robertson and her colleagues found that negative ideas about old age make people walk more slowly.

Our stereotypes can clearly alter our perceptions of what is happening. But luckily for us, our stereotypes can be reversed, as long as we don't just continue with blinkers on, and we unfocus to question our assumptions.

Great people are more flexible and creative. They think outside of focused categories. One way to train yourself to do this is to reflect on the stereotypes that you hold (e.g. narcissistic men or over-emotional women). Then, consciously, reverse your thinking. Say out loud, or write out the opposite of that stereotype. After you have done this, try solving an unrelated problem—you may just find a new solution!

The Need to Know

Sometimes we resist being unfocused because it is disorienting. Indeed, there's a scientific term for the natural human tendency to focus: the desire to put an end to openness in thinking is called "need for cognitive closure" (NCC).

In 1994, psychology researchers Daniel Webster and Arie Kruglanski pointed out five characteristics of people with high NCC: discomfort with ambiguity, preference for predictability, preference for order, decisiveness and closed-mindedness. On the surface, these attributes sound rational and clear-headed—perhaps the attributes you think you want in a leader—but in a world where things are constantly changing, this does not serve anybody. It's a formula for mediocrity.

High levels of NCC make it difficult to adapt to conflicts when incongruent tasks present themselves: there is less connectivity between key brain regions such as the short-term memory cup and other thought-control regions. That means that your brain's ability to switch things up is stymied by your underlying NCC. Just having this trait of wanting things to be done can hamper your mental flexibility when you need it.

To train yourself away from a need for cognitive closure and towards flexibility in thinking, create time in your week for low NCC activities. What are some safe chances that you could take where you would definitely not know the end result? You could choose a topic that really interests you, and look it up and take notes on it even though it has no actual relevance to your life right now. This kind of activity will get your brain used to the idea of low NCC and will help you become more alert and mentally flexible.

Imagining with the Brain in Mind

Great people don't just intend to be great—they imagine it, with precision, and tinker with their imaginations until they get it right. When you commit to your imagination, you have committed to unfocusing from reality.

Rather than aiming for goals, you create them. Rather than following a focused path, you make one in your imagination.

As early as 1995, neurologist Marc Jeannerod pioneered the study of how imagery impacts the brain. He found that when you imagine moving, you actually stimulate vital movement circuits in the brain. Imagery warms up your brain to take action. It offers a leg up to your intention. Since then, numerous studies have demonstrated that imagery can help people move again after a stroke has impaired their movement: simply *imagining* improved mobility or use of a now-useless limb helped these people regain movement. And in 2015, brain researcher Chang-Hyun Park and his colleagues confirmed that imagery stimulates the "action" brain, and because the action brain is involved in actual movement, it helps people move—whether they be an elderly person needing to gain better mobility or healthy young athletes wanting to improve their performance.

Try this: choose one to three images that represent a goal you want to achieve. If you want optimal health, imagine yourself running a marathon and crossing the finish line. If you want a fulfilling relationship, imagine yourself completely satisfied as you are lying next to someone. And if you want more money, imagine something believable and satisfying that you would do with that money, like writing a cheque out to your favourite charity, buying your mum a house, or going on a very exciting holiday. If you choose something that creates overt conflict for you, such as a sum of money that is so great, you don't really believe you can get it, you run the risk of unconsciously sabotaging your efforts.

You don't have to choose an image initially. Dabbling in many images will help you decide on one that works.

Play with first- and third-person perspectives. Many brain-imaging studies have shown that your brain is more powerfully stimulated by first-person than third-person images—i.e. imagining actually doing something, rather than watching yourself doing something. First-person images make you feel like you are in an actual situation, but they can also make you more anxious because they are so real. So if first-person images make you anxious, start with third-person images first. Better yet, use both —this will serve to give you different "camera angles" of the same situation.

The Power of the Underdog in the Imagination

There are five types of imagery that you can use in your quest for greatness: winning, coming from behind, working on a specific weakness, seeing a strategy on a board in front of you, or feeling excited about getting what you want.

In 2009, kinesiology professor Craig Hall and his colleagues examined 345 athletes to see which types of imagery improved their confidence at crunch time. They found that only two types of imagery actually improved

---

confidence: working on your specific weaknesses and imagining coming from behind. Dabbling in these two kinds of images will help you feel the confidence that you need for your greatness pursuits.

When you imagine something, engage all of your senses. Try to feel what you would feel in that situation, and imagine the tastes if relevant, or the smell if that pertains to the situation. Make it as real as you can. Imagining in these many ways makes you less anxious and more confident. Also, ensure that your image is clearly delineated and rewarding. What colours do you see? How does this make you feel? Is your image in 3-D? All this taken together really helps clarify your image so that your brain can use it as a blueprint to conjure up a plan to take you there.

A Hawk's-Eye View

Ray Kurzweil is the director of engineering at Google. He is one of the world's most famous futurists. A stunning 86 per cent of his predictions about the future have been correct. In 1999, he predicted that personal computers would come in a variety of shapes and ten years later, that they would be wearable. He also predicted that portable computers would be a trend by 2009. In 2000, he predicted very high bandwidth wireless communication to the internet at all times by 2010. That year, he also correctly predicted that in ten years, computers would tap into a worldwide mesh forming vast supercomputers and memory banks. He was right on all accounts.

Currently, Kurzweil predicts that search engines will soon provide spontaneous feedback to us. If we look up a new restaurant opening, for instance, Kurzweil's imagined new and improved search engine will remind us when it opens, and might even send us a menu. It will act as an ancillary brain. Even more boldly, Kurzweil predicts that we will one day have nanobots made from our DNA scurrying through our bloodstreams. These nanobots will connect us to the cloud and we will be able to send email and photos directly from our brains.

If you examine his thinking carefully, you will see that he has a very focused and intricate knowledge of people and machines. But in addition to this, he is able to project out into the future to imagine the tipping point when exponential progress will occur. Unfocus, when it activates the DMN, sets up your slow-wave rhythms, and helps you create possible versions of the future. But how does Kurzweil unfocus to come up with such radical ideas, and how can he be correct so often?

Freeman Dyson, a theoretical physicist and mathematician, suggested an explanation. He divided natural scientists into hawks that fly above the confusing particularity of nature and the frogs that muck around in the messy details. Kurzweil is one of those hawks, content to unfocus from time to time to see the big picture. When he does, he is able to project possibilities far into the future.

It's becoming the hawk and asking big-picture questions that will bring you closer to your greatness. And you don't have to be predicting flying drones and nanobots either. You can ask big questions about your life, and talk about them. You could ask, "If I look at the greatest exponential opportunity in my business in the next six months, what would that be?"

For Bezos, unfocus takes the form of what he calls the "regret minimisation framework". There are three steps to this philosophy that anybody could utilise: project your life forward to when you are 80 years old; ask your 80-year-old self if you regret now that you didn't try out your big idea; then ask yourself if you'd regret leaving your job, your unpaid bonus, and leaving your stability behind in order to pursue your passion. When you take this long-term perspective, you awaken the hawk in your thinking.

Your brain can be a crystal ball because of the DMN. It's unfocus that will activate this network. It will get the connections within itself buzzing, and it will turn on the connections between the DMN and different brain regions that put puzzle pieces together to predict the future. Rather than sticking with the complete puzzles of the past, you play with the puzzle pieces of the future, stare at each possible picture, and rearrange the pieces until they make sense.

"To Be, or Not to Be..."

In normal waking consciousness, you think logically, plan, analyse and follow up on your intentions with action. In so doing, you capitalise on only a small amount of your brain's resources. But there is a higher level of intelligence that governs your decision-making, removes brain biases, and clears your mind of the usual obstructions that prevent your access to your own greatness. Called transcendental awareness, it circumvents the distracting and misleading effects of ongoing mental chatter, and helps you to have better thought control and make better decisions.

The essence of transcendental awareness involves "being" and not "doing". And there are many practices that can help you reach this state. Perhaps the best studied of all is mindfulness— a practice in which you focus on your breath, gently ignoring your mental chatter. You use your breath as the point of focus to return to each time your mind wanders into the chatter. With this practice (20 minutes twice a day is a standard recommendation), you learn how to deepen your self-awareness, control your emotions, and then transcend yourself to see and experience yourself as part of the greater universal whole. You can also practise mindfulness by using a technique known as open monitoring, in which you simply receive all thoughts, feelings and sensations without judgment instead simply monitoring them.

Aside from mindfulness meditation, transcendental meditation, which is a mantra-based meditation, Qi

Gong meditation and even several forms of prayer have shown some psychological benefit as well. Don't be discouraged if you can't sit still, because there are walking forms of meditation, too. Also, if you really can't sit still for too long, try an app called "headspace", which is an interactive form of meditation.

People often think of meditation—whether mantra- or breath-focused—as a kind of hyper-focus. But in fact, the focus you give your mantra or your breath leads to a wonderful kind of unfocus, and it is in this unfocus that there is transcendence of the self. You can see transcendental meditation on brain scans as a deactivation of the parietal lobe—a region associated with developing a sense of self. Disrupt or deactivate the sense of self and your sense of separateness from others is also minimised.

Mindfulness, on the other hand, stimulates regions in your brain responsible for empathy and social understanding, like the DMN, enhancing your connection with those around you, allowing you to have deeper insights about how you fit in a social context, and also, how that context can inform your own thinking. Even in children with ADHD, mindfulness meditation—focusing on your breath rather than your silent mental chatter—improves attention.

The Focus Triad

Three stages, from focus to unfocus, can move you towards transcendence.

In everyday life, you focus on your work, your chores, your children and your health. At best, this happens when you can stop all distractions and just look at what is in front of you. This is laser-sharp focus.

The second stage in the evolution of focus is a continuous flow of perception. In this state, you are not just removed from distractions but actually move much more deeply into concentration where you are not restless or troubled by your desires. Your attention is not just focused but sustained. You may, for example, be able to repeat a word in your head five times before your mind wanders off in another direction and you have to bring it back. But when you have mastered concentration, you continuously mention the word, and your mind will not wander anymore.

In the final state, the boundary between you and what you are concentrating on is completely lost. You are within, connected to that object. You and your word become one. If I ask you now what table is, for instance, you may describe it as an object that has four legs and a surface. But this is only using several words for one. In this final transcended state, when you look at the table, you experience its essence. In that state, you would see it and describe it very differently—you might fully comprehend it, say, as a collection of wood atoms that vibrate ever so slightly, remain bonded, and provide the potential energy necessary to resist the pull of gravity, should you place anything atop the horizontal vibrating atom collection. It's in such mind states that many scientific insights probably occur.

When all three states of consciousness happen at the same time, three types of attention coexist in different brain circuits. I call this the attention triad. In one room in your brain, the spotlight is on. In another, the recess lights are on. And in the third, light is streaming through the window making inside and outside indistinguishable. Talk about unfocus!

The widespread health benefits of meditation also help to sustain your greatness. Aside from stress reduction, meditation may also be able to increase the actual duration of your life. In 2009, molecular biologist Elizabeth Blackburn was awarded the Nobel Prize for discovering protective caps on chromosomes called telomeres. She has also discovered an enzyme ("telomerase") that protects the caps from the detrimental effects of aging. In an initial study conducted by Dr. Blackburn, a group of 30 volunteers went to the Shambhala Mountain Center in Northern Colorado for a three-month meditation retreat. With them, she found a 30 per cent increase in telomerase activity. Subsequently, many more studies have replicated this finding—no more telomere snipping with age if you meditate. You live longer!

Putting it all together for your personal greatness

All of these greatness principles can be found in three basic identities that you already likely possess.

The Inner Explorer

Some people will tell you that greatness is a mountain you have to climb. It may be—but it's not outside of you. Rather, it's a place that you have to find within yourself after clearing the fog that is in its way. You do this by reconstructing your personal narrative, re-examining your memories, allowing the many sides of yourself to surface, and by building an image of your future after tinkering with it over and over again. This is all about chipping away at the sculpture of you. That's what will reveal your greatness.

Years of indoctrination by formal education, social values and early-life insults may dupe you into thinking that greatness is beyond your reach. No matter what your age is, I'm here to tell you unequivocally that this is wrong. Greatness is a universal truth. I have seen it emerge over and over again in the most unlikely people in my therapy and coaching practice.

Every person is responsible for his or her own greatness. There's nothing fancy to practise in this belief. Know that you're great. It's one of life's axioms. Just as certainly as the sun will shine and the waves on the ocean will ebb and flow, you've got to believe that you are great. And move on. If you doubt it, question the doubt. If you're afraid of it, question the fear. If you're in disbelief about it, question the disbelief. But never question the greatness.

Rather, unfocus. Think less. Take time off to go on a run. Spend time in relaxing activities that you enjoy.

The more you learn to daydream and eventually connect your daydreams to your desires and spontaneous realisations, the closer you will get to your overall goals. Greatness, in that sense, is a lifestyle.

The Search Engineer

"Search engine optimisation" (SEO) is a way to organise the content of your web page so that it shows up higher in page ranks—the better your SEO, the more people will visit your page because it will come up first (or close to the top) in a search of a related term. (It's likely what helped Amazon become so successful!) But there's another kind of SEO called self-esteem optimisation which enhances your self-esteem. As opposed to simply protecting your self-esteem to maintain the status quo (called self-esteem maintenance—SEM), SEO can take your life to the next level.

For example, when Bezos left his job on Wall Street, his self-esteem would have been subjected to uncertainty. Had he "protected" it, he might have backtracked for SEM. Instead, he chose to optimise it—to acknowledge and live out his desires. To manage your self-esteem best, you need to go from SEM to SEO.

In some situations, it may not be obvious that you're stuck in SEM. For example, when you're downsizing and simplifying your life, it can take a huge burden off your shoulders. You may think you're optimising, but it could be that you're lowering the bar to handle the stress of life more effectively. You're self-handicapping! So, for every downsizing and simplifying decision in life, ask yourself, "What if I took my life to the next level *up*?" That's the kind of question you ask for SEO. But be prepared for your brain to fight back.

In my therapy and coaching practice, encouraging people to "up their game" often backfires at first. They dig their heels in even more—not realising that that's the SEM talking. SEM is often the superordinate goal—the goal above all other goals. It will race all other goals to the finish line unless you do something about this. When your brain says, "Why try?", it's a sign that your greatness is breaking down. You've got to build it up.

You acknowledge that there is a price to pay. Build an image of what you want and realise that your future is built from your mind and not your current circumstances. Try to dig into your paradoxes. Write out three stereotypes that confine you, and defy each one with a concrete behaviour. For instance, if you think you are "not a creative person", doodle for fifteen minutes a day and examine your doodles at the end of the month. You'll likely see things that you like, and certain ineffable patterns emerging.

When you examine SEM, you'll see how it keeps you in your unhealthy eating habits, away from the gym, stuck in a socio-economic bracket, stagnant in your relationships, and away from fun. SEO means you've decided to take your self-esteem apart, so that you can put it back together. Great people engage in SEO throughout their lives.

Consider this metaphor: when you work out, muscles actually tear before they repair to make you bigger and stronger. Similarly, self-esteem that comes apart in the right way can be reconstituted so that you feel much stronger and more prepared for success. In a sense, you submit to it. That's what positive disintegration is about.

Life's Olympian

When an Olympic figure skater moves on the ice, she must be focused to execute on her technical prowess, but when she leaps into the air she has to let go. Many elite athletes point to their ability to activate their unconscious mind in the most competitive and high-stress moments as the X factor that defines their places in history. They surrender!

This isn't as Zen as it may sound. When top-level athletes talk about learning to stop thinking, what they are really talking about is surrendering, and the process of releasing their minds from the stress of focusing on what they have learned. The brains of world-class gymnasts, for example, have particularly strong DMN connections compared to the general population. This makes sense, given that gymnasts often do things during which focus would be a liability. If you aren't sure if you are upside-down or right side up, if you are falling or flying, maybe it's better not to ask. Better to trust, to be mindful rather than vigilant, to surrender.

Whether you are a world-class athlete, a top-level strategist in a business, or simply an ordinary person trying to access your greatness, learning the mental competencies associated with a surrender mindset is critical. Greatness is something you surrender to when you push logic, memories and confusion about your contradictions out of the way.

The singer who belts out a note so high that it gives you chills, the firefighter who rescues a baby, the soccer player who dribbles the ball successfully to score a goal, or the runner who breaks through the tape at the finish line first—all of these people can only achieve these goals because they have learned to surrender to the moment that calls.

Keep in mind that it's often preferable to surf the waves than to control the ocean. Expertise isn't just about control. It's also about knowing when to give it up.

The problem with trying to be great is that every time you step onto your surfboard, the waves may knock you down. If this happens over and over again, you might even give up trying to surf. Yet anyone who has surfed would tell you that if you get back on that board, you'll make it eventually. Some days will be rougher than others. You may pack up the surfboard, but you always return. That's positive disintegration in action. Take time off to be with your mind—go for a stroll. Any top performer will tell you that downtime is as important as "on" time. So release your goals from time to time. Just be present.

Sometimes it's hard to talk about "presence" without sounding too abstract. But I'm talking about something simpler. Just practise letting go of your goals periodically. Unfocus on them. Maybe you don't want to make all that money this year, or to get that promotion. Maybe you do. But bring things in and out of focus and you will feel more connected to them. Staying focused on goals means that unfocus can't work its magic for you.

In a sense, this whole book has been about your greatness. To resolve your horizontal conflicts, to shift vertically to your higher self, to escape the trappings of memory, and to build a future without resistance from reality, remember to incorporate the unfocused competencies in this table.

Focused Mindset	Unfocused Mindset Shift
You've got to be constantly "on the case" to be great	Positive disintegration allows you to reconfigure your life continuously
Don't be hypocritical	Relax into your paradoxes and own them
Purpose requires a goal	Purpose will lead you to

your goal—activate it with crises and spontaneity

Keep your eye on the ball at all times

Practise surrendering to your spontaneity

Be realistic

Change your reality with your imagination

Conclusion

THE THINK-LESS MANIFESTO

"A lot of people in our industry haven't had very diverse experiences. So they don't have enough dots to connect, and they end up with very linear solutions without a broad perspective on the problem. The broader one's understanding of the human experience, the better design we will have."

Steve Jobs

I cdnuolt blveiee that I cluod aulaclty uesdnatnrd what I was rdanieg. Were you surprised that you were able to comprehend the garbled words in that sentence? According to psychologist Graham Rawlinson, all you need is the first and last letter in place, and your brain will automatically unscramble the rest to spell out the word correctly. Notwithstanding some caveats and exceptions, this illustrates one of the basic tenets of this book: that your brain does not have to logically focus on every component in sequence in order to understand what is happening. The context and connecting ideas can help it make sense of things.

So it is with the information, advice and strategies I've laid out in the preceding chapters. You can and should absorb the material that interests or inspires you, and come back to the rest when you feel yourself stuck or stymied by too much focus in one or more arenas of your life. That said, most people find it a helpful support to have the foundational principles of the unfocused mindset laid out all in one place.

Whether you're an individual looking to improve your life, or a company leader looking to engage your employees to improve profits, use these overarching credos as a guide. If you are lost as you wander back and forth from focus, they will remind you of why you committed to these changes in the first place. And they will help you to reset your cognitive rhythm too.

Practise Self-Forgiveness

You won't ever try anything in life if you can't forgive yourself when you fail. The fact that you're trying implies that you are willing to fail, and when you do, you will dig yourself out of the hole and keep going.

Can you imagine what would happen, if, every time you took a wrong turn while driving, you just gave up on your journey and sat there regretting it without ever moving again—or if you just kept cursing yourself while driving on? You probably wouldn't get very far without driving yourself batty!

In a sense, it suits us to idle, at least unconsciously. Scholars of unconscious motivations have pointed out that when we live in guilt, it gives us unconscious licence to avoid living life fully—to stagnate, in order to defy the march to our inevitable mortality. But this strategy doesn't work. Death will meet us anyway. So why not learn to course correct and move forward in life with greater vitality?

Self-forgiveness is part of the rejuvenation or refuelling process. You can be wrong, make a mistake, and learn from that mistake by exploring it; you can, and sometimes should, even regret your actions. But in order to discover anything new, to stop repeating prior traumas, you have to move on.

Self-forgiveness is not just brushing something aside. It is a deep realisation and acceptance that you are not perfect—and apparently were not designed to be. Your life can still be excellent, beautiful and great. Errors are not stop signs—they are signals for a detour. Sometimes, these detours pay off if you allocate your attention to what's possible rather than self-blame. Possibility thinking will help you get there.

Consider two examples from the world of pharmacology: the drug minoxidil was developed for the treatment of high blood pressure, but it also happened to cause hair growth, and once scientists realised that this "side effect" could actually be a desired effect for other conditions, they developed it as a topical application for male-pattern baldness. The common blood thinner, warfarin, was first used to kill rats by causing them to bleed, before scientists realised that same reaction could be harnessed in a life-extending way, hence its development into a blood-thinning drug that could help dissolve dangerous blood clots in humans.

Focus makes you think of side effects as just that, side effects. Unfocus makes you ask, "If I take my mind off the obvious for a moment, how might this side effect give me a better result?" Managed effectively, conflicts build brain capacity, and errors signify the need to change course. It was Einstein, after all, who reminded us that a person who has never made any mistakes has never tried anything new.

After more than two decades of studying and researching the brain, the one thing that I am convinced of, is that we are "wired funny". As rich as the experience of being human is, it is also fraught with things that don't make sense. Why does loving come with so much pain? Why does hard work come with varied gain? Why are we not wired to just connect and help each other rather than look to our differences—even fighting about them—to find ourselves?

These inevitable contradictions are dazzlingly confusing. That's why we can be humble about being human—and why it makes sense to recognise our frequently faulty brain wiring and turn to our many-sided selves when we're looking for answers. The mother who recognises that her organisational skills can just as easily be applied to running a business, or the business owner who recognises that her skills can just as easily be applied to running a house—these are the people who lead themselves and others with purpose to the proverbial promised land where they can be curious, adaptable and free. There, they will find their greatness.

Be Light

Consider how it feels when a helium balloon is let loose. If that balloon is tied to a line of string and you are holding the other end, you can delight in knowing it will rise but remain in your grasp. But what happens if it unexpectedly escapes? You'll likely know that mild feeling of panic when it floats out of reach. It's one thing to be flying high, another altogether to be drifting aimlessly, disconnected from the ground.

The call to one's own freedom is strong, yet few heed it, and when they do, they often feel untethered. Armed with the tools to unfocus that you now have, you can be sure that as you build and rebuild your life with cognitive rhythm, the glowing octopus of a default mode network (DMN) will help you put the puzzle pieces for possible new life scenarios together.

Not only does life include a sort of inertia, or heaviness, that holds us in place (like the person holding the balloon), we also seek out that heaviness so that we don't feel that we are flitting meaninglessly from one thing to another. Even though we say we want to be happy and free, we also want to feel grounded. Being grounded is fine if it means that we are being sensible. But it's not if we're grounded like a ship in dry dock, or a child who is forbidden to leave the house.

There's clearly an upside to having a schedule, family, friends and a stable job. But as much as these elements can bring profound meaning and comfort, we may be unconsciously using them to weigh ourselves down. As the Danish philosopher Søren Kierkegaard argues, too much freedom and too many possibilities make us anxious. He calls this the "dizziness of freedom". It creates a rebound reaction in which we hunker down with focus and hold onto our life's possessions and circumstances even more.

In the same way that you cannot swim until you surrender to the water and let it keep you afloat, you cannot have freedom unless you give in to the lightness that comes with it. Relieve yourself of too much heaviness before it becomes a burden. You have a choice.

There appear to be two arguments about whether we have the freedom to choose. Some people believe we have no free will to choose. Others believe that we can be agents of our own freedom—we have some ability to choose where we want to go, and what we want to do. To people on each side, the alternative seems absurd. But the truth is, the freedom to choose exists on a spectrum depending on what you are choosing. You can't choose your parents, for example. But you can choose how you relate to them. Just the belief that you have a choice, however, will activate your brain to start making changes and decisions. Even if it is stretched by stress, you now know how to reactivate your brain's spring coils.

Unfocus circuits play a major role in helping you escape the confines of the environment to access your own ingenuity for solutions. By updating what you know gradually, freedom will become less intimidating.

Let Life Add Up

Take any of the individuals I have highlighted in this book. You could conclude that any one of them got to their goals by using possibility thinking and sheer determination. That would be true, but it would only be a partial or relative truth, because every one of them also had struggles, doubts and failures along the way— who's to say that these adversities did not motivate these people even more?

Most of what you think is true is true to some extent only. Rarely are things that absolute. Loving someone unconditionally, being completely motivated, being the greatest that you can be—they are all usually relative truths. As jarring and infrequent as "partial truths" may sound, they are more the norm than the exception. It's important to accept partial truths because, being a far more reliable and representative guide, they can lead you to the greatness you're looking for.

Even computers are now programmed for partial truths. Rather than using binary computer logic based on "yes" and "no" answers, programmers who are developing artificial intelligence now increasingly use a kind of logic called "fuzzy logic", which more closely approximates how the brain works because it is based on degrees of truth. With fuzzy logic, a computer, much like a brain, aggregates information that is more or less true; it uses these approximations to get to a more accurate answer. You don't focus on each fact, just as you don't focus on the jumbled letters I showed you earlier. Instead, you think what you think and move on.

Embrace Complexity

Simple intentions are easy to understand. Need to go for a walk? Put on a pair of sneakers and go walking. Hungry? Make some food and eat dinner. For simple actions, you need what we call "simple cognition". It's easy to be clear with your intentions and act. Yet, for more complex things like "wanting to be happy", "wanting to be rich" or "wanting to be great", simple intentions are not enough. Either those goals or the paths toward them are often too obscure. And even when you think you're clear, you're frequently not.

First and foremost, an increasing number of studies have demonstrated that, for primary intentions, there is not one centre or circuit in the brain. Depending on your action—whether it is to speak, subtract or move your hand—intentions activate different brain circuits.

Rather than being a single function, "intention" is the resulting force that promotes action depending on the alignment of your memories, ideas, emotions and thoughts. If, in the balance of things, you still think that something is impossible or that you don't have the faculties to achieve it, success will continue to be out of reach despite your hard efforts. First, you have to align these various elements to build an intention. Unfocus will help you do that.

One of the most interesting aspects of complex cognition is that your "consciousness" may not just be a result of actual brain circuits interacting with each other. There may be largely invisible magnetic forces at play as well.

There are many reasons to assume that consciousness is electromagnetic. In 2016, biophysicist Abraham R. Lipoff pointed out that brain cells are able to generate electricity across their membranes and magnetic fields around them. Also, haemoglobin is magnetic, and when it runs through brain circuits, it could also contribute to this electromagnetic effect.

These forces cannot be seen, yet they impact your brain profoundly. To understand this, think of how you cannot see a magnetic field, but if you brought a magnet to a metal fridge, you would instantly see it in action. Your brain's electromagnetic field can be altered by unfocus techniques such as mindfulness which start with focus, and then lead to unfocused states.

Dare to Leap

The famous "Double Slit Experiment" demonstrated conclusively how electrons—the tiny "particles" in your brain—behave. To understand this experiment, imagine being in front of a plate in which there are two big holes large enough for tennis balls to pass through. Now imagine a screen behind this plate, so that when you fire tennis balls through the holes, they will hit the screen. If you were shooting tennis balls straight through the holes they would most likely hit the screen in line with the holes, right? But in the double slit experiment, when you fire electrons through slits (rather than using tennis balls and correspondingly-sized holes) something different happens. Instead of seeing the electrons hit the screen in line with the slits, you will see that the electron "hits" form bands all across the screen. The range of places that they hit is far broader than the size and positions of the holes.

After thinking long and hard about this, scientists have deduced that when electrons go through the slits, they behave like waves travelling towards the screen. The waves are distorted and spread outwards from their initial trajectory, like the concentric circles you might see if you dropped a rock into a pond. In the same way that the rocks will create outwardly moving circles in a pond, the electron beams that go through the double slits create concentric circles moving outwards toward the screen. As there are electrons travelling through each slit, and the two concentric circle formations are getting bigger and bigger as they move toward the screen, at some point, the lines of both crisscross each other (think of dropping two rocks side by side into that pond, and how the ripples from each overlap). Eventually more and more wave lines intersect on the way to the screen.

The bands on the screen correspond to where the waves intersect and combine; the blank spaces where they cancel each other out (a peak meets a trough). There are lots of points of intersection, so there are many bands on the screen. But here's where the story gets even stranger.

If you were to place a measuring device that observes the electrons as they pass through the slit (a metaphor for focus), the electrons stop behaving like waves and instead act like particles—like the tennis balls. You see them hitting the screen only directly in front of the slits. If you turn the device off (a metaphor for unfocus), they start behaving like waves again, and you see bands.

It's as if the electrons "know" whether you are watching them. Even stranger is that scientists later demonstrated that you could move the measuring device so far away and present it for so little time that there would not be enough time for the electrons to "detect" it. Yet 93 per cent of the time, they behave like particles when they are observed. How this occurs is still a mystery. But it's fair to say that electrons can be in more possible places when they are not being observed.

Now, we know that this phenomenon represents much of what quantum physics is about. And we know too that you can't apply principles that govern the behaviour of small particles like electrons to larger objects like humans willy-nilly. Yet when you appreciate that electrons are what we're made up of, and that the very particles that make up our brains can change when unobserved, it gives you reason to pause, and a deep respect for unfocus and the unknown.

Suppressing self-doubt is far inferior to replacing it with the acceptance of mystery, possibility thinking, intuition, spontaneity and operating from your psychological centre of gravity. When you do, you unfocus from the existing evidence (or lack of evidence) for success, and you use your brain to visualise and simulate templates of the future that you can explore. By accepting and accelerating on a more mysterious path, you don't allow focus to limit your possibilities or draw you down.

See Beads on a Chain, Not Isolated Buoys at Sea

It is a biological reality that our brains are all connected. There are holes in your skull (eyes, ears, nose, mouth, skin) and a brain within it—your brain is open to the world. Our heads are more like multiple beads joined by an invisible thread than single buoys floating out at sea. There's plenty of evidence to suggest that in addition to being a series of beads linked by a thread, our brains may be part of one bigger chain called universal consciousness.

Just because you can't "see" this universal consciousness" doesn't mean that it doesn't exist. For example, we believe that we can reliably see the world around us with our eyes, yet every human being has a literal blind spot in the eye so that it is possible to completely miss something. Similarly, any sound that has a frequency of 17,400 Hz can only be heard by teenagers. If you are over eighteen, you are unlikely to hear it. And similar limitations apply to taste, touch, and smell as well. The world is filled with more information than our senses will process. Mirror neurons are proof of our instant connection. These are brain circuits in *your* head that are turned on when they "reflect" (like a mirror) *my* movement, intention and emotions when you are near me.

Your brain can form a picture of what is going in my brain without any effort at all on your part. Somehow, something between you and me "transmits" this information. Call this air, radio waves, or whatever you like—a line of communication is open between you and me, and the effect is instant. Watch a figure skater leap into the air, and you feel magnificent because your brain is mounting a response as if you were doing the same— but it's below the threshold for movement or suppressed, which is why you're not leaping off the couch. The same goes for a person whose smile is contagious—your mirror neurons are reflecting the intention and emotion in your own brain automatically.

We can also synchronise our brains with one another automatically. In 2015, psychologist Yulia Golland and colleagues showed that when people watch a movie together, their brain waves become synchronised. The more synchronised their brain waves are, the more closely tied to each other their emotional states are. Even when people are not deliberately connected with each other, just being in the same physical space synchronises their physiology.

All of these ideas suggest that a "communication line"

exists between us—an "internet" connecting our brains.

When you look at the world, do you see it as a *collection* or *connection* of many things? Your perceptions would have you believe that the world is a collection of many things. However, when you suspend your perceptions, you see the world as a connection of things, and as one giant coordinated universe. Great minds are able to move from focus to unfocus by seeing the world as a collection and then as a connection. They move back and forth between the two with ease.

Our tendency to see things as a collection of separate things can be traced back to infancy when our brains develop the ability to differentiate ourselves from others. When infants first learn how to grasp things, like their mother's thumb, this heralds their first experience of a "self" as separate from "other". Neurons in the parietal cortex are largely responsible for this experience when they are adequately developed. And as we grow, we continue to see the world as objects outside of ourselves, and we think that this is a fact of life set in stone. It's not. Remember how meditation can change this?

Focus cannot help us see the connections in this "Internet of Things". No matter how hard we look for a tangible sign of it, we won't see it. That's why we need to rely on ways of "seeing" that are beyond perception. We need to settle into unfocus for this connection to become more apparent.

Replace Evolution

A long time ago, evolutionary biologists recognised that the human body evolved over time. When certain things become unnecessary, the body does away with them. And when new competencies are needed, the body scrambles to develop them. I believe that unfocus is a relatively new brain habit that has evolved to reclaim the glories of the Renaissance and also meet the demands of an ever-changing world—a new and modern Renaissance.

The brain does not, however, simply pull a new and clear function out of a hat. It develops its advances through tinkering. As evolution tinkers with our brains to endow us with the capacity to unfocus, we need to learn how to leverage this capacity to make the best of it.

But we are faster than evolution in many respects. And in any case, we can't wait for evolution to catch up with the changing world that we are creating.

Instead, we have to work *with* evolution. We must realise that our survival brains are simply fuelling fear and taking us away from opportunity. We must challenge the survival brain with possibility thinking and a brain that is more willing to understand the vast possibilities of the world by being in cognitive rhythm.

These mindset shifts can only occur when we take over from evolution—with the full power, productivity and passion that this manifesto declares for new, raw human potential.

THE THINK-LESS MANIFESTO

Practise self-forgiveness
Be light
Let life add up
Embrace complexity
Dare to leap
Be part of the Internet of Things
Challenge the survival brain

About the Author

SRINI PILLAY, MD, is a Harvard-trained and practising psychiatrist, brain-imaging researcher, and a brain-based technology innovator. Currently a part-time assistant professor at Harvard Medical School, he is also an invited faculty member in the executive education programmes at Harvard Business School and Duke Corporate Education. He is the founder and CEO of NeuroBusiness Group, an executive coaching, consultant and technology business, which was named one of the top 20 leadership training Movers and Shakers in the world by Training Industry. His previous book, *Life Unlocked: 7 Revolutionary Lessons to Overcome Fear*, won a "Books for a Better Life" Award. Born in Durban, South Africa, he lives in Newton, Massachusetts.

ACKNOWLEDGEMENTS

I am deeply indebted and grateful to the team that has allowed this book to become a reality.

The concept and book would probably have remained in my imagination were it not for the brilliant, incisive, and "nail on the head" mentality of my agent, Celeste Fine. Celeste saw my pressing need to encourage all people to find greatness within their own complexity—at a time when the term complexity bordered on profanity. With her nurturing sense of belief and promise and her deep-lying sensitivities and intellectual faculties, she helped me bring this book to life.

Before *Think Less* was born, Celeste asked me to engage in a monologue for an hour, in order to see what I was doing and why I loved my life and work so much. After hearing my seemingly endless ramblings, she looked at me and said, "Unfocus—you have to write about why unfocus is such a good idea, and how people can make it work for themselves in their lives. You've done it. Why not share it?" Celeste is not simply a representative. She knows deeply who her writers are. She advocated for me, and also read, thought, wondered, and pondered with me throughout this process. With never a wasted word, she is a master of communication, incorrigibly her own, and as inspiring of "self-ownership" as one could possibly be. Her entire team, including John Maas and Sarah Passick, helped me stay with this book, even when, at times, the concept seemed to have run away into obscurity.

In fact, it might have, were it not for the mind-blowing experience of working with my editor, Marnie Cochran. I'm not sure where to start—with her brilliant sensibility that makes every word want to blossom into the fullness that it can be, or slip into a space that was just waiting for it? Or with her light-hearted depth, so clearly obvious in her relentless dedication to the clarity of the writing? Or with my very large luck and good fortune that she did not give in to her probably quite frequent temptations to wash her hands of what at times was a book that seemed to want to become ether, or a mirror of all-too intense aspects of humanity that would have obscured its core message? Marnie, thank you for your amazing talent and your supreme understanding and professionalism in working with me so adaptively and collaboratively, even when my words were untamed, far too irreverent, or simply caught up in the excitement of themselves. Thank you for bothering to talk, listen, understand, change, or stay your course when you believed in it, and for working with me in articulating the immense power of unfocus. And so much thanks, too, to Liz Stein and Janet Biehl, who worked with us to help polish the words on the page.

Then there are all the people in my life who have tolerated my obsession with this book and my social media outreach to the world, despite their intense need for privacy. I acknowledge them in these brief mentions: To Uma—you are magic beyond compare, a stalwart presence of love, understanding, and critical feedback, and a bastion of support and faith in ethereal and transcendent ways. To Rajiv—your iconoclastic presence and gifts of insight have been so enlightening, and your tireless ability to accompany me and let me accompany you in neurotic entanglements personify unfocus. To Rajan—thank you for covering for me like a "mindguard", allaying my anxieties about our family, my choices, myself, and showing me the belief that has inspired this book to its completion. To my parents, Raz and Sava, I owe so much gratitude. They are in every intention and word in this book, and inextricably linked with my psyche— my mom, still my greatest fan, and a veritable miracle to behold; my dad, passed, yet ever present in my work ethic and reminders to reset to "no-nonsense".

To Paula, whose patience, inspiration, intelligence, work ethic, and dedication I have benefited from. And to Vicky and Irina, for helping me manage my life.

And how can I forget the unsung heroes of this process in my extended family and among my friends— Uncle Bobby, Mano, Shan, Jaya, Babes, Shunna, Jean, Bob, Pragasen, Brandon, Mahadev, Dennis, Stephen, Daphne, Phillip, JT, Daron, Zach, Brenda, and Gideon, people whose love, dedication, presence, support, and "beingness" have touched and supported this book in intangible yet essential and fundamental ways.

I grew up in a family of characters, with cousins who evolve out of that same matrix too: Boonch, Thumbiemama, Boyamama, Perima, Dayamama, Surya, Sagrie, Prakash, Monty, Pinglan, Naveen, Loges, Bashni, Georgie, Devan, Doris, Anna, Aggie—a potpourri of names and diversity of characters, but a foundational experience in my understanding of nondual consciousness. For that I am immensely grateful.

No book gets written without its teachers in mind either. I must thank and acknowledge Dr. P. D. Naidoo, one of my first inspirations to study the brain; Dr. Margaret Nair, for inspiring me to pursue an education in psychiatry; Dr. Shervert Frazier, for guiding me out of many dark holes, often in reverie, before his untimely recent passing; Dr. Bruce Cohen, for setting me on the path that was to become my academic life; Dr. Ross Baldessarini, for encouraging me to always question; Drs. Debbye Yurgelun-Todd and Perry Renshaw, for including me in the world's most innovative brain-imaging centre of its time at Harvard; Dr. Bill Carter, for seeing in me something that I am, often before I do, and often surprisingly too; Dr. Les Havens, for bothering to manifest as a human on earth, when you clearly had other things to do; and, of course, Dr. Jonathan Cole, for believing in me and the unfocus process, and for opening the doors to my home and my identity's place of rest and reinvention, in America. Also, I would be remiss if I were not to mention my colleagues from downtown—Dr. Maurizio Fava, for helping me do my initial research, and Drs. John Herman and Jerry Rosenbaum, for being there soon after I graduated, and for offering to be there if ever I needed them.

Finally, none of this would be possible if it were for not for my patients, coaching clients, and online community, who teach me and remind me endlessly that life hides in secret places; that "self" as we see it is an illusion; that we owe it to ourselves to find ourselves in ways that logic alone could never reveal. I bow to you, feeling now a place of reverence that I call God—a force that I humbly submit to, whatever it is—in deep and profound gratitude.

Think Less, Learn More is not just meant to be a book; it is meant to herald a new and invigorated movement. In reading this book, I hope that you will be inspired to own and manifest your identity as an adventurer, and if you already do, to take it to another level.

We are wired to be self-aware, but also to wander into ourselves, so that we may taste the magic of being alive and rise to the occasion of this opportunity to truly live—tinkering along the way!

ENDNOTES

INTRODUCTION: LEAVING THE CULT OF FOCUS

p11 **One Friday night in 1983** K. Mullis, "Polymerase Chain Reaction", Dr. Kary Banks Mullis, n.d.: http://www.karymullis.com/pcr.shtml.

p11 **"My little silver Honda's"** K. Mullis, Dancing Naked in the Minefield (New York: Vintage Books, 1998), pp. 3–4.

p12 **Dr. Kary Banks Mullis** "Biography", Dr. Kary Banks Mullis, n.d.: http://www.karymullis.com/biography.shtml.

p15 **inattentional blindness,** wherein C. Kreitz, P. Furley, et al., "The Influence of Attention Set, Working Memory Capacity, and Expectations on Inattentional Blindness", Perception 45, no. 4 (2016): 386–99.

p15 **police officer in Boston** C. F. Chabris, A. Weinberger, et al., "You Do Not Talk About Fight Club If You Do Not Notice Fight Club: Inattentional Blindness for a Simulated Real-World Assault", Iperception 2, no. 2 (2011): 150–53.

p16 **invisible gorilla** experiment D. J. Simons and C. F. Chabris, "Gorillas in Our Midst: Sustained Inattentional Blindness for Dynamic Events", Perception 28, no. 9 (1999): 1059–74.

p17 **too much or hyperfocus** B. Hahn, A. N. Harvey, et al., "Hyperdeactivation of the Default Mode Network in People with Schizophrenia When Focusing Attention in Space", Schizophrenia Bulletin (February 28, 2016).

p17 **long-term discounting** C. Chen and G. He, "The Contrast Effect in Temporal and Probabilistic Discounting", Frontiers in Psychology 7 (2016): 304.

p17 **loss of caring** C. N. Dewall, R. F. Baumeister, et al., "Depletion Makes the Heart Grow Less Helpful: Helping as a Function of Self-Regulatory Energy and Genetic Relatedness", Personality and Social Psychology Bulletin 34, no. 12 (December 2008): 1653–62.

p18 **Rosabeth Moss Kanter** R. M. Kanter, "Innovation: The Classic Traps", Harvard Business Review 84, no. 11 (2006): 154.

p19 **After obtaining his Ph.D.** E. Yoffe, "Is Kary Mullis God?" Esquire 122, no. 1 (1994): 68.

p22 **Unfocusing reduces amygdala activation** K. McRae, B. Hughes, et al., "The Neural Bases of Distraction and Reappraisal", Journal of Cognitive Neuroscience 22, no. 2 (2010): 248–62.

p22 **the frontopolar cortex** A. E. Green, M. S. Cohen, et al., "Frontopolar Activity and Connectivity Support Dynamic Conscious Augmentation of Creative State", Human Brain Mapping (2014), conference abstract.

p22 **anterior insula activity** H. C. Lou, M. Nowak, and T. W. Kjaer, "The Mental Self", Progress in Brain Research 150 (2005): 197–204.

p22 **prefrontal cortex activity** A. Golkar, E. Johansson, et al., "The Influence of Work-Related Chronic Stress on the Regulation of Emotion and on Functional Connectivity in the Brain", PLoS One 9, no. 9 (2014): e104550.

p22 **improves long-term memory** T. Amer, K. W. Ngo, and L. Hasher, "Cultural Differences in Visual Attention: Implications for Distraction Processing", British Journal of Psychology (2016), epub. ahead of print.

p22 **default mode network** A. Kucyi, M. J. Hove, et al., "Dynamic Brain Network Correlates of Spontaneous Fluctuations in Attention", Cerebral Cortex (2016), epub. ahead of print.

p22 **in diseases like Alzheimer's** L. L. Beason-Held, T. J. Hohman, et al., "Brain Network Changes and Memory Decline in Aging", Brain Imaging and Behavior (2016), epub. ahead of print.

p23 **DMN that is not synchronized** K. Mevel, G.Chételat, et al., "The Default Mode Network in Healthy Aging and Alzheimer's Disease", International Journal of Alzheimer's Disease 2011 (2011): http://dx.doi.org/10.4061/2011/535816.

p23 **Reduced connectivity in the unfocus** S. Sandrone and M. Catani, "Journal Club: Default-Mode Network Connectivity in Cognitively Unimpaired Patients with Parkinson Disease", Neurology 81, no. 23 (2013): e172–75.

p23 **build cognitive reserve** R. S. Wilson, C. F. Mendes de Leon, et al., "Participation in Cognitively Stimulating Activities and Risk of Incident Alzheimer Disease", Journal of the American Medical Association 287 (2002): 742–48.

p23 **protect your thinking brain** C. Fabrigoule, L. Letenneur, et al., "Social and Leisure Activities and Risk of Dementia: A Prospective Longitudinal Study", Journal of the American Geriatrics Society 43 (1995): 485–90; C. Helmer, D. Damon, et al., "Marital Status and Risk of Alzheimer's Disease: A French Population-Based Cohort Study", Neurology 53 (1999): 1953–58; J. Verghese, R. B. Lipton, et al., "Leisure Activities and the Risk of Dementia in the Elderly", New England Journal of Medicine 348, no. 25 (2003): 2508–16; X. Zhang, C. Li, and M. Zhang, "Psychosocial Risk Factors of Alzheimer's Disease", Zhonghua Yi Xue Za Zhi 79 (1999): 335–38.

Endnotes

CHAPTER 1: THE BEAT OF YOUR BRAIN

p29 **brains manage focus and unfocus** D. Gui, S. Xu, et al., "Resting Spontaneous Activity in the Default Mode Network Predicts Performance Decline During Prolonged Attention Workload", NeuroImage 120 (October 15, 2015): 323–30.

p30 **Your brain shut downs** M. Tanaka, A. Ishii, and Y. Watanabe, "Neural Effects of Mental Fatigue Caused by Continuous Attention Load: A Magnetoencephalography Study", Brain Research 1561 (May 2, 2014): 60–66.

p30 **in mini–mental journeys** M. A. Killingsworth and D. T. Gilbert, "A Wandering Mind Is an Unhappy Mind", Science 330, no. 6006 (November 12, 2010): 932.

p30 **a brain cell's resting voltage** J. E. Dowling, Creating Minds: How the Brain Works (New York: W. W. Norton, 1999), p. 22; M. A. Persinger, "Brain Electromagnetic Activity and Lightning: Potentially Congruent Scale-Invariant Quantitative Properties", Frontiers in Integrative Neuroscience 6 (2012): 19.

p30 **100 billion brain cells** S. Herculano-Houzel, "The Human Brain in Numbers: A Linearly Scaled-up Primate Brain", Frontiers in Human Neuroscience 3 (2009): 31.

p31 **your brain's attention fluctuates** A. Kucyi, M. J. Hove, et al., "Dynamic Brain Network Correlates of Spontaneous Fluctuations in Attention", Cerebral Cortex (February 13, 2016).

p31 **continuum from more to less** N. H. Liu, C. Y. Chiang, and H. C. Chu, "Recognizing the Degree of Human Attention Using EEG Signals from Mobile Sensors", Sensors (Basel) 13, no. 8 (2013): 10273–86.

p31 **Gamma waves are the odd** X. Jia and A. Kohn, "Gamma Rhythms in the Brain", PLoS Biology 9, no. 4 (April 2011): e1001045.

p31 **Faster than even beta waves** J. W. Kim, B. N. Kim, et al., "Desynchronization of Theta-Phase Gamma-Amplitude Coupling During a Mental Arithmetic Task in Children with Attention Deficit/Hyperactivity Disorder", PLoS One 11, no. 3 (2016): e0145288.

p31 **Being a peak performer** M. Graczyk, M. Pachalska, et al., "Neurofeedback Training for Peak Performance", Annals of Agricultural and Environmental Medicine 21, no. 4 (2014): 871–75; S. di Fronso, C. Robazza, et al., "Neural Markers of Performance States in an Olympic Athlete: An EEG Case Study in Air-Pistol Shooting", Journal of Sports Science and Medicine 15, no. 2 (June 2016): 214–22; T. Hulsdunker, A. Mierau, and H. K. Struder, "Higher Balance Task Demands Are Associated with an Increase in Individual Alpha Peak Frequency", Frontiers in Human Neuroscience 9 (2015): 695.

p32 **Georg Philipp Telemann** S. Zohn, Music for a Mixed Taste: Style, Genre and Meaning in Telemann's Instrumental Works (New York: Oxford University Press, 2008), p. 20.

p32 **Benjamin Franklin invented** L. Gensel, "The Medical World of Benjamin Franklin", Journal of the Royal Society of Medicine 98, no. 12 (December 2005): 534–38; M. W. Jernegan, "Benjamin Franklin's 'Electrical Kite' and Lightning Rod", New England Quarterly 1, no. 2 (1928): 180–96.

p32 **the frontoparietal circuit** S. Vossel, J. J. Geng, and G. R. Fink, "Dorsal and Ventral Attention Systems: Distinct Neural Circuits but Collaborative Roles", Neuroscientist 20, no. 2 (April 2014): 150–59.

p32 **central executive network** L. E. Sherman, J. D. Rudie, et al., "Development of the Default Mode and Central Executive Networks across Early Adolescence: A Longitudinal Study", Developmental Cognitive Neuroscience 10 (October 2014): 148–59.

p33 **The brain circuit that allows** D. Tomasi, N. D. Volkow, et al., "Dopamine Transporters in Striatum Correlate with Deactivation in the Default Mode Network During Visuospatial Attention", PLoS One 4, no. 6 (2009): e6102.

p33 **"Do Mostly Nothing"** A. Mohan, A. J. Roberto, et al., "The Significance of the Default Mode Network (DMN) in Neurological and Neuropsychiatric Disorders: A Review", Yale Journal of Biology and Medicine 89, no. 1 (2016): 49–57.

p33 **one of the greatest consumers** I. Neuner, J. Arrubla, et al., "The Default Mode Network and EEG Regional Spectral Power: A Simultaneous fMRI-EEG Study", PLoS One 9, no. 2 (2014): e88214.

p33 **connected with the focus circuits** A. Karten, S. P. Pantazatos, et al., "Dynamic Coupling between the Lateral Occipital-Cortex, Default-Mode, and Frontoparietal Networks During Bistable Perception", Brain Connectivity 3, no. 3 (2013): 286–93; T. Piccoli, G. Valente, et al., "The Default Mode Network and the Working Memory Network Are Not Anti-Correlated During All Phases of a Working Memory Task", PLoS One 10, no. 4 (2015): e0123354.

p33 **a mix of brainwaves** F. Lopes de Silva, "Neural Mechanisms Underlying Brain Waves: From Neural Membranes to Networks", Electroencephalography and Clinical Neurophysiology 79, no. 2 (1991): 81–93; Neuner, Arrubla, et al., "Default Mode Network"; W. Gao, J. H. Gilmore, et al., "The Dynamic Reorganization of the Default-Mode Network During a Visual Classification Task", Frontiers in Systems Neuroscience 7 (2013): 34; X. Di and B. B. Biswal, "Dynamic Brain Functional Connectivity Modulated by Resting-State Networks", Brain Structure and Function 220, no. 1 (January 2015): 37–46; R. N. Spreng, W. D. Stevens, et al., "Default Network

Activity, Coupled with the Frontoparietal Control Network, Supports Goal-Directed Cognition", NeuroImage 53, no. 1 (October 15, 2010): 303–17.

p34 **It's we who stop this** G. Bush, "Attention-Deficit/Hyperactivity Disorder and Attention Networks", Neuropsychopharmacology 35, no. 1 (January 2010): 278–300; M. Schecklmann, A. C. Ehlis, et al., "Diminished Prefrontal Oxygenation with Normal and Above-Average Verbal Fluency Performance in Adult ADHD", Journal of Psychiatric Research 43, no. 2 (December 2008): 98–106.

p34 **Unfocus circuits bring on** M. Drolet, R. I. Schubotz, and J. Fischer, "Authenticity Affects the Recognition of Emotions in Speech: Behavioral and fMRI Evidence", Cognitive, Affective and Behavioral Neuroscience 12, no. 1 (March 2012): 140–50; C. G. Davey, J. Pujol, and B. J. Harrison, "Mapping the Self in the Brain's Default Mode Network", NeuroImage 132 (May 15, 2016): 390–97.

p34 **What's more they can be trained** K. L. Hyde, J. Lerch, et al., "Musical Training Shapes Structural Brain Development", Journal of Neuroscience 29, no. 10 (March 11, 2009): 3019–25; L. Jancke, "Music Drives Brain Plasticity", F1000 Biology Reports 1 (2009): 78.

p34 **Fritz Reiner,** P. Hart, Fritz Reiner: A Biography (Evanston, IL: Northwestern University Press, 1994); H. Edgar, "CSO Unveils Fritz Reiner Bust at Symphony Center", Chicago Maroon (June 15, 2016): http://chicagomaroon.com/2016/06/15/cso-unveils-fritz-reiner-bust-at-symphony-center/; "The Forgotten Great Conductors", Gramophone (October 12, 2013): http://www.gramophone.co.uk/features/focus/the-forgotten-great-conductors.

p35 **"You're not men"** G. Stein, "Fritz Reiner: A Marriage of Talent and Terror", Dr. Gerald Stein: Blogging About Psychotherapy from Chicago (October 12, 2013): https://drgeraldstein.wordpress.com/tag/our-strengths-are-our-weaknesses/.

p36 **The Many Notes of Your** A. Anticevic, M. W. Cole, et al., "The Role of Default Network Deactivation in Cognition and Disease", Trends in Cognitive Sciences 16, no. 12 (December 2012): 584–92.

p36 **a distraction filter** M. Ziaei, N. Peira, and J. Persson, "Brain Systems Underlying Attentional Control and Emotional Distraction During Working Memory Encoding", NeuroImage 87 (February 15, 2014): 276–86; T. Piccoli, G. Valente, et al., "The Default Mode Network and the Working Memory Network Are Not Anti-Correlated During All Phases of a Working Memory Task", PLoS One 10, no. 4 (2015): e0123354.

p36 **builds mental flexibility** D. Vatansever, A. E. Manktelow, et al., "Cognitive Flexibility: A Default Network and Basal Ganglia Connectivity Perspective", Brain Connectivity 6, no. 3 (April 2016): 201–7; A. W. Sali, S. M. Courtney, and S. Yantis, "Spontaneous Fluctuations in the Flexible Control of Covert Attention", Journal of Neuroscience 36, no. 2 (January 13, 2016): 445–54.

p36 **connects you more deeply** C. G. Davey, J. Pujol, and B. J. Harrison, "Mapping the Self in the Brain's Default Mode Network", NeuroImage 132 (May 15, 2016): 390–97; P. Qin, S. Grimm, et al., "Spontaneous Activity in Default-Mode Network Predicts Ascription of Self-Relatedness to Stimuli", Social Cognitive and Affective Neuroscience 11, no. 4 (April 2016): 693–702.

p37 **activates "social connection" circuits** W. Li, X. Mai, and C. Liu, "The Default Mode Network and Social Understanding of Others: What Do Brain Connectivity Studies Tell Us", Frontiers in Human Neuroscience 8 (2014): 74; R. B. Mars, F. X. Neubert, et al., "On the Relationship between the 'Default Mode Network' and the 'Social Brain,' " Frontiers in Human Neuroscience 6 (2012): 189.

p37 **integrates the past, present** M. Konishi, D. G. McLaren, et al., "Shaped by the Past: The Default Mode Network Supports Cognition That Is Independent of Immediate Perceptual Input", PLoS One 10, no. 6 (2015): e0132209; Y. Ostby, K. B. Walhovd, et al., "Mental Time Travel and Default-Mode Network Functional Connectivity in the Developing Brain", Proceedings of the National Academy of Sciences 109, no. 42 (October 16, 2012): 16800–4.

p37 **express your unique self** R. E. Beaty, M. Benedek, et al., "Creativity and the Default Network: A Functional Connectivity Analysis of the Creative Brain at Rest", Neuropsychologia 64C (September 20, 2014): 92–98; N. C. Andreasen, "A Journey into Chaos: Creativity and the Unconscious", Mens Sana Monographs 9, no. 1 (January 2011): 42–53.

p38 **dredge up intangible memories** J. Yang, X. Weng, et al., "Sustained Activity within the Default Mode Network During an Implicit Memory Task", Cortex 46, no. 3 (March 2010): 354–66; T. Ino, R. Nakai, et al., "Brain Activation During Autobiographical Memory Retrieval with Special Reference to Default Mode Network", Open Neuroimaging Journal 5 (2011): 14–23.

p39 **maintain the status quo** S. M. Fleming, C. L. Thomas, and R. J. Dolan, "Overcoming Status Quo Bias in the Human Brain", Proceedings of the National Academy of Sciences 107, no. 13 (March 30, 2010): 6005–9.

p39 **cognitive dissonance**, which is K. Izuma, M. Matsumoto, et al., "Neural Correlates of Cognitive Dissonance and Choice-Induced Preference Change", Proceedings of the National Academy of Sciences 107, no. 51 (December 21, 2010): 22014–19.

p40 **Switch cost comes in the** S. Yin, T. Wang, et al., "Task-Switching Cost and Intrinsic Functional Connectivity in the Human Brain: Toward Understanding Individual Differences in Cognitive Flexibility", PLoS One 10, no. 12 (2015): e0145826; P. S. Cooper, P. M. Garrett, et al., "Task Uncertainty Can Account for Mixing and Switch Costs in Task-Switching", PLoS One 10, no. 6 (2015): e0131556.

p40 **called spreading of alternatives** E. Harmon-Jones, C. Harmon-Jones, et al., "Left Frontal Cortical Activation and Spreading of Alternatives: Tests of the Action-Based Model of Dissonance", Journal of Personality and Social Psychology 94, no. 1 (January 2008): 1–15.

p40 **professor Issidoros Sarinopoulos** I. Sarinopoulos, D. W. Grupe, et al., "Uncertainty During Anticipation Modulates Neural Responses to Aversion in Human Insula and Amygdala", Cerebral Cortex 20, no. 4 (April 2010): 929–40.

p41 **focus casts a magic spell** B. R. Payne, J. J. Jackson, et al., "In the Zone: Flow State and Cognition in Older Adults", Psychology and Aging 26, no. 3 (September 2011): 738–43.

p41 **more psychologically comfortable** S. B. Ostlund and B. W. Balleine, "On Habits and Addiction: An Associative Analysis of Compulsive Drug Seeking", Drug Discovery Today: Disease Models 5, no. 4 (Winter 2008): 235–45.

p43 **feeling more drained** M. A. Boksem, T. F. Meijman, and M. M. Lorist, "Effects of Mental Fatigue on Attention: An ERP Study", Brain Research: Cognitive Brain Research 25, no. 1 (September 2005): 107–16.

p43 **they either choke or just** R. Yu, "Choking Under Pressure: The Neuropsychological Mechanisms of Incentive-Induced Performance Decrements", Frontiers of Behavioral Neuroscience 9 (2015): 19.

p43 **making the same mistake** M. C. Stevens, K. A. Kiehl, et al., "Brain Network Dynamics During Error Commission", Human Brain Mapping 30, no. 1 (January 2009): 24–37.

p44 **quickly or repeatedly overwhelmed** A. F. Arnsten, "Stress Signalling Pathways That Impair Prefrontal Cortex Structure and Function", Nature Reviews Neuroscience 10, no. 6 (June 2009): 410–22.

p44 **settling is a sign** T. Thompson and A. Richardson, "Self-Handicapping Status, Claimed Self-Handicaps and Reduced Practice Effort Following Success and Failure Feedback", British Journal of Educational Psychology 71, pt. 1 (March 2001): 151–70.

p46 **Reverie is a form** T. H. Ogden, "Reverie and Interpretation", Psychoanalytic Quarterly 66, no. 4 (October 1997): 567–95.

p46 **you can use reverie** J. Smallwood and J. Andrews-Hanna, "Not All Minds That Wander Are Lost: The Importance of a Balanced Perspective on the Mind-Wandering State", Frontiers in Psychology 4 (2013): 441.

p47 **projecting into the future** R. N. Spreng, R. A. Mar, and A. S. Kim, "The Common Neural Basis of Autobiographical Memory, Prospection, Navigation, Theory of Mind, and the Default Mode: A Quantitative Meta-Analysis", Journal of Cognitive Neuroscience 21, no. 3 (March 2009): 489–510.

p47 **it must not be stressful** R. L. McMillan, S. B. Kaufman, and J. L. Singer, "Ode to Positive Constructive Daydreaming", Frontiers in Psychology 4 (2013): 626.

p48 **usefulness of self-talk** E. Kross, E. Bruehlman-Senecal, et al., "Self-Talk as a Regulatory Mechanism: How You Do It Matters", Journal of Personality and Social Psychology 106, no. 2 (February 2014): 304–24.

p48 **value of reframing your thoughts** D. Cutuli, "Cognitive Reappraisal and Expressive Suppression Strategies Role in the Emotion Regulation: An Overview on Their Modulatory Effects and Neural Correlates", Frontiers in Systems Neuroscience 8 (2014): 175.

p49 **Psychologist Daniel Wegner** D. M. Wegner, "Ironic Processes of Mental Control", Psychological Review 101, no. 1 (1994): 34–52; D. M. Wegner, "How to Think, Say, or Do Precisely the Worst Thing for Any Occasion", Science 325, no. 5936 (2009): 48–50.

p49 **a "do not" instruction** D. M. Wegner, R. Erber, and S. Zanakos, "Ironic Processes in the Mental Control of Mood and Mood-Related Thought", Journal of Personality and Social Psychology 65, no. 6 (December 1993): 1093–104.

p49 **use your body to activate** M. Oppezzo and D. L. Schwartz, "Give Your Ideas Some Legs: The Positive Effect of Walking on Creative Thinking", Journal of Experimental Psychology, Learning, Memory, and Cognition 40, no. 4 (July 2014): 1142–52.

p49 **One person may want to** R. A. Atchley, D. L. Strayer, and P. Atchley, "Creativity in the Wild: Improving Creative Reasoning through Immersion in Natural Settings", PLoS One 7, no. 12 (2012): e51474.

p49 **Regardless of the technique** J. Xu, A. Vik, et al., "Nondirective Meditation Activates Default Mode Network and Areas Associated with Memory Retrieval and Emotional Processing", Frontiers in Human Neuroscience 8 (2014): 86.

p52 **Ana Luisa Pinho** A. L. Pinho, O. de Manzano, et al., "Connecting to Create: Expertise in Musical Improvisation Is Associated with Increased Functional Connectivity between Premotor and Prefrontal Areas", Journal of Neuroscience 34, no. 18 (April 30, 2014): 6156–63.

p53 **psychologist Anika Maraz** A. Maraz, O. Kiraly, et al., "Why Do You Dance? Development of the Dance Motivation Inventory (DMI)", PLoS One 10, no. 3 (2015): e0122866.

p54 **John Elfreth Watkins** E. Watkins, "What May Happen in the Next Hundred Years?" Ladies' Home Journal (1900): 8.

p55 **may not always be correct** S. Sandrone, "The Brain as a Crystal Ball: The Predictive Potential of Default Mode Network", Frontiers in Human Neuroscience 6 (2012): 261.

p55 **neuroscientist Julia Mossbridge** J. Mossbridge, P. Tressoldi, and J. Utts, "Predictive Physiological Anticipation Preceding Seemingly Unpredictable Stimuli: A Meta-Analysis", Frontiers in Psychology 3 (2012): 390.

p56 **an active role in this prediction** C. S. Soon, A. H. He, et al., "Predicting Free Choices for Abstract Intentions", Proceedings of the National Academy of Sciences 110, no. 15 (April 9, 2013): 6217–22.

p56 **some kind of unconscious mirroring** M. Iacoboni, I. Molnar-Szakacs, et al., "Grasping the Intentions of Others with One's Own Mirror Neuron System", PLoS Biology 3, no. 3 (March 2005): e79.

p56 **theories based on quantum physics** S. Hameroff, "How Quantum Brain Biology Can Rescue Conscious Free Will", Frontiers in Integrative Neuroscience 6 (2012): 93.

p56 **Children who learn to play** E. A. Miendlarzewska and W. J. Trost, "How Musical Training Affects Cognitive Development: Rhythm, Reward and Other Modulating Variables", Frontiers in Neuroscience 7 (2013): 279.

CHAPTER 2: CONJURING CREATIVITY

p59 **Brazilian artist Vik Muniz** V. Muniz, "Art with Wire, Sugar, Chocolate and String", TED (April 2007): https://www.ted.com/talks/vik _muniz _makes_art_with_wire_sugar/transcript?language=en.

p59 **peanut butter and jam** M. Schwendener, "Smile and Say 'Peanut Butter,' Mona Lisa", New York Times (March 2, 2007): http://www .nytimes. com/2007/03/02/arts/design/02muni.html?_r=0.

p60 **brings potential conflicts** Erkan, "10 Most Creative Artworks Made from Unexpected Materials By Vik Muniz", Most 10 (February 19, 2013): http://www.themost10.com/creative-artworks-unexpected-materials/.

p61 **researcher Melissa Ellamil** M. Ellamil, C. Dobson, et al., "Evaluative and Generative Modes of Thought During the Creative Process", NeuroImage 59, no. 2 (January 16, 2012): 1783–94.

p62 **hired Edelman Berland** Edelman Berland (for Adobe), "Seeking Creative Candidates: Hiring for the Future" Adobe (September 2014): http://www.images.adobe.com/content/dam/Adobe/en/education/pdfs/creative-candidates-study-0914.pdf?scid =social33220386.

p62 **situations of uncertainty** J. S. Mueller, S. Melwani, and J. A. Goncalo, "The Bias Against Creativity: Why People Desire but Reject Creative Ideas", Psychological Science 23, no. 1 (January 1, 2012): 13–17.

p63 **when you focus exclusively** M. Gilead, N. Liberman, and A. Maril, "From Mind to Matter: Neural Correlates of Abstract and Concrete Mindsets", Social Cognitive and Affective Neuroscience 9, no. 5 (May 2014): 638–45.

p63 **fast and unconscious reorganisation** S. M. Ritter and A. Dijksterhuis, "Creativity—The Unconscious Foundations of the Incubation Period", Frontiers in Human Neuroscience 8 (2014): 215.

p64 **you surrender to the chaos** D. Safan-Gerard, "Chaos and Control in the Creative Process", Journal of the American Academy of Psychoanalysis 13, no. 1 (January 1985): 129–38.

p64 **a state of tension** M. Faust and Y. N. Kenett, "Rigidity, Chaos and Integration: Hemispheric Interaction and Individual Differences in Metaphor Comprehension", Frontiers in Human Neuroscience 8 (2014): 511; N. C. Andreasen, "A Journey into Chaos: Creativity and the Unconscious", Mens Sana Monographs 9, no. 1 (January 2011): 42–53.

p65 **"Philosophy of science"** Attributed to R. Feynman, quoted by S. Weinberg, in D. Overbye, "Laws of Nature, Source Unknown", New York Times (December 2007).

p65 **Kevin Dunbar's research** K. Dunbar, "How Scientists Really Reason: Scientific Reasoning in Real World Laboratories", in R. Sternberg and J. Davidson, eds., The Nature of Insight (Cambridge, MA: MIT Press, 1995), pp. 365–96.

p66 **Charles Limb is a doctor** C. J. Limb and A. R. Braun, "Neural Substrates of Spontaneous Musical Performance: An fMRI Study of Jazz Improvisation", PLoS One 3, no. 2 (2008): e1679.

p67 **behaviour expert Kenneth Resnicow** K. Resnicow and S. E. Page, "Embracing Chaos and Complexity: A Quantum Change for Public Health", American Journal of Public Health 98, no. 8 (August 2008): 1382–89.

p68 **Arno Penzias and Robert Wilson** "Penzias and Wilson Discover Cosmic

Microwave Radiation", PBS, 1965: http://www.pbs.org/wgbh /aso/ da-tabank/entries/dp65co.html; R. Schoenstein, "The Big Bang's Echo", All Things Considered, NPR, May 17, 2005: http://www .npr.org/templates/ story/story.php?storyId=4655517; "June 1963: Discovery of the Cosmic Microwave Background", APS News, July 2002: https://www.aps.org/publications/apsnews/200207/history.cfm.

p70 **like a mind pop** L. Zhang, W. Li, et al., "The Association between the Brain and Mind Pops: A Voxel-Based Morphometry Study in 256 Chinese College Students", Brain Imaging and Behavior 10, no. 2 (June 2016): 332–41.

p70 **Yet in fact inspiration** V. C. Oleynick, T. M. Thrash, et al., "The Scientific Study of Inspiration in the Creative Process: Challenges and Opportunities", Frontiers in Human Neuroscience 8 (2014): 436.

p72 **A natural way to prompt** G. M. Morriss-Kay, "The Evolution of Human Artistic Creativity", Journal of Anatomy 216, no. 2 (February 2010): 158–76.

p73 **"simplified semantic structures"** D. Landy, C. Allen, and C. Zednik, "A Perceptual Account of Symbolic Reasoning", Frontiers in Psychology 5 (2014): 275.

p73 **Metaphors are also implicit comparisons** O. Vartanian, "Dissociable Neural Systems for Analogy and Metaphor: Implications for the Neuroscience of Creativity", British Journal of Psychology 103, no. 3 (August 2012): 302–16.

p74 **The higher the quality** M. Benedek, R. Beaty, et al., "Creating Metaphors: The Neural Basis of Figurative Language Production", NeuroImage 90 (April 15, 2014): 99–106.

p75 **"split thinking" or "bundling"** E. Jauk, M. Benedek, and A. C. Neu bauer, "Tackling Creativity at Its Roots: Evidence for Different Patterns of EEG Alpha Activity Related to Convergent and Divergent Modes of Task Processing", International Journal of Psychophysiology 84, no. 2 (May 2012): 219–25.

p76 **signals from gut bacteria** L. Galland, "The Gut Microbiome and the Brain", Journal of Medicinal Food 17, no. 12 (December 2014): 1261–72.

p76 **Parkinson's disease—a disorder** E. Svensson, E. Horvath-Puho, et al., "Vagotomy and Subsequent Risk of Parkinson's Disease", Annals of Neurology 78, no. 4 (October 2015): 522–29.

p76 **psychologist Tony McCaffrey** T. McCaffrey, "Innovation Relies on the Obscure: A Key to Overcoming the Classic Problem of Functional Fixedness", Psychological Science 23, no. 3 (March 2012): 215–18.

p77 **"Openness to experience"** W. Li, X. Li, et al., "Brain Structure Links Trait Creativity to Openness to Experience", Social Cognitive and Affective Neuroscience (April 7, 2014): 191–98; B. Shi, D. Y. Dai, and Y. Lu, "Openness to Experience as a Moderator of the Relationship between Intelligence and Creative Thinking: A Study of Chinese Children in Urban and Rural Areas", Frontiers in Psychology 7 (2016): 641; S. B. Kaufman, L. C. Quilty, et al., "Openness to Experience and Intellect Differentially Predict Creative Achievement in the Arts and Sciences", Journal of Personality (December 8, 2014): 248–58.

p77 **"normal" people** D. Wood, S. D. Gosling, and J. Potter, "Normality Evaluations and Their Relation to Personality Traits and Well-Being", Journal of Personality and Social Psychology 93, no. 5 (November 2007): 861–79.

p44 **when you have openness** R. E. Beaty, S. B. Kaufman, et al., "Personality and Complex Brain Networks: The Role of Openness to Experience in Default Network Efficiency", Human Brain Mapping 37, no. 2 (February 2016): 773–79.

p77 **A freak accident** C. Kino, "Where Art Meets Trash and Transforms Life", New York Times (October 21, 2010): http://www.nytimes .com /2010/10/24/arts/design/24muniz.html?_r=0.

p78 **Intuition is your brain's ability** E. Nahmias, J. Shepard, and S. Reuter, "It's OK If 'My Brain Made Me Do It': People's Intuitions About Free Will and Neuroscientific Prediction", Cognition 133, no. 2 (November 2014): 502–16.

p78 **form an intuition network** T. Zander, N. K. Horr, et al., "Intuitive Decision Making as a Gradual Process: Investigating Semantic Intuition-Based and Priming-Based Decisions with fMRI", Brain and Behavior 6, no. 1 (January 2016): e00420; K. G. Volz, R. Rubsamen, and D. Y. von Cramon, "Cortical Regions Activated by the Subjective Sense of Perceptual Coherence of Environmental Sounds: A Proposal for a Neuroscience of Intuition", Cognitive Affective and Behavioral Neuroscience 8, no. 3 (September 2008): 318–28.

p78 **"serial hypothesis testing"** R. C. Wilson and Y. Niv, "Inferring Relevance in a Changing World", Frontiers in Human Neuroscience 5 (2011): 189.

p79 **is "predictive inference"** A. K. Seth, K. Suzuki, and H. D. Critchley, "An Interoceptive Predictive Coding Model of Conscious Presence", Frontiers in Psychology 2 (2011): 395.

p80 **a mind pop activates** L. Zhang, W. Li, et al., "The Association Between the Brain and Mind Pops: A Voxel-Based Morphometry Study in 256 Chinese College Students", Brain Imaging and Behavior 10, no. 2 (June 2016): 332–41.

Endnotes

p81 **famous Stanford commencement speech** S. Jobs, "You've Got to Find What You Love", Commencement Address at Stanford University, June 12, 2005: http://news.stanford.edu/2005/06/14/jobs -061505/.

p81 **scientists' and artists' brains** N. C. Andreasen and K. Ramchandran, "Creativity in Art and Science: Are There Two Cultures?" Dialogues in Clinical Neuroscience 14, no. 1 (March 2012): 49–54.

p82 **Henri Poincaré, a mathematician** A. Miller, Einstein, Picasso: Space, Time, and the Beauty That Causes Havoc (New York: Basic Books, 2002), pp. 1–5.

p83 **organisational psychologist Kevin Eschleman** K. J. Eschleman, J. Madsen, et al., "Benefiting from Creative Activity: The Positive Relationships Between Creative Activity, Recovery Experiences, and Performance-Related Outcomes", Journal of Occupational and Organizational Psychology 87, no. 3 (September 2014): 579–98.

p50 **professor Robert Root-Bernstein** R. S. Root-Bernstein, M. Bernstein, and H. Garnier, "Correlations Between Avocations, Scientific Style, Work Habits, and Professional Impact of Scientists", Creativity Research Journal 8, no. 2 (April 1995): 115–37.

p85 **example of Kirin Sinha** J. Chu, "Getting a Move On in Math", MIT News (December 23, 2013): http://news.mit.edu/2013/getting-a-move-on-in-math-1223.

p85 **The ancient Greeks considered** W. Eamon, "The Invention of Discovery", William Eamon (January 16, 2014): http://williameamon .com/?p=972.

p86 **psychologists Matthew Killingsworth** M. A. Killingsworth and D. T. Gilbert, "A Wandering Mind Is an Unhappy Mind", Science 330, no. 6006 (November 12, 2010): 932.

p86 **"what is a novel but"** O. Pamuk, Other Colors (New York: Vintage, 2008), p. 7.

p87 **Called "volitional daydreaming"** R. L. McMillan, S. B. Kaufman, and J. L. Singer, "Ode to Positive Constructive Daydreaming", Frontiers in Psychology 4 (2013): 626.

p87 **psychologist Benjamin Baird** B. Baird, J. Smallwood, et al., "Inspired by Distraction: Mind Wandering Facilitates Creative Incubation", Psychological Science 23, no. 10 (October 1, 2012): 1117–22.

p89 **To overcome writer's block** P. Huston, "Resolving Writer's Block", Canadian Family Physician 44 (January 1998): 92–97.

p89 **professor Angela K. Leung** A. K. Leung, S. Kim, et al., "Embodied

Metaphors and Creative 'Acts,' " Psychological Science 23, no. 5 (May 1, 2012): 502–9.

p90 **fluid arm movements** M. L. Slepian and N. Ambady, "Fluid Movement and Creativity", Journal of Experimental Psychology: General 141, no. 4 (November 2012): 625–29.

p91 **sleep as coming in two phases** P. McNamara, P. Johnson, et al., "REM and NREM Sleep Mentation", International Review of Neurobiology 92 (2010): 69–86.

p91 **works its magic** S. M. Ritter, M. Strick, et al., "Good Morning Creativity: Task Reactivation During Sleep Enhances Beneficial Effect of Sleep on Creative Performance", Journal of Sleep Research 21, no. 6 (December 2012): 643–47.

p92 **Dreaming—the ultimate** D. Kahn, "Brain Basis of Self: Self-Organization and Lessons from Dreaming", Frontiers in Psychology 4 (2013): 408.

p57 **Carl Jung argued** S. Khodarahimi, "Dreams in Jungian Psychology: The Use of Dreams as an Instrument for Research, Diagnosis and Treatment of Social Phobia", Malaysian Journal of Medical Science 16, no. 4 (October 2009): 42–49.

p92 **Paul McCartney reportedly** S. Turner, A Hard Day's Write: The Stories Behind Every Beatles Song, 3rd ed. (New York: Harper, 2005).

p92 **Albert Einstein famously dreamed** T. McIsaac, "5 Scientific Discoveries Made in Dreams", Epoch Times (June 4, 2015): http://www.theepochtimes .com/n3/1380669-5-scientific-discoveries-made-in-dreams/.

p91 **sleep expert Matthew Walker** M. P. Walker and R. Stickgold, "Overnight Alchemy: Sleep-Dependent Memory Evolution", Nature Reviews Neuroscience 11, no. 3 (March 2010): 218; author reply on 18.

p93 **Napping is a great way** S. C. Mednick, D. J. Cai, et al., "Comparing the Benefits of Caffeine, Naps and Placebo on Verbal, Motor and Perceptual Memory", Behavioural Brain Research 193, no. 1 (November 3, 2008): 79–86.

p94 **researcher Felipe Beijamini** F. Beijamini, S. I. Pereira, et al., "After Being Challenged by a Video Game Problem, Sleep Increases the Chance to Solve It", PLoS One 9, no. 1 (2014): e84342.

p94 **psychiatrist Sara Mednick** D. J. Cai, S. A. Mednick, et al., "REM, Not Incubation, Improves Creativity by Priming Associative Networks", Proceedings of the National Academy of Sciences 106, no. 25 (June 23, 2009): 10130–34.

p94 **created four conditions** A. J. Tietzel and L. C. Lack, "The Recuperative Value of Brief and Ultra-Brief Naps on Alertness and Cognitive Performance", Journal of Sleep Research 11, no. 3 (September 2002): 213–18.

p95 **Haruki Murakami sleeps** M. Currey, Daily Rituals: How Artists Work (New York: Knopf, 2013).

p97 **Creativity is as much perspiration** V. C. Oleynick, T. M. Thrash, et al., "The Scientific Study of Inspiration in the Creative Process: Challenges and Opportunities", Frontiers in Human Neuroscience 8 (2014): 436.

p97 **immerse yourself in a completely different** D. Dumas and K. N. Dunbar, "The Creative Stereotype Effect", PLoS One 11, no. 2 (2016): e0142567.

p98 **Rosa Aurora Chavez** R. A. Chavez, "Imagery as a Core Process in the Creativity of Successful and Awarded Artists and Scientists and Its Neurobiological Correlates", Frontiers in Psychology 7 (2016): 351.

CHAPTER 3: DYNAMIC LEARNING IN A BRAVE NEW WORLD

p100 **"Fuckup Nights" is a phenomenon** "What Is Fuckup Nights?" Fuckup Nights, n.d.: http://fuckupnights.com; C. D. Von Kaenel, "Failure Has Never Been More Successful", Fast Company (November 14, 2014): http://www.fastcompany.com/3038446/innovation-agents/failure-has-never-been-more-successful.

p101 **Yet it's so common** D. Gage, "The Venture Capital Secret: 3 Out of 4 Start-Ups Fail", Wall Street Journal (September 20, 2012): http://www.wsj.com/articles/SB10000872396390443720204578004980476 429190; C. Nobel, "Why Companies Fail—and How Their Founders Can Bounce Back", Harvard Business School: Working Knowledge (March 7, 2011): http://hbswk.hbs.edu/item/why-companies-failand-how-their-founders-can-bounce-back.

p101 **sad or frustrated** J. Goldman and J. McCarthy, "Job Market Optimism Up Sharply in Northern America, Europe", Gallup (May 21, 2015): http://www.gallup.com/poll/183380/job-market- optimism -sharply-northern-america- europe. aspx.

p101 **rather than failure,** A. C. Edmondson, "Strategies of Learning from Failure", Harvard Business Review 89, no. 4 (April 2011): 48–55, 137; M. Lindstrom, "The Truth About Being 'Done' Versus Being 'Perfect,' " Fast Company (April 25, 2012): http://www.fastcompany.com/3001533/truth-about-being-done-versus-being- perfect;R.Asghar, "Why Silicon Valley's 'Fail Fast' Mantra Is Just Hype", Forbes (July 14, 2014): http://www.forbes.com/sites/robasghar/2014/07/14/why-silicon-valleys-fail-fast-mantra- is-just-hype/#46b8da722236.

p102 **Brightworks School, and** its "Brightworks: An Extraordinary School", Brightworks, n.d.: http://www.sfbrightworks.org.

p105 **physics Peter Galison E. Keto,** "Visual Research: Galison Brings Together Art and Science in Scholarship, Filmmaking", Harvard Crimson (April 26, 2016): http://www.thecrimson.com/article /2016 /4 /26 /galison-profile/.

p105 At **MIT there is a "Hobby Shop"** T. Moroney, "MIT Hobby Shop Spawns Offbeat Creations Like 'Hairball,'" Bloomberg (May 21, 2014): http://www.bloomberg.com/news/articles/2014-05- 21/mit-hobby-shop-spawns-offbeat-creations-like-hairball- .

p105 **Google's hiring practice** A. Bryant, "In Head-Hunting, Big Data May Not Be Such a Big Deal", New York Times, June 19, 2013: http://www .ny-times.com/2013/06/20/business/in-head-hunting-big-data-may-not-be-such-a-big-deal.html?partner=socialflow&smid=tw-nytimes bus iness&_r=0.

p106 **No wonder then, that the DMN** M. E. Raichle, "The Restless Brain: How Intrinsic Activity Organizes Brain Function", Philosophical Transactions of the Royal Society of London. Series B: Biological Sciences 370, no. 1668 (May 19, 2015).

p107 **psychologist named Jackie Andrade** J. Andrade, "What Does Doodling Do?" Applied Cognitive Psychology 24, no. 1 (2008): 100–106.

p110 **One Laptop Per** Child D. Talbot, "Given Tablets but No Teachers, Ethiopian Children Teach Themselves", MIT Technology Review (October 29, 2012): https://www.technologyreview.com/s/506466/given-tab-lets-but-no-teachers-ethiopian-children-teach-themselves/.

p112 **stick with investing** P. Lynch, One Up on Wall Street: How to Use What You Already Know to Make Money in the Market (New York: Simon & Schuster, 1989).

p113 **The best way to tap** C. G. Davey, J. Pujol, and B. J. Harrison, "Mapping the Self in the Brain's Default Mode Network", NeuroImage 132 (May 15 2016): 390–97; P. Qin, S. Grimm, et al., "Spontaneous Activity in Default-Mode Network Predicts Ascription of Self-Relatedness to Stimuli", Social Cognitive and Affective Neuroscience 11, no. 4 (April 2016): 693–702.

p113 **Meditation, listening to music** J. Xu, A. Vik, et al., "Nondirective Meditation Activates Default Mode Network and Areas Associated with Memory Retrieval and Emotional Processing", Frontiers in Human Neuro-science 8 (2014): 86; V. A. Taylor, V. Daneault, et al., "Impact of Meditation Training on the Default Mode Network During a Restful State", Social Cognitive and Affective Neuroscience 8, no. 1 (January 2013): 4–14; E. A. Vessel, G. G. Starr, and N. Rubin, "Art Reaches Within: Aesthetic Experience, the Self and the Default Mode Network", Frontiers in Neuroscience 7 (2013): 258; E. A. Vessel, G. G. Starr, and N. Rubin, "The Brain on Art: Intense Aesthetic Experience Activates the Default Mode Network", Frontiers in Human Neuroscience 6 (2012): 66; L. K. Miles, K. Karpinska, et al., "The Meandering Mind: Vection and Mental Time Travel", PLoS One 5, no. 5 (2010): e10825.

p113 **And exercise too, which** C. E. Krafft, J. E. Pierce, et al., "An Eight Month Randomized Controlled Exercise Intervention Alters Resting State Synchrony in Overweight Children", Neuroscience 256 (January 3, 2014): 445–55; M. W. Voss, R. S. Prakash, et al., "Plasticity of Brain Networks in a Randomized Intervention Trial of Exercise Training in Older Adults", Frontiers in Aging Neuroscience 2 (2010).

p114 **brain researcher Christopher Davey** Davey, Pujol, and Harrison, "Mapping the Self."

p115 **Psychologist Martin Seligman** M. E. Seligman, "Learned Helplessness", Annual Review of Medicine 23 (1972): 407–12.

p116 **psychologist Carol Dweck** C. S. Dweck and E. L. Leggett, "A Social-Cognitive Approach to Motivation and Personality", Psychological Review 95, no. 2 (1988): 256.

p116 **David Franklin and Daniel Wolpert** D. W. Franklin and D. M. Wolpert, "Computational Mechanisms of Sensorimotor Control", Neuron 72, no. 3 (November 3, 2011): 425–42.

p120 **"systematic forecasting"**, as J. M. Stogner, "Predictions Instead of Panics: The Framework and Utility of Systematic Forecasting of Novel Psychoactive Drug Trends", American Journal of Drug and Alcohol Abuse 41, no. 6 (2015): 519–26.

p121 **Neuroscientist Moshe Bar** M. Bar, "The Proactive Brain: Memory for Predictions", Philosophical Transactions of the Royal Society B 364, no. 1521 (May 12, 2009): 1235–43.

p125 **mental simulation**, R. E. Beaty, S. B. Kaufman, et al., "Personality and Complex Brain Networks: The Role of Openness to Experience in Default Network Efficiency", Human Brain Mapping 37, no. 2 (February 2016): 773–79.

p127 **neuroscientist Matthias Gruber** M. J. Gruber, B. D. Gelman, and C. Ranganath, "States of Curiosity Modulate Hippocampus-Dependent Learning via the Dopaminergic Circuit", Neuron 84, no. 2 (October 22, 2014): 486–96.

p128 **Dean Mobbs, a pyschology professor** D. Mobbs, C. C. Hagan, et al., "Reflected Glory and Failure: The Role of the Medial Prefrontal Cortex and Ventral Striatum in Self vs Other Relevance During Advice-Giving Outcomes", Social Cognitive and Affective Neuroscience 10, no. 10 (October 2015): 1323–28.

p129 **used brain imaging to** J. B. Engelmann, C. M. Capra, et al., "Expert Financial Advice Neurobiologically 'Offloads' Financial Decision-Making Under Risk", PLoS One 4, no. 3 (2009): e4957.

p130 **Oxford University researchers** C. B. Frey and M. A. Osborne, "The Future of Employment: How Susceptible Are Jobs to Computerisation?" (Oxford, U.K.: Oxford Martin Programme on Technology and Employment, 2013): http://www.oxfordmartin ox.ac.uk/downloads/academic/future-of-employment.pdf.

p130 **World Economic Forum** "The Future of Jobs: Employment, Skills and Workforce Strategy for the Fourth Industrial Revolution", World Economic Forum (2016): 13–15: http://www3.weforum.org/docs/Media/WEF_Future_of_Jobs_embargoed.pdf.

p130 **Tech-No-Logic has made** "The Robotic Private Chef that Frees Your Cooking Time", One Cook, n.d.: http://onecook4.me.

p130 **Momentum Machines has made** M. McNeal, "Rise of the Machines: The Future Has Lots of Robots, Few Jobs for Humans" Wired (April 2015): http://www.wired.com/brandlab/2015/04/rise-machines-future-lots-robots-jobs-humans/.

p131 **entrepreneur Kevin Ashton** A. Wood, "The Internet of Things Is Revolutionising Our Lives, but Standards Are a Must", Guardian (March 31, 2015): https://www.theguardian.com/media-network/2015/mar/31/the-internet-of-things-is-revolutionising-our-lives-but-standards-are-a-must.

p131 **"We want Google to be"** N. Saint, "Google Launches Google Instant, Search Results That Stream Instantly As You Type", Business Insider (September 8, 2010): http://www.businessinsider.com /google-search-event-live-2010-9.

CHAPTER 4: SUPERTASKING

p135 **"wobbly brain syndrome"** W. C. Clapp, M. T. Rubens, et al., "Deficit in Switching Between Functional Brain Networks Underlies the Impact of Multitasking on Working Memory in Older Adults", Proceedings of the National Academy of Sciences 108, no. 17 (April 26, 2011): 7212–17.

p135 **Kep Kee Loh** K. K. Loh and R. Kanai, "Higher Media Multi-Tasking Activity Is Associated with Smaller Gray-Matter Density in the Anterior Cingulate Cortex", PLoS One 9, no. 9 (2014): e106698.

p136 **Psychologists Jason Watson** J. M. Watson and D. L. Strayer, "Super taskers: Profiles in Extraordinary Multitasking Ability", Psychonomic Bulletin and Review 17, no. 4 (August 2010): 479–85.

p137 **what is working right** J. Duncan and D. J. Mitchell, "Training Refines Brain Representations for Multitasking", Proceedings of the National Academy of Sciences 112, no. 46 (November 17, 2015): 14127–28; M.K. Rothbart and M. I. Posner, "The Developing Brain in a Multitasking World",

Developmental Review 35 (March 1, 2015): 42–63;A. Verghese, K. G. Garner, et al., "Prefrontal Cortex StructurePredicts Training-Induced Improvements in Multitasking Performance", Journal of Neuroscience 36, no. 9 (March 2, 2016): 2638–45.

p137 **cognitive rhythm** H. Koshino, T. Minamoto, et al., "Anterior Medial Prefrontal Cortex Exhibits Activation During Task Preparation but Deactivation During Task Execution", PLoS One 6, no. 8 (2011): e22909; M. Moayedi, T. V. Salomons, et al., "Connectivity-Based Parcellation of the Human Frontal Polar Cortex", Brain Structure and Function 220, no. 5 (September 2015): 2603–16.

p137 **A little stress—called eustress** M. Kumar, S. Sharma, et al., "Effect of Stress on Academic Performance in Medical Students: A Cross Sectional Study", Indian Journal of Physiology and Pharmacology 58, no. 1 (January–March 2014): 81–86.

p138 **One recent study compared** J. M. Soares, A. Sampaio, et al., "Stress Impact on Resting State Brain Networks", PLoS One 8, no. 6 (2013): e66500.

p138 **numerous things you could do** J. E. van der Zwan, W. de Vente, et al., "Physical Activity, Mindfulness Meditation, or Heart Rate Variability Biofeedback for Stress Reduction: A Randomized Controlled Trial", Applied Psychophysiology and Biofeedback 40, no. 4 (December 2015): 257–68.

p138 **normalise DMN function** J. Xu, A. Vik, et al., "Nondirective Meditation Activates Default Mode Network and Areas Associated with Memory Retrieval and Emotional Processing", Frontiers in Human Neuroscience 8 (2014): 86; C. J. Boraxbekk, A. Salami, et al., "Physical Activity over a Decade Modifies Age-Related Decline in Perfusion, Gray Matter Volume, and Functional Connectivity of the Posterior Default-Mode Network: A Multimodal Approach", NeuroImage 131 (May 1, 2016): 133–41.

p138 **use self-talk to reframe** Y. Kivity and J. D. Huppert, "Does Cognitive Reappraisal Reduce Anxiety? A Daily Diary Study of a Micro-Intervention with Individuals with High Social Anxiety", Journal of Consulting and Clinical Psychology 84, no. 3 (March 2016): 269–83; T. Shore, K. C. Kadosh, et al., "Investigating the Effectiveness of Brief Cognitive Reappraisal Training to Reduce Fear in Adolescents", Cognition and Emotion (June 13, 2016): 1–10.

p138 **deactivating your amygdala** A. Zilverstand, M. A. Parvaz, and R. Z. Goldstein, "Neuroimaging Cognitive Reappraisal in Clinical Populations to Define Neural Targets for Enhancing Emotion Regulation. A Systematic Review", NeuroImage (June 8, 2016); X. Xie, S. Mulej Bratec, et al., "How Do You Make Me Feel Better? Social Cognitive Emotion Regulation and the Default Mode Network", NeuroImage 134 (July 1, 2016): 270–80; J. Ferri, J. Schmidt, et al., "Emotion Regulation and Amygdala-Precuneus Connectivity: Focusing on Attentional Deployment", Cognitive, Affective and Behavioral Neuroscience (July 21, 2016); M. Quirin, M. Kent, et al., "Integration of Negative Experiences: A Neuropsychological Framework for Human Resilience", Behavioral and Brain Sciences 38 (2015): e116.

p139 give yourself this joyful G. L. Poerio, P. Totterdell, et al., "Social Daydreaming and Adjustment: An Experience-Sampling Study of Socio-Emotional Adaptation During a Life Transition", Frontiers in Psychology 7 (2016): 13; J. B. Banks and A. Boals, "Understanding the Role of Mind Wandering in Stress-Related Working Memory Impairments", Cognition and Emotion (May 4, 2016): 1–8; W. C. Taylor, K. E. King, et al., "Booster Breaks in the Workplace: Participants' Perspectives on Health-Promoting Work Breaks", Health Education Research 28, no. 3 (June 2013): 414–25; B. W. Mooneyham and J. W. Schooler, "Mind Wandering Minimizes Mind Numbing: Reducing Semantic-Satiation Effects through Absorptive Lapses of Attention", Psychonomic Bulltin and Review 23, no. 4 (August 2016): 1273–79.

p139 companies like Google J. B. Stewart, "Looking for a Lesson in Google's Perks", New York Times (March 15, 2013): http://www .nytimes. com/2013/03/16/business/at-google-a-place-to-work-and-play.html.

p139 cognitive neuroscientist E. L. Maclin E. L. Maclin, K. E. Mathewson, et al., "Learning to Multitask: Effects of Video Game Practice on Electrophysiological Indices of Attention and Resource Allocation", Psychophysiology 48, no. 9 (September 2011): 1173–83.

p140 Kinesiologist Joaquin Anguera J. A. Anguera, J. Boccanfuso, et al., "Video Game Training Enhances Cognitive Control in Older Adults", Nature 501, no. 7465 (September 5, 2013): 97–101.

p140 This alliance of the conscious H. Pashler and J. C. Johnston, "Attentional Limitations in Dual Task Performance", in H. Pashler, ed., Attention (Studies in Cognition) (New York: Psychology Press, 1998), p. 155.

p140 Like Georgie Hyde-Lees R. Ellman, Yeats: The Man and The Masks (New York: W. W. Norton, 1948), p. 224.

p141 Sir Arthur Conan Doyle A. Conan Doyle, The New Revelation (Auckland, New Zealand: Floating Press, 2010).

141 psychologist Wilma Koutstaal W. Koutstaal, "Skirting the Abyss: A History of Experimental Explorations of Automatic Writing in Psychology", Journal of the History of the Behavioral Sciences 28 (1992): 5–27.

p141 voluntarily switch your state Z. Lin and S. He, "Seeing the Invisible: The Scope and Limits of Unconscious Processing in Binocular Rivalry", Progress in Neurobiology 87, no. 4 (April 2009): 195–211; J. Lisman and E. J. Sternberg, "Habit and Nonhabit Systems for Unconscious and Conscious Behavior: Implications for Multitasking", Journal of Cognitive Neuroscience 25, no. 2 (February 2013): 273–83.

p141 **"seeing" and "guiding"** V. van Polanen and M. Davare, "Interactions Between Dorsal and Ventral Streams for Controlling Skilled Grasp", Neuropsychologia 79, pt. B (December 2015): 186–91.

p142 **a mixed bag** J. A. Bargh and E. Morsella, "The Unconscious Mind", Perspectives on Psychological Science 3, no. 1 (January 2008): 73–79; W. Meredith-Owen, "Jung's Shadow: Negation and Narcissism of the Self", Journal of Analytical Psychology 56, no. 5 (November 2011): 674–91.

p142 **stirring the unconscious** J. Schimel, T. Psyszczynski, et al., "Running from the Shadow: Psychological Distancing from Others to Deny Characteristics People Fear in Themselves", Journal of Personality and Social Psychology 78, no. 3 (March 2000): 446–62.

p143 **One way to activate** J. Sayers, "Marion Milner, Mysticism and Psychoanalysis", International Journal of Psycho-Analysis 83, pt. 1 (February 2002): 105–20.

p143 **Marion Milner explains** M. Milner, On Not Being Able to Paint (New York: Routledge, 2010).

p143 **Psychologist Robert Burns** S. Juan, "Why Do We Doodle?" Register (October 13, 2006): http://www.theregister.co.uk/2006/10/13 /the _odd_ body_doodling/.

p144 **hesitate to doodle** C. Magazine and D. Greenberg, Presidential Doodles: Two Centuries of Scribbles, Scratches, Squiggles, and Scrawls from the Oval Office (New York: Basic Books, 2006).

p144 **Albrecht Dürer, also doodled** G. D. Schott, "Doodling and the Default Network of the Brain", Lancet 378, no. 9797 (September 24, 2011): 1133–34.

p144 **"Try to pose for yourself"** T. Dostoyevsky and D. Patterson, Winter Notes on Summer Impressions (Evanston, IL: Northwestern University Press, 1997), p. 49.

p144 **Daniel Wegner's research** D. M. Wegner, "Ironic Processes of Mental Control", Psychological Review 101, no. 1 (January 1994): 34–52.

p144 **four months of musical training** S. Seinfeld, H. Figueroa, et al., "Effects of Music Learning and Piano Practice on Cognitive Function, Mood and Quality of Life in Older Adults", Frontiers in Psychology 4 (2013): 810.

p144 **It can also increase your overall IQ** E. A. Miendlarzewska and W. J. Trost, "How Musical Training Affects Cognitive Development: Rhythm, Reward and Other Modulating Variables", Frontiers in Neuroscience 7 (2013): 279; K. Hille, K. Gust, et al., "Associations between Music Education, Intelligence, and Spelling Ability in Elementary School", Advances in Cognitive Psychology 7 (2011): 1–6.

p144 **When we examine brain images** C. Y. Wan and G. Schlaug, "Music Making as a Tool for Promoting Brain Plasticity Across the Life Span", Neuroscientist 16, no. 5 (October 2010): 566–77; L. Jancke, "Music Drives Brain Plasticity", F1000 Biology Reports 1 (2009): 78.

p145 **called serial processing** R. Fischer and F. Plessow, "Efficient Multitasking: Parallel Versus Serial Processing of Multiple Tasks", Frontiers in Psychology 6 (2015): 1366.

p146 **neuroscientist Omar Al-Hashimi** O. Al-Hashimi, T. P. Zanto, and A. Gazzaley, "Neural Sources of Performance Decline During Continuous Multitasking", Cortex 71 (2015): 49–57.

p148 **researcher, Hansjörg Neth** H. Neth, S. S. Khemlani, and W. D. Gray, "Feedback Design for the Control of a Dynamic Multitasking System: Dissociating Outcome Feedback from Control Feedback", Human Factors 50, no. 4 (2008): 643–51.

p152 **Todd Kelley and Steven Yantis** T. A. Kelley and S. Yantis, "Neural Correlates of Learning to Attend", Frontiers in Human Neuroscience 4 (2010): 216.

p154 **neuroscientist Wesley Clapp** W. C. Clapp, M. T. Rubens, and A. Gazzaley, "Mechanisms of Working Memory Disruption by External Interference", Cerebral Cortex 20, no. 4 (2010): 859–72.

p156 **neuroscientist Jaak Panksepp** J. Panksepp, "Can PLAY Diminish ADHD and Facilitate the Construction of the Social Brain?" Journal of the Canadian Academy of Child and Adolescent Psychiatry 16, no. 2 (2007): 57–66.

p158 **psychologist Arie Kruglanski** A. W. Kruglanski and G. Gigerenzer, "Intuitive and Deliberate Judgments Are Based on Common Principles", Psychological Review 118, no. 1 (2011): 97–109.

CHAPTER 5: GETTING UNSTUCK

p165 **pops into your head** L. Kvavilashvili and G. Mandler, "Out of One's Mind: A Study of Involuntary Semantic Memories", Cognitive Psychology 48, no. 1 (January 2004): 47–94.

p165 **get more emotionally neutral** J. H. Mace, "Involuntary Autobiographical Memory Chains: Implications for Autobiographical Memory Organization", Frontiers in Psychiatry 5 (2014): 183; J. H. Mace, Involuntary Memory (Malden, MA: Wiley-Blackwell, 2007).

p166 **increase your brain opioids** J. K. Zubieta, J. A. Bueller, et al., "Placebo Effects Mediated by Endogenous Opioid Activity on Mu-Opioid Receptors",

Journal of Neuroscience 25, no. 34 (August 24, 2005): 7754–62; A. Piedimonte, F. Benedetti, and E. Carlino, "Placebo-Induced Decrease in Fatigue: Evidence for a Central Action on the Preparatory Phase of Movement", European Journal of Neuroscience 41, no. 4 (February 2015): 492–97; F. Benedetti, E. Carlino, and A. Pollo, "How Placebos Change the Patient's Brain", Neuropsychopharmacology 36, no. 1 (January 2011): 339–54; A. Pollo, E. Carlino, et al., "Preventing Motor Training Through Nocebo Suggestions", European Journal of Applied Physiology and Occupational Physiology 112, no. 11 (November 2012): 3893–903.

p166 **called attention shifting** D. R. Johnson, "Emotional Attention Set-Shifting and Its Relationship to Anxiety and Emotion Regulation", Emotion 9, no. 5 (October 2009): 681–90; D. Di Nocera, A. Finzi, et al., "The Role of Intrinsic Motivations in Attention Allocation and Shifting", Frontiers in Psychology 5 (2014): 273.

p167 **"Buying" into this idea** J. Groopman, "The Anatomy of Hope", Permanente Journal 8, no. 2 (Spring 2004): 43–47.

p167 **try affect labelling** E. Constantinou, M. Van Den Houte, et al., "Can Words Heal? Using Affect Labeling to Reduce the Effects of Unpleasant Cues on Symptom Reporting", Frontiers in Psychology 5 (2014): 807; S. H. Hemenover, A. A. Augustine, et al., "Individual Differences in Negative Affect Repair", Emotion 8, no. 4 (August 2008): 468–78.

p167 **putting up a barrier** M. D. Lieberman, N. I. Eisenberger, et al., "Putting Feelings into Words: Affect Labeling Disrupts Amygdala Activity in Response to Affective Stimuli", Psychological Science 18, no. 5 (May 2007): 421–28; S. J. Torrisi, M. D. Lieberman, et al., "Advancing Understanding of Affect Labeling with Dynamic Causal Modeling", NeuroImage 82 (November 15, 2013): 481–88.

p168 **reframing your emotions calms** J. M. Cisler, B. A. Sigel, et al., "Changes in Functional Connectivity of the Amygdala During Cognitive Reappraisal Predict Symptom Reduction During Trauma-Focused Cognitive-Behavioral Therapy Among Adolescent Girls with Post-Traumatic Stress Disorder", Psychological Medicine (August 15, 2016): 1–11; J. Ferri, J. Schmidt, et al., "Emotion Regulation and Amygdala-Precuneus Connectivity: Focusing on Attentional Deployment", Cognitive, Affective and Behavioral Neuroscience (July 21, 2016); C. E. Waugh, P. Zarolia, et al., "Emotion Regulation Changes the Duration of the Bold Response to Emotional Stimuli", Social, Cognitive and Affective Neuroscience (May 19, 2016).

p169 **using focused techniques** Y. Zhai and Y. Zhu, "Study of Effect on Solution-Focused Approach in Improving the Negative Emotion of Surgical Patients in Department of Vascular Surgery", Pakistan Journal of Pharmaceutical Sciences 29, 2 Suppl. (March 2016): 719–22; M. J. Rohrbaugh and V. Shoham, "Brief Therapy Based on Interrupting Ironic Processes: The Palo Alto Model", Clinical Psychology (New York) 8, no. 1 (2001): 66–81.

p170 **This is reflected in** "Fisher Sees Stocks Permanently High", New York Times (October 16, 1929): http://query.nytimes .com/ gst/abstract.html?res=9806E6DF1639E03ABC4E52DFB6678382639EDE&legacy=true; V. Navasky, "Tomorrow Never Knows", New York Times Magazine (September 29, 1996): http://www.nytimes.com/1996/09/29/magazine/tomorrow-never- knows. html; J. Sanburn, "Top 10 Failed Predictions: Four-Piece Groups with Guitars Are Finished", Time (October 21, 2011): http://content.time .com/time/specials/packages/article/0,28804,2097462_2097456 _2097466 ,00.html; H. Davies, The Beatles: The Authorized Biography (Nw York: McGraw-Hill, 1968); U. Saiidi, "Here's Why the Majority of Brexit Polls Were Wrong", CNBC (July 4, 2016): http://www.cnbc.com /2016/07/04/ why-the-majority-of-brexit-polls-were-wrong.html; J. Edwards, "Pollsters Now Know Why They Were Wrong About Brexit", Business Insider (July 24, 2016): http://www.businessinsider.com/pollsters-know-why-they-were-wrong -about-brexit-2016-7; S. Lohr and N. Singer, "How Data Failed Us in Calling an Election", New York Times (November 10, 2016): https://www. nytimes.com/2016/11/10/technology/the-data-said-clinton-would-win-why-you-shouldnt-have-believed-it.html.

p172 **psychologist Charles S. Carver** C. S. Carver and S. L. Johnson, "Authentic and Hubristic Pride: Differential Relations to Aspects of Goal Regulation, Affect, and Self-Control", Journal of Research in Personality 44, no. 6 (December 2010): 698–703.

p173 **your brain's compass** J. Boedecker, T. Lampe, and M. Riedmiller, "Modeling Effects of Intrinsic and Extrinsic Rewards on the Competition between Striatal Learning Systems", Frontiers in Psychology 4 (2013): 739.

p173 **extrinsic rewards play a role** J. S. Carton, "The Differential Effects of Tangible Rewards and Praise on Intrinsic Motivation: A Comparison of Cognitive Evaluation Theory and Operant Theory", Behavior Analysis 19, no. 2 (Fall 1996): 237–55.

p173 **moment things become** K. Murayama, M. Matsumoto, et al., "Neural Basis of the Undermining Effect of Monetary Reward on Intrinsic Motivation", Proceedings of the National Academy of Sciences 107, no. 49 (December 7, 2010): 20911–16.

p173 **orient and motivate you** S. Reiss, "Extrinsic and Intrinsic Motivation at 30: Unresolved Scientific Issues", Behavior Analysis 28, no. 1 (2005): 1–14.

p175 **Releasing focus makes it "glow"** Y. Ostby, K. B. Walhovd, et al., "Mental Time Travel and Default-Mode Network Functional Connectivity in the Developing Brain", Proceedings of the National Academy of Sciences 109, no. 42 (October 16, 2012): 16800–4.

p175 **called autonoetic consciousness** J. R. Andrews-Hanna, "The Brain's Default Network and Its Adaptive Role in Internal Mentation", Neuroscientist 18, no. 3 (June 2012): 251–70.

p175 **spontaneous thoughts are** A. Berkovich-Ohana and J. Glicksohn, "The Consciousness State Space (Css): A Unifying Model for Consciousness and Self", Frontiers in Psychology 5 (2014): 341.

p175 **a sign that you** B. J. Baars, "Spontaneous Repetitive Thoughts Can Be Adaptive: Postscript on 'Mind Wandering,'" Psychological Bulletin 136, no. 2 (March 2010): 208–10.

p175 **that's a good thing** C. E. Giblin, C. K. Morewedge, and M. I. Norton, "Unexpected Benefits of Deciding by Mind Wandering", Frontiers in Psychology 4 (2013): 598.

p175 **Your conscious brain processes** T. Nørretranders, The User Illusion: Cutting Consciousness Down to Size (New York: Viking, 1998); T. D. Wilson, Strangers to Ourselves: Discovering the Adaptive Unconscious (Cambridge, MA: Harvard University Press, 2002); A. Dijksterhuis, "Think Different: The Merits of Unconscious Thought in Preference Development and Decision Making", Journal of Personality and Social Psychology 87, no. 5 (November 2004): 586–98.

p176 **can be less accurate** L. M. Augusto, "Unconscious Knowledge: A Survey", Advances in Cognitive Psychology 6 (2010): 116–41; P. C Trimmer, A. I. Houston, et al., "Mammalian Choices: Combining Fast-but-Inaccurate and Slow-but-AccurateDecision-MakingSystems", Proceedings of the Royal Society B Biological Sciences 275, no. 1649 (October 22, 2008): 2353–61.

p177 **brain researcher Luigi F. Agnati** L. F. Agnati, D. Guidolin, et al., "The Neurobiology of Imagination: Possible Role of Interaction-Dominant Dynamics and Default Mode Network", Frontiers in Psychology 4 (2013): 296.

p179 **"decided to drop out"** S. Jobs, " 'You've Got to Find What You Love,' Jobs Says", News Stanford (June 14, 2005): http://news.stanford.edu/2005/06/14/jobs-061505/.

p179 **at an ashram** A. Gowen, "Inside the Indian Temple That Draws America's Tech Titans", Washington Post (October 31, 2015): https://www.washingtonpost.com/world/asia_pacific/inside-the-indian-temple-that-draws-americas-tech-titans/2015/10/30/03b646d8-7cb9-11e5-bfb6-65300a5ff562_story.html.

p179 **he founded Apple** N. Rawlinson, "History of Apple, 1976–2016: The Story of Steve Jobs and the Company He Founded", Macworld (April 1, 2016): http://www.macworld.co.uk/feature/apple/history-of-apple-steve-jobs-what-happened-mac-computer-3606104/.

p179 **Bill Gates still takes** R. A. Guth, "In Secret Hideaway, Bill Gates Ponders Microsoft's Future", Wall Street Journal (March 28, 2005): http://www.wsj.com/articles/SB111196625830690477.

p180 **Bryce Huebner and Robert D. Rupert** B. Huebner and R. D. Rupert, "Massively Representational Minds Are Not Always Driven by Goals, Conscious or Otherwise", Behavioral and Brain Sciences 37, no. 2 (April 2014): 145–46.

p181 **allows your predictive brain** M. Bar, "The Proactive Brain: Memory for Predictions", Philosophical Transactions of the Royal Society of London. Series B: Biological Sciences 364, no. 1521 (May 12, 2009):. 1235–43; S. L. Mullally and E. A. Maguire, "Memory, Imagination, and Predicting the Future: A Common Brain Mechanism?" Neuroscientist 20, no. 3 (June 2014): 220–34.

p182 **"complete" and "whole"** C. G. Davey, J. Pujol, and B. J. Harrison, "Mapping the Self in the Brain's Default Mode Network", NeuroImage 132 (May 15, 2016): 390–97.

p181 **fuels your path** J. F. Cornwell, B. Franks, and E. T. Higgins, "Truth, Control, and Value Motivations: The 'What,' 'How,' and 'Why' of Approach and Avoidance", Frontiers in Systems Neuroscience 8 (2014): 194.

p182 **"When I let go"** L. Tzu, Tao Te Ching (New York: Dover, 1997).

p182 **biologist Alexander Fleming** "Discovery and Development of Penicillin",American Chemical Society, n.d.: http://www.acs.org/con tent /acs/en/education/whatischemistry/landmarks/flemingpeni cillin.html; B. L. Ligon, "Penicillin: Its Discovery and Early Development",Seminars in Pediatric Infectious Disease 15, no. 1 (January 2004): 52–57.

p183 **Henk van Steenbergen** H. van Steenbergen, G. P. Band, et al., "Hedonic Hotspots Regulate Cingulate-Driven Adaptation to Cognitive Demands", Cerebral Cortex 25, no. 7 (July 2015): 1746–56.

p185 **psychologist Jack Brehm** J. W. Brehm, "Postdecision Changes in the Desirability of Alternatives", Journal of Abnormal Psychology 52, no. 3 (May 1956): 384–89.

p185 **psychologist Robert E. Knox** R. E. Knox and J. A. Inkster, "Postdecision Dissonance at Post Time", Journal of Personality and Social Psychology 8, no. 4 (April 1968): 319–23.

p186 **dopamine D4 receptor gene** R. P. Ebstein and R. H. Belmaker, "Saga of an Adventure Gene: Novelty Seeking, Substance Abuse and the Dopamine D4 Receptor (D4DR) Exon III Repeat Polymorphism", Molecular Psychiatry 2, no. 5 (September 1997): 381–84; J. Benjamin, L. Li, et al., "Population and Familial Association Between the D4 Dopamine Receptor Gene and Measures of Novelty Seeking", Nature Genetics 12, no. 1 (January 1996): 81–84.1

p186 **tries to stay stuck** L. Schwabe and O. T. Wolf, "Stress Prompts Habit

Behavior in Humans", Journal of Neuroscience 29, no. 22 (June 3, 2009): 7191–98.

p187 **psychologist Nicholas Spanos** N. P. Spanos, R. J. Stenstrom, and J. C. Johnston, "Hypnosis, Placebo, and Suggestion in the Treatment of Warts", Psychosomatic Medicine 50, no. 3 (May–June 1988): 245–60.

p187 **"biochemical battle strategies."** T. S. Sathyanarayana Rao, M. R. Asha, et al., "The Biochemistry of Belief", Indian Journal of Psychiatry 51, no. 4 (October–December 2009): 239–41.

p188 **limits as horizons** S. Yoshimura, Y. Okamoto, et al., "Neural Basis of Anticipatory Anxiety Reappraisals", PLoS One 9, no. 7 (2014): e102836.

p189 **Yale psychologist Jerome Singer** R. L. McMillan, S. B. Kaufman, and J. L. Singer, "Ode to Positive Constructive Daydreaming", Frontiers in Psychology 4 (2013): 626.

p190 **brain's emotional centres** P. Feng, Y. Zheng, and T. Feng, "Resting-State Functional Connectivity between Amygdala and the Ventromedial Prefrontal Cortex Following Fear Reminder Predicts Fear Extinction", Social Cognitive and Affective Neuroscience 11, no. 6 (June 2016): 991–1001; C. J. Reppucci and G. D. Petrovich, "Organization of Connections between the Amygdala, Medial Prefrontal Cortex, and Lateral Hypothalamus: A Single and Double Retrograde Tracing Study in Rats", Brain Structure and Function 221, no. 6 (July 2016): 2937–62.

p190 **neurologist Antonio Damasio** A. Damasio, Descartes' Error: Emotion, Reason, and the Human Brain (New York: Penguin, 1995).

p191 **John Cassavetes**, J. Loewen, "John Cassavetes from A Personal Journey with Martin Scorsese Through American Movies", YouTube: https://www.youtube.com/watch?v=UR3jKqsMI_c.

CHAPTER 6: FROM DISENCHANTMENT TO
GREATNESS

p193 **a son was born** "Jeff Bezos Biography", Biography, n.d.: http://www.biography.com/people/jeff-bezos-9542209.
p193 **married a Cuban** "Jeff Bezos Biography", Famous People, n.d.: http://www.thefamouspeople.com/profiles/jeff-bezos-4868.php.

p193 **boy never saw** J. Yarow, "The Astonishing Story of Jeff Bezos' Biological Father Who Didn't Even Know Bezos Existed Until the End of Last Year", Business Insider (October 10, 2013): http://www.businessinsider.com/jeff-bezos-biological-father-2013-10.

p193 **took it apart** K. Russell, "The 9 Most Interesting Facts About Jeff Bezos from the Big New Amazon Book", Business Insider (November 18, 2013): http://www.businessinsider.in/The-9-Most-Interesting-Facts-About-Jeff-Bezos-From-The-Big-New-Amazon-Book/arti cleshow/25996451.cms?format=slideshow.

p193 **rigged an electric alarm** "Jeff Bezos Fun Facts", Celebrity Fun Facts (August 20, 2016): http://www.celebrityfunfacts.com/jeff-bezos/f67m89/.

p194 **an automatic gate-closer** J. Ostdick, "e-vangelist", Success (June 30, 2011): http://www.success.com/article/e-vangelist.

p194 **a book on "bright minds"**, N. Carlson, "Jeff Bezos: Here's Why He Won", Business Insider (May 16, 2011): http://www.businessinsider.com/jeff-bezos-visionary-2011-4.

p194 **the "Dream Institute"** "Bezos Biography", Biography.

p194 **person of the year** "Bezos Biography", Famous People.

p195 **America's best leaders** D. LaGasse, "America's Best Leaders: Jeff Bezos, Amazon.com CEO", U.S. News & World Report (November 19, 2008): http://www.usnews.com/news/best-leaders/articles /2008 /11/19/americas-best-leaders-jeff-bezos-amazoncom-ceo.

p195 **businessperson of the year** "2012 Business Person of the Year", Fortune(November 16, 2012): http://fortune.com/2012/11/16/2012 -businessperson-of-the-year/.

p195 **fourth-wealthiest person** "The Richest People in America", Forbes (August 20, 2016): http://www.forbes.com/forbes-400/gallery/jeff-bezos.

p195 **second-best CEO** "The Best Performing CEOs", Harvard Business Review (November 2015): 49–59.

p195 **consistency of thought** A. W. Kosner, "Jeff Bezos on How to Change Your Mind", Forbes (October 19, 2012): http://www.forbes.com /sites/anthonykosner/2012/10/19/jeff-bezos-on-people-who-are-right-a-lot-vs-wrong-a-lot-has-he-got-it-right/#92c790762ed3.

p195 **brain can change** C. M. van Heugten, R. W. Ponds, and R. P. Kessels, "Brain Training: Hype or Hope?" Neuropsychological Rehabilitation 26, nos. 5–6 (October 2016): 639–44.

p196 **origin of this focus** Ibid.; A. P. Jha, J. Krompinger, and M. J. Baime, "Mindfulness Training Modifies Subsystems of Attention", Cognitive, Affective and Behavioral Neuroscience 7, no. 2 (June 2007): 109–19.

p197 **more-generous CEOs** P. Dey, "9 Most Generous CEOs of Our Time", Best Mankind, n.d.: http://www.bestmankind.com/most-generous-ceos-of-our-time/; J. Kantor and D. Streitfeld, "Inside Amazon: Wrestling Big Ideas in a Bruising Workplace", New York Times (August 16, 2015): http://www.nytimes.com/2015/08/16/technology /inside-amazon-wrestling-big-ideas-in-a-bruising-workplace.html.

p198 **also quite playful** A. Deutschman, "Inside the Mind of Jeff Bezos", Fast Company (August 1, 2004): http://www.fastcompany.com /50106 / inside-mind-jeff-bezos.

p198 **be stubborn and flexible** Ibid.

p198 **sometimes sell something** Ibid.

p198 **"pleasure" chemicals being released** A. S. Sprouse-Blum, G. Smith, et al., "Understanding Endorphins and Their Importance in Pain Management", Hawaii Medical Journal 69, no. 3 (March 2010): 70–71.

p199 **direct your attention** B. Salehi, M. I. Cordero, and C. Sandi, "Learning Under Stress: The Inverted-U-Shape Function Revisited", Learning and Memory 17, no. 10 (October 2010): 522–30.

p199 **love and hatred** E. Meaux and P. Vuilleumier, "Facing Mixed Emotions: Analytic and Holistic Perception of Facial Emotion Expressions Engages Separate Brain Networks", NeuroImage 141 (July 5, 2016): 154–73; H. E. Heshfield, S. Scheibe, et al., "When Feeling Bad Can Be Good: Mixed Emotions Benefit Physical Health across Adulthood", Social Psychological and Personality Science 4, no. 1 (January 2013): 54–61; S. Zeki and J. P. Romaya, "Neural Correlates of Hate", PLoS One 3, no. 10 (2008): e3556.

p199 **also connects you** I. Molnar-Szakacs and L. Q. Uddin, "Self-Processing and the Default Mode Network: Interactions with the Mirror Neuron System", Frontiers in Human Neuroscience 7 (2013): 571.

p200 **reward centre is activated** A. S. Heller, C. M. van Reekum, et al., "Sustained Striatal Activity Predicts Eudaimonic Well-Being and Cortisol Output", Psychological Science 24, no. 11 (November 1, 2013): 2191–200.

p200 **100 most influential** "The 100 Most Influential People", Time (April 21, 2016): http://time.com/collection/2016-time-100/.

p202 **Called self-handicapping** M. Zuckerman and F. F. Tsai, "Costs of Self-Handicapping", Journal of Personality 73, no. 2 (April 2005): 411–42.

p202 **Make self-handicapping a habit** H. Takeuchi, Y. Taki, et al., "Anatomical Correlates of Self-Handicapping Tendency", Cortex 49, no. 4 (April 2013): 1148–54.

p202 **Kazimierz Dabrowski**, K. Dabrowski, "On Positive Disintegration. An Outline of the Theory Concerning the Psychological Development of

Man through Unbalanced States, Nervous States, Neuroses and Psychoses",
Annales Medico-Psychologiques 117, no. 2 (November 1959): 643–68; K.
Dabrowski, "Remarks on Typology Based on the Theory of Positive Disinte-
gration", Annales Medico-Psychologiques 118, no. 2 (October 1960): 401–6.

p203 **Billie Jean King** B. J. King, Pressure Is a Privilege: Lessons I've Learned
from Life and the Battle of the Sexes (New York: LifeTime Media, 2008).

p203 **depends on three factors** W. Tillier, "The Basic Concepts of Dabrowski's Theory of Positive Disintegration", in W. Tillier, ed., Perspectives
on the Self: Proceedings of the Second Biennial Conference on Dabrowski's
Theory of Positive Disintegration (unpublished, 1996): 5–14.

p203 **Gifted students often** S. Mendaglio, "Dabrowski's Theory of Positive
Disintegration: Some Implications for Teachers of Gifted Students", AGATE
15, no. 2 (Fall 2002): 14–22.

p203 **referred to as "dynamisms"** Ibid.

p204 **state of positive disintegration** W. Tillier, "Dabrowski 101: The Theory
of Positive Disintegration", Positive Disintegration (December 6, 2014):
http://positivedisintegration.com/Dabrowski101.pdf.

p205 **psychologist Andrea Berger** A. Berger, G. Tzur, and M. I. Posner, "In-
fant Brains Detect Arithmetic Errors", Proceedings of the National Academy
of Sciences 103, no. 33 (August 15, 2006): 12649–53.

p207 **brain's control regions relax** C. J. Limb and A. R. Braun, "Neural
Substrates of Spontaneous Musical Performance: An fMRI Study of Jazz
Improvisation", PLoS One 3, no. 2 (2008): e1679; M. C. Anderson, K. N.
Ochsner, et al., "Neural Systems Underlying the Suppression of Unwanted
Memories", Science 303, no. 5655 (January 9, 2004): 232–35.

p207 **the improvisation circuit** A. Engel and P. E. Keller, "The Perception
of Musical Spontaneity in Improvised and Imitated Jazz Performances", Frontiers in Psychology 2 (2011): 83.

p207 **Jazz musicians, for example** R. E. Beaty, "The Neuroscience of Musical
Improvisation", Neuroscience and Biobehavioral Reviews 51 (April 2015):
108–17.

p208 **consultant Andrew Campbell** A. Campbell, J. Whitehead, and S.
Finkelstein, "Why Good Leaders Make Bad Decisions", Harvard Business
Review 87, no. 2 (February 2009): 60–66,109.

p208 **lists of related words** D. R. Cann, K. McRae, and A. N. Katz, "False
Recall in the Deese-Roediger-McDermott Paradigm: The Roles of Gist and
Associative Strength", Quarterly Journal of Experimental Psychology (Hove)
64, no. 8 (August 2011): 1515–42.

p208 **able to remember** J. Storbeck and G. L. Clore, "With Sadness Comes Accuracy; with Happiness, False Memory: Mood and the False Memory Effect", Psychological Science 16, no. 10 (October 2005): 785–91.

p208 **psychologists Youssef Ezzyat** Y. Ezzyat and L. Davachi, "Similarity Breeds Proximity: Pattern Similarity Within and Across Contexts Is Related to Later Mnemonic Judgments of Temporal Proximity", Neuron 81, no. 5 (March 5, 2014): 1179–89.

p210 **gastroenterologist Jin-Yong Kang** J. Y. Kang, K. G. Yeoh, et al., "Chili—Protective Factor Against Peptic Ulcer?" Digestive Diseases and Sciences 40, no. 3 (March 1995): 576–79.

p210 **the active ingredient** M. N. Satyanarayana, "Capsaicin and Gastric Ulcers", Critical Reviews in Food Science and Nutrition 46, no. 4 (2006): 275–328.

p210 **researcher Martijn Mulder** M. J. Mulder, E. J. Wagenmakers, et al., "Bias in the Brain: A Diffusion Model Analysis of Prior Probability and Potential Payoff", Journal of Neuroscience 32, no. 7 (February 15, 2012): 2335–43.

p211 **researcher Mariela Jaskelioff** M. Jaskelioff, F. L. Muller, et al., "Telomerase Reactivation Reverses Tissue Degeneration in Aged Telomerase-Deficient Mice", Nature 469, no. 7328 (January 6, 2011): 102–6.

p212 **David Sinclair** D. Sinclair, A. P. Gomes, N. L. Price, et al., "Declining Nad(+) Induces a Pseudohypoxic State Disrupting Nuclear-Mitochondrial Communication During Aging", Cell 155, no. 7 (December 19, 2013): 1624–38.

p212 **geneticist George Church** G. Church, "Where Do We Go from Here?" Future of Genetic Medicine IX (March 3, 2016): https://www.scripps.org/sparkle-assets/documents/brochure_future_of_genomic_medicine_ix.pdf.

p212 **doctoral student Daniela Aisenberg** D. Aisenberg, N. Cohen, et al., "Social Priming Improves Cognitive Control in Elderly Adults—Evidence from the Simon Task", PLoS One 10, no. 1 (2015): e0117151.

p213 **doctoral student Deirdre Robertson** D. A. Robertson, G. M. Savva, et al., "Negative Perceptions of Aging and Decline in Walking Speed: A Self-Fulfilling Prophecy", PLoS One 10, no. 4 (2015): e0123260.

p213 **researchers Daniel Webster** D. M. Webster and A. W. Kruglanski, "Individual Differences in Need for Cognitive Closure", Journal of Personality and Social Psychology 67, no. 6 (December 1994): 1049–62.

p214 **High levels of NCC** Y. Tanaka, J. Fujino, et al., "Are Ambiguity Aversion and Ambiguity Intolerance Identical? A Neuroeconomics Investigation", Frontiers in Psychology 5 (2014): 1550.

p215 **neurologist Marc Jeannerod** M. Jeannerod and J. Decety, "Mental Motor Imagery: A Window into the Representational Stages of Action", Current Opinion in Neurobiology 5, no. 6 (December 1995): 727–32; M. Jeannerod, "Mental Imagery in the Motor Context", Neuropsychologia 33, no. 11 (November 1995): 1419–32.

p215 **brain researcher Chang-Hyun Park** C. H. Park, W. H. Chang, et al., "Which Motor Cortical Region Best Predicts Imagined Movement?" Neuro-Image 113 (June 2015): 101–10.

p216 **First-person images make you** H. J. Rice and D. C. Rubin, "I Can See It Both Ways: First-and Third-Person Visual Perspectives at Retrieval", Consciousness and Cognition 18, no. 4 (December 2009): 877–90; A. R. Sutin and R. W. Robins, "Correlates and Phenomenology of First and Third Person Memories", Memory 18, no. 6 (August 2010): 625–37.

p216 **professor Craig Hall** C. R. Hall, K. J. Munroe-Chandler, et al., "Imagery and Observational Learning Use and Their Relationship to Sport Confidence", Journal of Sports Sciences 27, no. 4 (2009): 327–37.

p217 **stunning 86 per cent** A. Knapp, "Ray Kurzweil Defends His 2009 Predictions", Forbes (March 21, 2012): http://www.forbes.com/sites/alex-knapp/2012/03/21/ray-kurzweil-defends- his-2009-predictions/.

p217 **he predicted that personal** D. Baer, "5 Amazing Predictions by Futurist Ray Kurzweil That Came True—And 4 That Haven't", Tech Insider (October 20, 2015): http://til.ink/2cY5gia.

p218 **provide spontaneous feedback** S. Rosenbush, "Google's Ray Kurzweil Envisions New Era of Search", Wall Street Journal blogs (February 4, 2014): http://blogs.wsj.com/cio/2014/02/04/googles-ray-kurzweil-envisions-new-era-of-search/.

p218 **nanobots made from** K. Miles, "Ray Kurzweil: In the 2030s, Nanobots in Our Brains Will Make Us 'Godlike,'" Huffington Post (October 1, 2015): http://www.huffingtonpost.com/entry/ray-kurzweil-nanobots-brain-god-like_us_560555a0e4b0af3706dbe1e2.

p218 **slow-wave rhythms** F. M. Carvalho, K. T. Chaim, et al., "Time-Perception Network and Default Mode Network Are Associated with Temporal Prediction in a Periodic Motion Task", Frontiers in Human Neuroscience 10 (2016): 268; S. Sandrone, "The Brain as a Crystal Ball: The Predictive Potential of Default Mode Network", Frontiers in Human Neuroscience 6 (2012): 261.

p218 **Freeman Dyson**, a theoretical J. Kagan, "Review: The Future of the Mind: The Scientific Quest to Understand, Enhance, and Empower the Mind", Cerebrum 2014 (May–June 2014): 7.

p219 **"regret minimisation framework"** M. Thompson, "Jeff Bezos—Regret Minimization Framework", YouTube (December 20, 2008): https://www.youtube.com/watch?v=jwG_qR6XmDQ.

p219 **a crystal ball** S. Sandrone, "The Brain as a Crystal Ball, the Predictive Potential of Default Mode Network" Frontiers in Human Neuroscience 6 (2012): 261.

p220 **Called transcendental awareness** D. R. Vago and D. A. Silbersweig, "Self-Awareness, Self-Regulation, and Self-Transcendence (S-Art): A Framework for Understanding the Neurobiological Mechanisms of Mindfulness", Frontiers in Human Neuroscience 6 (2012): 296.

p220 **mindfulness– a practice** C. Noone, B. Bunting, and M. J. Hogan, "Does Mindfulness Enhance Critical Thinking? Evidence for the Mediating Effects of Executive Functioning in the Relationship Between Mindfulness and Critical Thinking", Frontiers in Psychology 6 (2015): 2043.

p220 **known as open monitoring** D. P. Lippelt, B. Hommel, and L. S.Colzato, "Focused Attention, Open Monitoring and Loving Kindness Meditation: Effects on Attention, Conflict Monitoring, and Creativity—a Review", Frontiers in Psychology 5 (2014): 1083; H. Uusberg,A. Uusberg, et al., "Mechanisms of Mindfulness: The Dynamics of Affective Adaptation During Open Monitoring", Biological Psychology 118 (July 2016): 94–106.

p220 **transcendental meditation** K. W. Chen, C. C. Berger, et al., "Meditative Therapies for Reducing Anxiety: A Systematic Review and Meta-Analysis of Randomized Controlled Trials", Depression and Anxiety 29, no. 7 (July 2012): 545–62.

p221 **app called Headspace** A. Puddicome, "10 Minutes Could Change Your Whole Day", Headspace, n.d.: https://www.headspace.com/headspace-meditation-app.

p221 **deactivation of the parietal** Vago and Silbersweig, "Self-Awareness Self-Regulation"; E. Mohandas, "Neurobiology of Spirituality", Mens Sana Monographs 6, no. 1 (January 2008): 63–80;F. Travis, D. A. Haaga, et al., "A Self-Referential Default Brain State: Patterns of Coherence, Power, and Eloreta Sources During Eyes-Closed Rest and Transcendental Meditation Practice", Cognitive Processing 11, no. 1 (February 2010): 21–30.

p221 **empathy and social understanding** N. A. Farb, A. K. Anderson, and Z. V. Segal, "The Mindful Brain and Emotion Regulation in Mood Disorders", Canadian Journal of Psychiatry/Revue Canadienne de Psychiatrie 57, no. 2 (February 2012): 70–77; R. Simon and M. Engstrom, "The Default Mode Network as a Biomarker for Monitoring the Therapeutic Effects of Meditation", Frontiers in Psychology 6 (2015): 776.

p221 **children with ADHD** J. T. Mitchell, L. Zylowska, and S. H. Kollins,

"Mindfulness Meditation Training for Attention-Deficit/Hyperactivity Disorder in Adulthood: Current Empirical Support, Treatment Overview, and Future Directions", Cognitive and Behavioral Practice 22, no. 2 (May 2015): 172–91; L. Zylowska, D. L. Ackerman, et al., "Mindfulness Meditation Training in Adults and Adolescents with ADHD: A Feasibility Study", Journal of Attention Disorders 11, no. 6 (May 2008): 737–46.

p221 **Three stages from focus** S. Satchidananda, The Yoga Sutras of Patanjali (Buckingham, VA: Integral Yoga Publications, 1990): pp171–75.

p223 **widespread health benefits** P. H. Canter, "The Therapeutic Effects of Meditation", British Medical Journal 326, no. 7398 (May 17, 2003): 1049–50; H. Sharma, "Meditation: Process and Effects", Ayu 36, no. 3 (July–September 2015): 233–37.

p223 **biologist Elizabeth Blackburn** K. Harmon, "Work on Telomeres Wins Nobel Prize in Physiology or Medicine for 3 U.S. Genetic Researchers [Update]", Scientific American (October 5, 2009): http://www.scientificamerican.com/article/nobel-prize-medicine-2009-genetics/.

p223 **Shambhala Mountain Centre** Q. Conklin, B. King, et al., "Telomere Lengthening After Three Weeks of an Intensive Insight Meditation Retreat", Psychoneuroendocrinology 61 (November 2015): 26–27.

p225 **protecting your self-esteem** R. A. Josephs, J. K. Bosson, and C. G. Jacobs, "Self-Esteem Maintenance Processes: Why Low Self-Esteem May Be Resistant to Change", Personality and Social Psychology Bulletin 29, no. 7 (July 2003): 920–33; A. D. Hermann, G. Leonardelli, and R. M. Arkin, "Self-Doubt and Self-Esteem: A Threat from Within", Personality and Social Psychology Bulletin 28 (2002): 395–408.

p227 **brains of world-class gymnasts** R. Huang, M. Lu, et al., "Long-Term Intensive Training Induced Brain Structural Changes in World Class Gymnasts", Brain Structure and Function 220, no. 2 (March 2015): 625–44; B. Wang, Y. Fan, et al., "Brain Anatomical Networks in World Class Gymnasts: A DTI Tractography Study", NeuroImage 65 (January 15, 2013): 476–87; J. Wang, M. Lu, et al., "Exploring Brain Functional Plasticity in World Class Gymnasts: A Network Analysis", Brain Structure and Function (September 29, 2015).

p231 **psychologist Graham Rawlinson** G. E. Rawlinson, "The Significance of Letter Position in Word Recognition", unpublished Ph.D. thesis, University of Nottingham, U.K., 1976.

p233 **licence to avoid living fully** R. H. Lehto and K. F. Stein, "Death Anxiety: An Analysis of an Evolving Concept", Research and Theory for Nursing Practice 23, no. 1 (2009): 23–41; L. Razinsky, Freud, Psychoanalysis and Death (Cambridge, U.K.: Cambridge University Press, 2014).

p233 **Self-forgiveness is part** D. E. Davis, M. Y. Ho, et al., "Forgiving the Self and Physical and Mental Health Correlates: A Meta-Analytic Review", Journal of Counseling Psychology 62, no. 2 (April 2015): 329–35.

p233 **The drug minoxidil** A. G. Messenger and J. Rundegren, "Minoxidil: Mechanisms of Action on Hair Growth", British Journal of Dermatology 150, no. 2 (February 2004): 186–94.

p233 **blood thinner warfarin** D. Wardrop and D. Keeling, "The Story of the Discovery of Heparin and Warfarin", British Journal of Haematology 141, no. 6 (June 2008): 757–63.

p234 **conflicts build brain capacity** M. C. Stevens, K. A. Kiehl, et al., "Brain Network Dynamics During Error Commission", Human Brain Mapping 30, no. 1 (January 2009): 24–37.

p236 **philosopher Søren Kierkegaard** S. Kierkegaard, The Concept of Anxiety (Princeton, NJ: Princeton University Press, 1981).

p236 **belief in having** E. Filevich, P. Vanneste, et al., "Brain Correlates of Subjective Freedom of Choice", Consciousness and Cognition 22, no. 4 (December 2013): 1271–84.

p236 **Unfocus circuits play** I. Molnar-Szakacs and L. Q. Uddin, "Self-Processing and the Default Mode Network: Interactions with the Mirror Neuron System", Frontiers in Human Neuroscience 7 (2013): 571; S. Sandrone, "Self Through the Mirror (Neurons) and Default Mode Network: What Neuroscientists Found and What Can Still Be Found There", Frontiers in Human Neuroscience 7 (2013): 383; F. Travis, D. A. Haaga, et al., "A Self-Referential Default Brain State: Patterns of Coherence, Power, and Eloreta Sources During Eyes-Closed Rest and Transcendental Meditation Practice", Cognitive Processing 11, no. 1 (February 2010): 21–30.

p237 **"fuzzy logic", which** S. S. Godil, M. S. Shamim, et al., "Fuzzy Logic: A 'Simple' Solution for Complexities in Neurosciences?" Surgical Neurology International 2 (2011): 24.

p238 **for more complex things** P. Dayan, "Simple Substrates for Complex Cognition", Frontiers in Neuroscience 2, no. 2 (December 2008): 255–63.

p238 **not one centre or circuit** S. Uithol, D. C. Burnston, and P. Haselager, "Why We May Not Find Intentions in the Brain", Neuropsychologia 56 (April 2014): 129–39.

p238 **success will continue** J. A. Mangels, B. Butterfield, et al., "Why Do Beliefs About Intelligence Influence Learning Success? A Social Cognitive Neuroscience Model", Social Cognitive and Affective Neuroscience 1, no. 2 (September 2006): 75–86.

p239 **aspects of complex cognition** B. Libet, "The Neural Time Factor in Conscious and Unconscious Events", Ciba Foundation Symposium 174 (1993): 123–37,discussion 37–46;B. Libet, C. A. Gleason, et al., "Time of Conscious Intention to Act in Relation to Onset of Cerebral Activity (Readiness-Potential): The Unconscious Initiation of a Freely Voluntary Act", Brain 106, pt. 3 (September 1983): 623–42.

p239 **biophysicist Abraham R. Liboff** A. R. Liboff, "Magnetic Correlates in Electromagnetic Consciousness", Electromagnetic Biology and Medicine 35, no. 3 (2016): 228–36.

p239 **The famous "Double Slit Experiment"** I. Orion and M. Laitman, "The Double-Slit Experiment and Particle-Wave Duality: Toward a Novel Quantum Interpretation", Journal of Modern Physics 1, no. 1 (2010): 90–92; E. Strambini, K. S. Makarenko, et al., "Geometric Reduction of Dynamical Nonlocality in Nanoscale Quantum Circuits", Scientific Reports 6 (2016): 18827.

p241 **hide the device** "This Will Mindfuck You: The Double-Slit Experiment", High Existence, n.d.: http://highexistence.com/this-will-mind fuck-you-the-double-slit-experiment/.

p242 **our brains are all** R. S. Bobrow, "Evidence for a Communal Consciousness",Explore (New York) 7, no. 4 (July–August 2011): 246–48; W. Hirstein, "Mindmelding: Connected Brains and the Problem of Consciousness", Mens Sana Monographs 6, no. 1 (January 2008): 110–30.202 reliably see the world P. A. Miller, G. Wallis, et al., "Reducing the Size of the Human Physiological Blind Spot through Training", Current Biology 25, no. 17 (August 31, 2015): R747–48.

p242 **any sound that has** G. A. Gates and J. H. Mills, "Presbycusis", Lancet 366, no. 9491 (September 24–30,2005): 1111–20; L. Kenney, "Try It: Can You Hear These Sounds Only Young People Hear?" Yahoo (March 3, 2015): https://www.yahoo.com/beauty/try-it-can-you-hear-these-sounds-only-young-112627654778.html.

p243 **form a picture** V. Gallese, L. Fadiga, et al., "Action Recognition in the Premotor Cortex", Brain 119, pt. 2 (April 1996): 593–609; V. Gallese, C. Keysers, and G. Rizzolatti, "A Unifying View of the Basis of Social Cognition", Trends in Cognitive Sciences 8, no. 9 (September 2004): 396–403; V. Gallese and C. Sinigaglia, "Understanding Action with the Motor System", Behavioral and Brain Sciences 37, no. 2 (April 2014): 199–200; M. Iacoboni, I. Molnar-Szakacs,et al., "Grasping the Intentions of Others with One's Own Mirror Neuron System", PLoS Biology 3, no. 3 (March 2005): e79.

p243 **psychologist Yulia Golland** Y. Golland, Y. Arzouan, and N. Levit-Binnun,"The Mere Co-Presence: Synchronization of Autonomic Signals and Emotional Responses Across Co-Present Individuals Not Engaged in Direct Interaction", PLoS One 10, no. 5 (2015): e0125804.

p244 **Neurons in the parietal** S. Kaplan, "Grasping at Ontological Straws: Overcoming Reductionism in the Advaita Vedanta—Neuroscience Dialogue", Journal of the American Academy of Religion 77, no. 2 (2009): 238–74.

p245 **human body evolved** F. Jacob, "Evolution and Tinkering", Science 196, no. 4295 (June 10, 1977): 1161–66.

INDEX

Index